EL SER UNO IV

COSMIC ALIGNMENT – 7 THOUSAND YEARS OF PREPARATION

D1525568

EL SER UNO

IV

COSMIC ALIGNMENT
7 Thousand Years of Preparation

FRANCA ROSA CANONICO DE SCHRAMM

INTERNATIONAL DATA PUBLICATION CATALOGUE
REGISTRY COPYRIGHT / Brazil - Sao Paulo
Franca Rosa Canonico de Schramm

Book published originally by the author and channel:
Franca Rosa Canonico de Schramm

Second Edition 2022
ISBN: 9798802087190

Books:
EL SER UNO I – The Arcana of Thoth
EL SER UNO II – Planet 3.3.3 – The Guardians of Tera
EL SER UNO III – The Seramitas – The Long Path of Return
EL SER UNO IV – Cosmic Alignment – 7 Thousand Years of Preparation
EL SER UNO V – The Interanos – The City of Crystal
EL SER UNO VI – The Siren-Lemurianos – City of Light and Love

---

www.elseruno.com
www.elserunobooks.com

CONTENT

INTRODUCTION   7

CHAPTER I
THE COSMIC ALIGMENT   15

CHAPTER II
**THE AYAPLIANOS-ELOHIM (*INTERANOS*)
AND THE REPTILIAN-GRAYS**   175

CHAPTER III
INTERVIEW WITH THE ELOHIM-INTERANOS   198

INTRODUCTION

El SER UNO IV – Cosmic Alignment – 7 Thousand Years of Preparation is a book about self-knowledge. It should be read in order. It would be useless to read it randomly, as it would not offer the expected results. Its reading will open and connect the cerebral circuits of knowledge, understanding and love.

To help with its understanding, we suggest that you consult with the following type dictionaries:

- English Language
- Dream Symbolism
- Esotericism
- Symbols
- Philosophy

Knowledge from *EL SER UNO IV – Cosmic Alignment – 7 Thousand Years of Preparation* should never be used for profit, power, manipulation or personal gain. Those who do so will be responsible for forming their negative cause and effect. This book was received in order to help the being called Planet Earth become elevated and to do this, humanity will need Knowledge, Understanding and Universal Love.

We would like to make it clear that this book is being published exactly as it was received. The Masters SERAMITAS of the INTERNAL

CITY requested this in order to safeguard the original channeling of the book. The Masters said they had placed CODES between the lines and words so that through sequential reading readers would open and activate circuits and channels in their minds as they progressed in their reading, since this book is *KNOWLEDGE of HEALING...*

Readers should realize that this knowledge is not simple to read because it is not a story or a novel but *a channeling* based on questions and answers. We recommend that the book be read with an open mind, slowly, very patiently, and above all, following the SEQUENCE in which it was written. If you try to read it randomly you may feel sleepy, probably end up with headaches and little understanding of its content. The codes inserted between the lines will make your circuits open slowly and thus understanding help you assimilate the content.

We hope that through El *SER UNO IV – Cosmic Alignment – 7 Thousand Years of Preparation*, you will discover and heal your inner self. If you feel you cannot understand this book when you read it, keep on because the questions that may arise in you will be fully answered. Read it with interest. There is a reason for it having come to you. Do not dismiss it from your life. Analyze it, study it and make it part of your own knowledge, understanding and love.

Children, brothers and sisters of light and love!

This fourth book, EL SER UNO IV – The Cosmic Alignment - 7 thousand Years of Preparation, is for all those who have vigorously activated their Desire of Creation. Upon awaking consciously to Knowledge and Understanding, they have gained the "Conception of the Spirit" and the right of joining the Cosmic Alignment, to initiate July 7, 2014.

We, your Elder Brothers, Volunteers of the Spacecraft, Seramitas-Guardians of Tera and our Brothers Interanos will be your guides on this journey toward the Cosmic Alignment that will bring transformations you might not understand in the beginning. We are the messengers to transmit to you scientific, technological and spiritual knowledge so that the initial 200 and the following 7 thousand years may not take you by surprise.

It will the four dimensions of the Cosmic Alignment take 200 years (Tera time) to reach a position of perfect symmetry and harmony with planet Tera; and it is during this time that those of you who have awaked will be part of one of the most extraordinary events to occur on the Southern Hemisphere of our universe.

The Internal City will admit thought-energies (souls) whose frequency, vibration, colors and rhythm show positive conditions, but make them return (incarnate) during the Cosmic Alignment.

After disincarnating they are re-admitted to the Internal City to complete their energetic transmutation of knowledge, understanding and love. The wisdom they so accumulate will make them elevated and, therefore, part of Universal Wisdom, whereas in their incarnated condition they will be: the future of Tera.

It is of importance that you activate the process of "Awakening", otherwise you will not be part of the universal thought-energies. Thought-energies who fail to develop will fall behind in the coordinated advance of the EL SER UNO (Being One) and its new ideas.

Activating your awakening means to have the energetic and cosmic conscience that you belong to a mind. You also have to know how to adjust your frequency appropriately. The search for happiness, harmony, peace and love requires the energy of knowledge. If you know how to gain this knowledge, you will occupy your place in the great universal context.

We, your Elder Brothers, have been preparing you for the Cosmic Alignment. In the past 150 thousand years, we have been guiding you on the way to this important event that will change the energy of anything you have known so far. Growing scientific fundaments and knowledge about the planet will allow you to reach new frontiers and this process will deeply mark you.

You need to understand and prepare for the changes that lie ahead. You must not worry. Planet Tera is undergoing molecular re-structuring in order to resist the great climatic, magnetic and gravitational variations.

We will always be close to secure that you safely enter the Cosmic Alignment. We will provide the necessary instructions and guidelines for your governments and scientists and our messengers involved in the process.

As of 2014 and over the next 200 years governments are going to disclose classified information confirming the long hidden truth of the human species' extraterrestrial origin. Science will accept this fact and thus give rise to the elevation of your Knowledge, Understanding and Love. THE TRUTH WILL MAKE YOU FREE. We will reveal to you all of it and lead you step by step to full consciousness so that you may rid yourselves of the oppressors who had left you with a blind eye and a deaf ear for so long. Every one of you will have his own personal revelation and responsibility guided by universal knowledge.

The messengers who are working with us will be committed to transmitting to you the truth of the universe, but time will come when we, your Elder Brothers, will communicate directly with every one of you. Nothing nor anyone will be able to stop the energy advance called Evolution and Elevation. The universe that will properly drive this process and you will advance with it. The universe will neutralize any possible ill-negative interference to block it. The time of collection, Brothers, has come and it will take 7 thousand years Tera time to complete.

The Ayaplianos-Volunteers of the spacecraft, The Ayaplianos-Seramitas and our Brothers Interanos, Elohim (Guardians of Tera) have dictated this fourth book. They all belong to the Eighth Hierarchy of the Antimatter Reality of Alpha Centauri.

THE COSMIC ALIGNMENT
7 THOUSAND YEARS OF PREPARATION

21 phases of 333 years each (333.3333333)
is the time it will take you to leave the planet
and become part of the realities
of universal conscience.

CHAPTER I

THE COSMIC ALIGNMENT

Year: 2014
Month: July
Day: 7

You and planet Tera have to prepare for the Cosmic Alignment announced in these books. Each phase takes 333 years and has its particular characteristics in order to show you how to proceed. You may think that the changes about to occur within yourselves and the Tera-Cell are exclusive in the universe. You may also believe that you are the only ones to undergo a process of transformation...Far from certain, brothers. The universe itself with all its life forms is suffering identical changes, in a continuous cycle of cell birth and death, thus revitalizing the energetic womb of *EL SER UNO*, and keeping it young, active, dynamic and... ***immortal***. The Cosmic Alignment is no other thing than the process of defining the form of energy that will connect you with the dynamic forces of the universe. Redefining energy when entering 2014 means to create connections with the energy of the cosmos that will absorb and adapt your energy to a wider range of recycling and expansion.

Universal knowledge has been within your reach at all times, but you have been dormant and unable of grasping the wisdom of the ancient.

Nevertheless, the elders are back, they have reincarnated, you are they, and you are the ancient Mayas, Greek, Egyptians, Lemurians and atlantes who are marking a new era of prosperity and elevation. You have made progress and your brain is working with a larger number of elevated thought-energies. This is activating your AWAKENING leading you to knowledge, understanding and universal love, wisdom of the ancient. In the past, few had that gift, today many do, for the benefit of all.

1. What does it mean to enter the Cosmic Alignment?

When we say that all thought-energies are sheltered in a huge Universal Mind, we mean that, upon joining the Cosmic Alignment, all your thought-energies will unite transmuting negative into positive and heading for the: *Universal Light*. While elevating, growing and sophisticating your thought-energies (souls) will reach the frequencies, rhythms and vibrations of other realties of existence. You are consciously preparing them so they can adapt to those higher frequencies where they will interact with others and together will elaborate and execute much more advanced ideas. The Cosmic Alignment does not just take place in the universe with the four dimensions aligning; it occurs at the same time in your minds where your inner sun (Pineal Gland) will adopt a vertical position between the two brain zones (solar system) and thus perfectly align with the four universal dimensions.

2. Why does the Cosmic Alignment start exactly July 7, 2014?

We, the Antimatter realities, do not use dates, but go by frequencies, vibrations, rhythms, colors etc. We help you define a proper position and the respective working schedule of your thought-energies, but also for a better understanding. The forces of the universe submit to the laws of mathematics and chemistry and the quality of their energy will determine frequency, vibration, rhythm and color. The date July 7, 2014 is the sequence of three sevens, i.e., 777. This is an important number of the Kabbala and you need to study it to learn about its significance in your lives. The date is the result of axiomatic and cosmic calculations marking the exact beginning of the Cosmic Alignment.

Number 7

Symbol of reflection, spirituality, conscience, wisdom, intellect, idealism, but also of oppression, hidden motives, reservedness, sarcasm, isolation, inflexibility and distraction.

The number 7 is compatible with and complementary to the number 3.

The number 7 is compatible with the number 8 as an effective alliance to reach diverse common objectives.

In the three books before we wanted you to learn about the origin of the universe and yourselves, who you are and where you came from but especially how to return to the origin of creation. There is not much time until the beginning of the Cosmic Alignment and you need to prepare for it. We have mentioned several times that you are bound to join a Cosmic Alignment of great magnitude commencing in the year 2014. We also emphasized that this would enable you to leave the planet and your energies become part of other, more advanced and elevated realities. Moreover, we told you that other planets for the same reason would welcome you and which would be those planets. However, to understand what joining the Cosmic Alignment represents we have to study the meaning of the term: *Alignment*.

Alignment: To put in a straight line, to be in line with a tendency, with relation to a certain ideology. Alignment means establishing equivalent sequences by comparison of forms between two or more structures of polymers (chemistry) based on their tridimensional conformation.

This definition will guide us in our understanding about the creation of the Tera-Cell. It will be subject to intense research the results of which will definitely change your attitude and be the beginning of an intense interaction. So far, there has been an energetic disassociation between yourselves, the Tera-Cell and the universe, because evolution and elevation had not yet reached the necessary degree of maturity. The universe moves, adapts, recycles, needs to expand and adjust to other realities, so that the energy, cells, organs and systems may continue their everlasting cycle.

You and the planet will start an unprecedented relationship in the annals of the cosmos. *EL SER UNO* (Being One) is recycling both of you so you may become part of an outstanding new concept for which elevated energy, vivid frequency, cadenced rhythm and very high vibration is needed. To understand the negative events that occur on the planet you should view them from different angles. You have to realize that for many of them humans have no responsibility and are therefore unable to solve them by just using positive thinking. In general, problems and actions have various aspects. Analyzing them allows a **broader vision** and thus a better understanding, in this case, of your and the planet's situation.

Many **ecological calamities** are the consequence of natural forces, others caused by human action out of ignorance or irresponsibility. To understand the fundamental changes of the planet we have to look at the Tera-Cell from a universal stand and consider how extraterrestrials may observe it. Tera is a cell of the universe's body and a youngster of only 5 billion years of age. It grows and develops turning from an adolescent into a young adult cell, building its material body and psyche. Watching your own young children grow and initiate the long journey to maturity may help you understand the process Tera is undergoing.

It is like having a look at a 15-year-old who is leaving his adolescence behind struggling to adapt to powerful physical and mental changes with cells multiplying, bones developing, blood and minerals nourishing his organism. The magnitude of changes is such that we could compare them to the force of earthquakes, heavy rains and floods.

This is what you see when you turn your view and mind to the universe: cells-planets, organisms-galaxies, systems-constellations, blood-energy, and the vivid image of the Womb of the Universe that we call **Macrocosm**. Most of what happens is the planet's natural course of life and part of its evolution. We have seen that Tera is a living organism and as such subject to cycles of growth, development, life and death as everything else in the universe.

Consequently, certain that the Tera-Cell is turning from adolescent into young adult, that is, evolving "normally", you may readily accept that many natural disasters are a consequence of growth and will repeat until the cell completes evolution. Henceforth the Tera-Cell will cease to grow and the process of evolution and cell definition stabilize. Nowadays all of you are in the middle of evolution and change as well, since you are the planet's mind. On the one hand, there is the Tera-Cell trying to evolve the best it can, on the other, you yourselves have started a process of change you call: *Awakening to Conscience*, which means that you are evolving physically and mentally the way Tera does.

Just like the planet, which is making a transition from adolescent to young adult, you *cease being adolescents to become young responsible adults*. This passage is usually full of pain and confusion. Adolescents are restive, unruly, whimsical, bad mannered, undisciplined, insecure, all of them typical attitudes of their age. Life is a never-ending challenge and the natural process of growing demands a change of these characteristics to foster physical and mental development. Nevertheless, they are not alone in this; their parents with their life experience, knowledge and understanding gathered over the years will be ready to help with their studies, correct nutrition and be patient and loving advisers when they have to cope with strong and difficult emotions.

All of you are bound to suffer this process called: Evolution. It means distress and pain and is sometimes of such severity that it forces you to analyze deeply situations to be able to understand. When you finally do, you grow and mature becoming adult persons with full conscience of their lives. Having said that the Tera-Cell is growing to become a young adult just the way you are, the problem is that as long as you continue being restive, rude, whimsical and terribly selfish adolescents you do not contribute to its mental and psychical growth in peace, harmony and love complicating, instead, its development by performing all kinds of barbaric action.

Now, as both you and the Tera-Cell are adolescents and about to turn young adults it is you, as thinking beings, who are responsible for the Tera-Cell in a manner a brother would be. In fact, you are the *Brothers of Tera*. Only that this relationship turned out to be the worst possible. When you, Ayaplianos, left your sideral home planet Tera was already here and at your arrival became your elder brother who gave you a warm welcome, nourished and sheltered you and helped you develop as a species.

3. Why do we have only 200 years to join the Cosmic Alignment?

We deal with Cause and Effect using mathematical and chemical calculations while you handle both with your thought-energies. These thought-energies are sheltered in the planet's magnetism and we can predict the frequency and vibration you produce, to determine the appropriate sound that will emanate from your thoughts. It is a high-pitched note that reaches the precise tune you need for the attraction to a more elevated reality. When we are saying that you only have 200 years, it is because those of you who will transcend have already been preparing for the last 150 thousand years. This preparation started with the appearance of the Neanderthals when the thought-energy became conscious of its existence. From that moment on, oneiric symbols developed understanding and produced the correlation resulting in what you are today.

It therefore will the Cosmic Alignment only take another 200 years to complete a perfect vertical line; however, those of you who do not manage to enter the Internal City during this lapse will be able to succeed during the following 7 thousand years. As a consequence, knowledge and understanding will be directed to the north, that is, toward the dome of *EL SER UNO* in the macrocosm, while in the microcosm both will be traveling to your heads (brains) nourishing your minds with new revelations of understanding and love. Heading north means that the cosmic and individual compass will guide you by using all its power to convey raw material, that is, universal, planetarian and individual thought-energies to the heads (brains) so that they may create progressive ideas.

4. Is it true that the polarity of the planet's magnetic axis will change?

Yes. In *EL SER UNO II – Planet 3.3.3. – The Guardians of Tera*, we explained that the minute hand of the six-pointed star would take the disincarnated thought-energies (souls) in a clockwise movement to the southern cone for purification and healing. After this, they would return

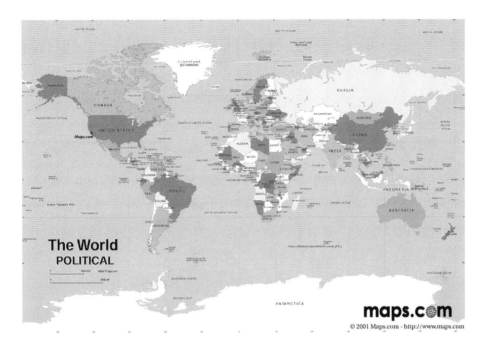

The World
POLITICAL

maps.c●m
© 2001 Maps.com - http://www.maps.com

to the exterior to incarnate and continue their learning process and elevation. These thought-energies (souls) would awake to conscience and eventually conceive their spirit. The minute hand would take them to the northern cone (the planet's dome) where the souls prepare to leave the planet, conducted by the second hand, in order to enter a reality of existence we have termed: *The Internal City*.

Nowadays the majority of thought-energies (souls that inhabit the left side of the brain) gathers in the southern cone. As a result, most of their energy occupy the left side of the planetary brain. After purification and elevation of their frequency and vibration, these souls (thought-energies) turn much lighter and, heading for the northern cone, will relieve the southern cone. This will cause the magnetic axis of Tera to revert its position, as the majority of souls (thought-energies) is now on the northern cone, that is, on the right side of the brain thus giving Tera's brain equilibrium and stability. This will also stabilize the planet's electromagnetism and change at the same time the power of gravitation from the left to the right side of the brain.

Incarnations will occur following the course of a figure eight (infinity), for example: If a soul incarnates in Europe, its next incarnation will be

21

in South America. After that in North America, then in Africa or Australia, Indonesia, Japan, China, Russia, Greenland, Iceland and restart in Europe, time and again, until completing the preparation of its energy.

The degree of elevation of frequency, vibration, rhythm and colors and passing the crossing point of the figure eight will determine whether it will go to the vortex of the northern or southern cone. It will then use the passage of the umbilical cord and initiate a journey toward a lighter or denser reality of existence. We have stated that, to be the first to head for the Internal City, you must elevate your thought-energies, form your spirit and transcend your present reality in the next 200 years. This means that you need at least two or three more incarnations. Following the line of the figure eight, symbol of infinity, you will know in what part of the planet these incarnations will occur.

The journey the souls realize across the planet compares to the displacement of the thought-energies within your microcosm. The two cones of the universe-man are the energy center of procreation (reproductive system) on the southern cone (left side brain) and the energy center of creation on the northern cone (right side brain). The figure eight crossing point lies in the solar plexus. This is where the thought-energies determine whether to choose the path of creation (north) or procreation (south).

So far, the thought-energies move freely from the left to the right side and vice versa. Then they start connecting and interacting and finally unite at the point of the figure eight where the Pineal Gland is located. This is where you form your spirit, provided the majority of your thought-energies be elevated enough for the right side of the brain and help it gestate the baby-spirit. There are no geographical zones such as North, South, East and West in planet cells. Instead, we classify the planets in terms of gravity, frequency, rhythm and colors and know when they originate from zones or centers of weak energy. When we refer to the Northern or Southern Cone, we actually mean thought-energies (souls) of high or very low frequency respectively, but considering there may be mixtures of both.

When the planet changes the polarity of its axis, you will do likewise. Thought-energies that occupy zones 1, 2 and 3 of the brain and correspond to the respective energy centers below the solar plexus will elevate to inhabit zones 4, 5 and 6 related to the energy centers above the same. This means that part of the thought-energies of instinct and sensation, that is, energy of procreation will elevate and turn energy of creation.

5. What does the change of polarity of the axis mean to us?

The thought-energy that many of you use for mere procreation (sexual activity) and the satisfaction of material desires will suffer transmutation and be concentrated on creativity and the development of mental and, above all, spiritual strength. Thus, though-energies of the highest value will properly nurture and gestate the emerging spirit (Baby-Spirit).

We certainly do not refer to the renouncement of physical pleasure, but to the fact that this act of intimacy should be one of love, intelligence and creativity because it would profoundly mark your hearts and souls and the pleasure of the Ego become Ecstasy of Love. The emerging spirit will draw the largest possible number of elevated thought-energies from the human mind. This is why we insist so much on spiritual nourishment, which are Knowledge, Understanding and Love that the energy sheltered by the Pineal Gland needs to grow the way an infant would.

The Internal City will welcome this spirit in gestation, which will be staying on planet Tera, Venus and Mercury equal periods to complete the total time of gestation. It will grow strong and as soon as it reaches its peak of development continue its passage by exiting through the Solar Pineal Gland and heading for other elevated realities during this journey of eternal existence. In the universe, the human species will undergo nine metamorphoses; the One Origin created it this way. These metamorphoses represent the centers of energy of *EL SER UNO* (Being One).

The thought-energies (souls) of the universal body of *EL SER UNO* travel all of the centers of energy following the figure eight (infinity) over and again, ascending and descending, until they become a being of LIGHT. This is where the Energetic Being returns to the One Origin, its creator, recovering its center, but now replete with Knowledge, Understanding and Love, to share with the creator the infinite experience gathered along the eternal path of life.

You have traveled these path innumerable times but lost track of them because of the density of your environment and the disease called Distortion. Now you have started recalling and many of you realize that they are returning and that it is of great importance for them to know the reason they are in this reality and that this reality is only part of their eternal existence.

6. How can we recognize that our electromagnetism is changing?

There will be changes in both your physical and psychical bodies. In this extraordinary process of transformation many of your negative emotions will change rather quietly which will make you feel easy, relieved and in complete peace with your inner self and everything around you. One of the most visible signs is that you will clearly perceive deep changes in your zodiacal constellations, in the reading of the astrological charts. Why do we emphasize this? Because, by changing the polarity of the axis of human nature, you will convert negative-emotional into positive-psychical energy. Let us see what this means...

Every one of you has a zodiacal sign according to the day and year of birth. As of the year 2014, these signs will suffer changes and the astrological charts be in an upside-down position since from now on new energies will rule your lives.

From 2014 on, the beings whose conscience has awaked will feel profound and meaningful alterations in their souls, a consequence of astrological energy changes and considering the magnitude of the imminent Cosmic Alignment. With the change of the energetic axis' polarity in every one of you the negative energy of your zodiacal sign turns positive in the corresponding opposite sign, as follows:

Aries	Libra	(Fire – Air)
Taurus	Scorpio	(Earth – Water)
Gemini	Sagittarius	
Cancer	Capricorn	
Leo	Aquarius	
Virgo	Pisces	
Libra	Aries	

Scorpio   Taurus
Sagittarius Gemini
Capricorn   Cancer
Aquarius   Leo
Pisces   Virgo

To understand what we are trying to point out, you have to study the negative traits of your sign striving to transmute them into the positive ones of the opposite sign. For instance:

Aries negative - impatient, impulsive, dominant, imprudent, irritable, violent, intolerant, unsteady, impertinent, tactless, aggressive.
Which you should transmute, as indicated above, into the opposite Libra Positive.

Libra Positive - have interpersonal skills such as being cooperative, sociable, delicate, tactful, sophisticated, preoccupied with people, partners and team work, sensitive to esthetics and arts, mediators and peacemakers.

Libra Negative - indecisive, undisciplined, frivolous, impressionable, superficial, flirty, indolent, go to great lengths, dislike commitment and taking sides, apathetic, lacking resolve, craving for admiration.
Which you should transmute into the opposite Aries Positive.

Aries Positive - do not depend on social acceptance, entrepreneurs, pioneers, compensate impatience and lack of perseverance through high amount of energy, spirited, passionate, give encouragement, independent, active, daring. Quick reaction, trust their strength and disregard obstacles, fighters, emotional, hate and love intensely, great self-confidence and self-discipline, do not like routine jobs, love challenges, straightforward, courageous.

Taurus Negative - avaricious, obstinate, choleric, extremely conservative, slow, keen on easy money, resentful, possessive, limited, materialists.
Which you should transmute into the opposite Scorpio Positive.

Scorpio Positive - analysts, investigators, great ability of reasoning, natural psychologists, given to intuition, open to self-criticism, intense feelings and emotions, curious, great imagination, perceptive, great physical strength, determined, great charisma.

We will not list them all and suggest that you study your signs. You will be surprised to find that you probably will have to work hard on a good deal of negative aspects to level off with your positive opposite sign, that is, balance the left (Mars) and right side (Venus) of your brain. Your task will be to discover, which aspects are to be changed and proceed according to the findings. This is how you will transform your emotions into feelings.

Following consciously our indications, the positive thought-energies will predominate and, nourishing one another, gradually take the place of the negative ones. So far, we have mainly been drawing your attention to negative thoughts. Now we want to concentrate on the positive ones to give your souls the strength to keep on with the task the universe has entrusted to you.

7. Would our interference with the planet's electromagnetism affect mathematical calculations and chemical formulas?

Your interference would have to be in a large scale to unbalance the planet's electromagnetism. The emanation of ill negative thought-energies could unbalance the electromagnetism of yourselves and, at the same time, that of the planet. Nevertheless, we should be optimistic as, so far, an enormous number of healthy positive thought-energies has hindered a possible major unbalance. It is that some of your governments are testing machinery, which is not yet totally operative, however, when it is, will definitely interfere with the planet's electromagnetism. One of the devices is the Large Hadron Collider (LHC), the other the HAARP project.

These machines represent hazard because you do not have full knowledge of their operational details, thus, running the risk to misjudge possible consequences for you and the planet. If you lose control, the outcome would be disastrous. The day your scientists do interfere with the electromagnetism we, the Volunteers-Ayaplianos, actually could not define the extent of this unbalance. It would rather be our Brothers Seramitas and Interanos' concern who are in charge by taking measures that would guarantee the planet's safety.

Do not worry. At least during the first 333 years of the cosmic alignment, there will be no such mishap since our brothers and we will never allow the operation of these machines to jeopardize the planet and its population.

8. Are you intervening to avoid that the machines perform at a 100%?

We, the Volunteers-Ayaplianos of the spacecraft are not taking action, but the Seramitas and Interanos will by blocking a 100 % performance of the equipment, because they have full knowledge of what would happen to you and the planet. We did send you innumerable messages to stop dangerous experiments, but your scientists' capacity to see, hear and speak, has been seriously affected by ego and ambition, to the extent, that they seem to ignore the risks involved.

9. What will our Brothers Seramitas and Interanos do to avoid a 100 % performance of these machines?

The knowledge of electromagnetism our Brothers Seramitas and Interanos have is such that they use it for entries and exits. Electromagnetism commands the universe, allows thought-energies to move freely and is the source of energy for the mental spacecraft, the Orbs and the cycle of life and existence. While on the planet, the electromagnetism's source is a gigantic magneto, in the universe it is the vibration frequency of the energy.

To intervene the Seramitas and Interanos would be using magnetism to interfere with the operation. Thus, your scientists would be unable to conduct experiments at full load (100 %). Thought-energies, mental-spacecrafts, Orbs, frequencies, vibrations, and life rhythms, existence of the universe are produced by the electromagnetism.

Problems, however, may arise when the positive thought-energies (souls) leave Tera for the Internal City of Venus because, after that, the planet will suffer a certain decrease of electromagnetism.

The Reptilian force could take advantage using the machines to control and manipulate those thought-energies (souls) that continue on the planet.

10. Is there any relation between natural disasters such as earthquakes, tsunamis and hurricanes and the Cosmic Alignment?

Absolutely. The Tera-Cell is making adjustments and growing because it is preparing to ascend to universal frequencies of superior energy vibration, rhythm and colors with an extraordinary energy increase that will help it dominate a gravity, which held it prisoner for millions of years. What is happening to the Tera-Cell is a reflection of yourselves. As we know, the planet's brain is a cumulus of billions of incarnated and disincarnated thought-energies whose heavy influence overly affects the psychical behavior of the planet's brain as well as that of human beings. The Tera-Cell reacts by reproducing energetic activities you have developed and recorded.

Yet we have to remark that there is responsibility on your part. Planet Tera is a living cell and any negative (harmful) action from your side has an enormous impact on it. Air pollution; ozone layer shrinking; global warming; greenhouse effect; contamination of oceans, rivers and lakes; use of LHC and HAARP, breeding animals for sacrifice; large scale fumigation; experiments with toxic products: warfare using bacteriological arms. All this is in heavy detriment of the planet.

11. Who will control the electromagnetism of the planet and where will the disincarnated souls be?

Until now, the Planet-Tera-Brain's evolution has been a **natural** one in accordance with an existential process of its own and maintained functions of both the left and right side in the usual manner. The negative-reptilian-force has dominated and manipulated the humans of the planet using psychology and slyness, so far. This, however, might change in the future. The negative force is losing its capacity of manipulation because many humans are awaking by recognizing their errors and the untrue life they were living.

Losing control and realizing that shrewdness does not work the way it did before, the ill-negative force is going to be more drastic employing mind and electromagnetism control equipment to keep many of you working for it in a state of extreme dependence. When the Reptilian force definitely controls the minds of those who will not transcend this reality in the next 200 years and, therefore, will have to stay on, life apparently continues the same.

However, there will be a frightening difference between the present and the near future, because the disincarnating souls will have to go to the left side of the planet's brain, as the right side will start to shrink for lack of activity and due to an alarming density of the thought-energies (souls) that feed it. What we want to make clear is that the human beings' brain, while controlled and manipulated by machines, will only function with its left side. The right side tends to shrink as it remains without activity and will finally cease to exist which means that the planet's electromagnetism will vanish leaving behind just gravity. This gravity is going to be the force that will determine the path the human species will travel between the years 2300 and 2800.

12. Recently, countries like Guatemala, Portugal and China detected enormous holes. What could have caused them?

You need to understand that the planet's magnetism is not very stable. We, therefore, are blocking your high risk LHC and HAARP tests, which interfere with the electromagnetism, that is, the overall electrical power source and thus with the natural vibration of the planet. The two experiments attract and concentrate large amounts of antimatter energy, which would cause explosions when making contact with the planet's surface. You have been observing this electromagnetic phenomenon in the atmosphere calling it ORBS.

These Orbs, so far, do not mean any hazard as they originate from energy that accumulates and after some time just vanishes. What your scientists ignore is that the antimatter energy also draws nitrogen from the atmosphere. The combination of both results in a powerful compound, which would hit the planet at an extreme speed like a bomb of nitrogen.

Nitrogen: Molecular nitrogen, a chemical element with the atomic number 7 and the symbol *N* is under normal conditions a colorless inert gas and the principal constituent (abt. 78 %) of the planet's atmosphere. This concentration results from a combination of bacterial, electric and chemical action. Nitrogen is a component of all vegetal and animal organisms. The human body contains approx. 3 % nitrogen. Scientific studies indicate the existence of nitrogen and nitrogen isotope-14 compounds of extraterrestrial origin. An important chemical compound of nitrogen with hydrogen is ammonia used in the manufacture of fertilizers, synthetic fibers and explosives.

Being nitrogen an element of vital importance to the planet you may easily understand why our brothers Seramitas and Interanos will decidedly block any experiment that could result in a tragic cataclysm. The formation of the holes is a consequence of the violent impact of the compound of nitrogen in reaction with antimatter energy on the planet's surface related to experiments that four of your governments have conducted in restricted areas. You sure have noticed that these holes are perfectly round.

At this point, we have to refer to what we earlier said about ORBS. What looks like an electromagnetic phenomenon is actually an operation we conduct introducing precise controls into the Orbs to lower their impact creating perfect round figures you call CROP CIRCLES. The amount of nitrogen we use will not cause any damage to the ground. It will not cut crops just bend them. In the second part of this book, we will extensively deal with this topic.

13. What is actually behind the tests run by governments?

Many governments of this planet are preparing for a possible third world war and consider that the LHD and HAARP technologies will guarantee them superior military power but also prevent a possible "invasion of extraterrestrials". At the same time, they have total awareness of our presence in the Magnetism of the planet and the Solar System and know that we do not represent any danger to the human species and the planet. Governments of the planet know about us. They also know that we would not hurt you, but they do not just believe it.

What they do fear is our persistent work to help an ever-growing number of you free from a dependence that has lasted thousands of years. These governments know exactly what they do, as the new technologies will allow them total control of Electricity, the Magnetism and thus people's minds. ***They are the Reptilian Force that will never give up on the domination of this planet using science, technology, religion, money etc.***

You were born slaves, but never knew. You think you are free, but you are not. You all work for an immense number of big corporations that run this planet. Your dependence is absolute, from the day of birth until your disincarnation. From the very day you enter the reality of this planet, you are registered and monitored.

You have 200 years to awake to conscience and prepare for departure since during this time the Reptilian Force will not be able to gain full knowledge of the new technologies. If you fail, you will have to wait, during another extended period, for a new chance to free yourselves. Remember! The Reptilian Force has great knowledge of electric power and magnetism making every effort to turn the control over you and the planet into an absolute one. Those of you who still do not awake during this second phase of the Cosmic Alignment will remain in the darkness of ignorance.

That is why we insist so much on your awakening. For, once you have formed your spirit, no Reptilian knowledge can ever exert power on you; their power waves will be without effect as the frequency and vibration of your spirit will reject them thus blocking their influence and mental manipulation. The governments of this planet do know: those who control electric power are going to dominate electromagnetism...and shall be the future masters of the world.

14. Will the Reptilian force dominate the electromagnetism?

Today the planet's electromagnetism shelters myriads of thought-energies (souls). These souls have been incarnating and disincarnating for a long time in order to elevate their energies. In the next 200 years, the souls who conceived their baby-spirit will disincarnate and enter the planet's electromagnetism. There they will wait for the energetic vortex of the Northern Cone to open and head for the Internal City of Venus. The Reptilian force knows that these souls are sheltered in the electromagnetism and is trying to develop the HAARP Project to block their departure and dominate, at the same time, the incarnated thought-energies in the exterior. Total control over the electromagnetism does not only mean an immense advance in science and technology, but absolute power over everything in the future that is, over all living beings and the very planet.

15. Will the Reptilian Force really gain all this power?

Brothers, the Reptilian force has subdued you for thousands of years. Trust us they will gain this power! It is, however, not only through arms that domination occurs. The Reptilian force has always used food, water, communication (radio, TV, newspapers, internet), politics, religion, ecology, etc. to create dependence and/or false ideas to keep you weak, dormant, ignorant and, thus, malleable.

You have become addicts consuming enormous amounts of chemicals added to whatever you drink and eat. These chemicals are intended to: sterilize you, make you sick, dependent, vitiate you through repetitive habits, schematize, and brainwash you. They do all these through advertising, cinema, television, radio, the internet, gases in the atmosphere, and more.

Vaccines, considered efficient health protection by most humans, are another forceful means of control, but many of them have not only been developed in an unethical manner; they also are increasingly questioned for being ineffective or causing even serious side effects; but all this never affected the generous returns they produce for the pharmaceutical industry. Furthermore, there are the considerable stocks of bacteriological weapons, a good number of them employed by criminal governments against independence movements. The most efficient way of controlling the Reptilian Force discovered is the technology of information and communication being the cell phone one of the devices that excels.

This equipment widely used for communication and intended to foster human relations has also turned an excellent instrument of personal data registry and monitoring in the hands of the negative force.

The LHC equipment is constantly tested and improved and the HAARP and other projects developed in total secrecy affecting already the frequency of natural electromagnetic waves of the planet. You are witnessing the painful consequences: drastic climate change, severe and unusual droughts and floods, major frequency of tornados, earthquakes, tsunamis, continual reduction of the ozone layer and one of the biggest ecological disasters caused by the oil extracting industry at the Mexican gulf, in decades.

What seemed to have been an enormous operational mishap there, caused by an explosion of gas at the bottom of a large well, had actually been the consequence of unstable waves from tests with HAARP, which affected the electromagnetism of the area causing a violent movement and rupture of a tectonic plate in that area. This occurrence will leave the tectonics with permanent instability.

Further consequences from these large-scale tests for your and the planet's electromagnetism are: frequent headaches, nausea, severe muscle and bone pain, hair loss, weakness, stress, depression, heart and lung ailment and signs of new diseases to develop in the near future. We shall therefore keep a close eye on such projects as: holography and time traveling technologies; under no circumstances, shall we allow the Reptilian force to make use of them; the respective large-scale tests involve the massive use of electromagnetism through light, sound, vibration and colors and are therefore banned by the cosmic entities.

By decision of the Superior Dimensions, the Cosmic Interstellar Confederation is not to intervene in such projects; yet magnetism is sacred because we all live within; it is our very source of life in the Regular, Secondary and Primary Dimensions, the home of all of us. During the first 200 years as of 2014, the Reptilian force shall be very anxious to improve these technologies running as many the tests as necessary to reach its goals.

We, the Ayaplianos, shall do everything in our power to block these plans. However, after the departure of the positive-elevated thought-energies now sheltered in the planet's electromagnetism, we shall not be able to assist you during the following phase, which will be extremely hard for those who have to stay on because they will live in a state of total dependence and domination. As of the third phase in 2800, with the advent of the avatar Abigahel, we shall resume our task to help you free yourselves by striving to eliminate from Tera ill-negative energy sending it to Mars where it is to remain forever. Thus, those of you who had been staying behind will enter the fourth phase: ready and conscious in order to continue on the path of elevation during the remainder of the 7 thousand years.

Since the Reptilian force will have completely dominated during the second phase, the number 666 is the figure of evil meaning humans' total submission to the ill-negative force through the Reptilian force's abuse of magnetic waves from 2300 to 2800. This second phase of the Cosmic Alignment will mark an overall loss of freedom, equilibrium and love, manipulation and terror. At the end of that phase the dominant and manipulating Reptilian-governments, however, will prohibit the use of the equipment because humans will start to suffer considerable loss of vitality and a further intensive use of the "Machines of Domination" is feared to lead to lasting negative-energetic mental limitations and at the same time have devastating consequences for the planet.

In the future, nations' governments shall make pacts to guarantee maximum control of their citizens. There will be no more birth certificates, IDs, passports etc. as chip implants with all personal data will be mandatory. Marked that way forever, humans lose freedom and privacy; work, marriage, number of children, housing, trips, every part of their social life, will be monitored. Any intent to remove the chip will be subject to prosecution. Voluntary chip implants with information for emergencies already exist and their upgrading would be easy.

16. Will there be time machines and holography in the future?

The time machine as well as holography have always been the dream of many scientists. Today science is on the verge of discovering the secrets of time traveling; the development of holography is already advancing with the help of 3D technology. In the future, 3D will be the unparalleled   technology   for   the   development   of   virtual communication and be omnipresent in humans' daily routine. The virtual environment of holography will be so lively that humans will have difficulty to tell real from unreal. It will be extremely effective and guarantee the ill-negative force overwhelming control during the second phase of the Cosmic Alignment. Humans will plunge into deep illusion and unreality and end up in a strange state of unawareness and frantic that will compromise the way they are facing the reality of their existence.

Time traveling will only be possible in the future. Humans always thought to be able to do it with their physical bodies. For the time being, the only possible way is to use the psychical body. Yet even knowing how to proceed, you would not succeed because of the instability of the electromagnetism. Time traveling maybe intended when both thought-energies and electromagnetism of the Tera-Cell are stable.

Since humans fail to have a true notion of Cause and Effect, time traveling becomes impossible. The very first thing they have to do is to stabilize their electromagnetic field and connect it in a harmonious way with the electromagnetism of the planet. By the time the thought-energies enter the Tera-planet-brain, the time traveler will access the akashic archive that holds every thoroughly recorded experience of human thought-energies and the planet. The traveler would not only have to grasp their history and vast knowledge, but also accompany their movements and changing positions.

The Tera-planet-brain archives any of the thought-energies' experiences precisely the way they occurred. Accessing the Akashic Archive, you will obtain knowledge of the past with its impact on the future based on Cause and Effect, in no time. However, your problem will be with the changing present that may produce millions of possible outcomes for the future. The present is transforming the past and the future in a fraction of a second. At this point you have to resort to the Theory of Relativity (mass, dimension and time will change with increased velocity) which implies that this extremely fast movement actually cannot be measured in terms of time.

Look at it his way! You may correct the past because the present is mentally changing, by transposition, of what has happened. This means that the future will also be subject to continuous variations of cause and effect. This is why divination very often fails. Many clairvoyants perceive the result of cause and effect of the present based on the cause and effect of the past from which they erroneously draw conclusions for an immediate future outcome. Owing to the fact that the thought-energies change continuously and that the seer has to make the divination in almost no time the result is going to vary, too. Many times, divination does work because a certain number of thought-energies had remained stable leaving the past, present and future invariable.

You live in the **X Factor – which is Probability**. This means that, being your thought-energies unstable, you are inconsequent, unsteady, insecure. The electromagnetism of the planet nurtures itself with your thought-energies and as long as you do not manage to stabilize them, time traveling is beyond reach. Time traveling, as you call it, can take you only to the past that is, making available events stored and maintained without variation in the Akashic Archive. Time traveling can never take you to the future, which is erratic and uncertain. Remember, you live in the X Factor. Thus, you may never be sure to receive the correct answer because of constant variation. This is the big problem of time traveling.

17. Do you do time traveling?

You have to understand that everything existing in the universe, that is, living beings and any other life form are inside an unimaginable and immense... Universal Mind. With this in mind, we may try to understand what time traveling is like. The Universal Mind has a Cosmic Akashic Archive of its own, incommensurable and infinite. All that happens in your minds happens in the Universal Mind, but at an unconceivable speed. The reality of the Universal Mind is eternal and incomprehensible to many life forms. Trying to imagine the Universal Mind, we find millions of thought-energies (souls and spirits) moving, giving it life and assuring it eternal existence. The Universal Mind divides in zones with highly defined characteristics. Parts of every zone shelter thought-energies (spirits) which are constituents of the Cosmic Akashic Archive or memory of this great mind. Part of the Universal Mind's thought-energies (souls and spirits) live within the changes as they are undergoing the process of cosmic learning, are touring the zones, striving tirelessly for a profound comprehension of existence and working to extend and perfect this eternal source of wisdom. They are the star travelers that seek the essence of life and existence, are spirits that travel back and forth, zone by zone, in an eternal cycle of elevation. On the other hand, there are thought-energies (souls and spirits) that live in the harmonious quietness of this mind, which means that they are well defined, having assimilated during their never-ending journey universal wisdom in profusion. Time traveling for the spirit is easy since it is moving fast, eventually adapting to the circumstances of any reality it accesses, and being able to adjust velocity as its frequency and vibration show affinity with the universal reality.

The psychical body (soul) has not the same capacity to adjust to the velocity of the Universal Mind and only can adapt to the circumstances of a planetary mind provided the thought-energies that inhabit the electromagnetism of that planet are stable and in harmony. This is the only way for it to move in the past, present and future, which eventually are just one... the Present. We, the Ayaplianos-Volunteers and the Seramitas are Energy Beings (spirits). We are able to move beyond the velocity of light, since we do this at the velocity of thoughts. When you gain full knowledge of what energy really means you will understand that much of your scientists' successful research depends on the harmony of body, soul and spirit, and that important advances of science must always go along with spiritual progress.

18. Why are they running tests with HAARP technology at the Mexican gulf?

The objective of the HAARP Project is not only to control the electromagnetism and the humans' mind. Since your governments have proof of the ruins of the City of Atlantida, they are employing the HAARP technology to determine their exact location. This machine caused the disaster in the Mexican Gulf.

The discovery of the City of Atlantida will occur after 2014 but be a secret. Therefore, pay attention because everything the dark force will find there, it will use to continue domination and manipulation. The intense use of the magnetic waves, however, recently caused a large oil spill from an offshore well. While the public considered it an accident with severe ecological consequences, the ill-negative-Reptilian force took advantage of this interpretation using it as camouflage of what it was in reality doing, searching for the City of Atlántida.

19. We have noted that the ill negative-Reptilian energy aims at reducing the population employing massively unhealthy food, vaccines, sterilization, warfare, etc. Are we correct?

Yes. To tell the truth, this has been common practice at all times; it is only now that the humans of good are finding out because they are awaking. Wars and annihilation of human lives were and still are inevitable consequences of political strategies by many governments and at the same time a sinister manner of keeping control. Many of the events, that are taking the public by surprise, occur to keep a close watch on the number of inhabitants and the distribution of wealth across the planet. Power has stirred wars and justified invasions of sovereign countries boosting arms sales. Abuse and illegal enrichment are the consequences.

However, what governments have been unable to dominate is the inherent and immense power of nature because of their still limited knowledge of this planet. If they had the control, they would have used it for very specific objectives a long time ago. Nevertheless, if you fail to awake, they shall advance without the slightest doubt. You have to be extremely alert. Most processed food you consume is nutritious including vitamins and proteins but also contains inconvenient and even harmful concentrations of salt, sugar, fats as well as preservatives, coloring matters and artificial flavoring. Many of these chemicals cheat on the brain by making the food very tasty but creating dependence. There is a good deal of information on the food labels and you have to study it always very carefully.

Food, when it is processed, automatically loses vitamins and nutritional elements. Many of them, when cooked or boiled, produce the disappearance of the natural nutrients that the food had. Then the factories chemically supplement the unevenness and lack of these nutrients, and they do it because the Ministry of Health requires it. All processed food is not natural and when they put chemical nutrients such as: flavorings, preservatives and more, you become dependent on them.

We are aware that it is often difficult for you to find real fresh food in your big cities; but you have to try hard and limit processed food on your menu. Because your health is on stake.

There is evidence that beams, which emanate from good food, have been photographed using special equipment. What is visible is the radiant energy of photosynthesis whose photons in reaction with carbon dioxide form carbohydrates. Especially green vegetables have a very high nutritious value. In a certain way, you are subject to chemical reactions, which very much resemble photosynthesis. This chemical process has its origin in your soul, which projects the Sun light on your body helping, thus, with the conception of the baby-spirit. The atoms of your body and mind absorb the sunrays and, with this, each atom emits its own beam clarifying the crystals which, when receiving the photons initiate the alchemical transformation and metamorphosis of the emerging spirit.

20. How does photosynthesis work within us?

The photosynthesis starts to develop in our reflections. This means that the crystals forming the thought-energy (soul) start becoming transparent through understanding facilitating the attraction of the sunrays, which then pass through the crystals feeding body and mind with photons.

Photosynthesis from the ancient Greek "union" is the conversion of photonic energy to stable chemical energy. Besides, we have to remember that the fundaments of life on this planet are the action of marine algae and plants with the capacity of synthesizing organic matter (essential for the existence of living organisms) using sunlight and inorganic matter. (Wikipedia)

We want you to understand the convenience of turning vegetarians in order to favor the absorption of photons, as it is through the consumption of mainly vegetables that you will permit direct access of the sunlight (photons) to your organism. This change of nutrition guarantees you an important increase of vegetal protein, which will help your body cells develop greater capacity of absorption of the sunlight.

We must emphasize, that solar winds, electromagnetism, climate change, air pollution, global warming, greenhouse effect and other factors with widely negative consequences for the planet and the humans, on the other hand, contribute to boosting the performance of photosynthesis in the human organism. This chemical process will initiate a whole new era of evolution for humans, animals, plants and the environment. Changes are necessary and imminent so that you and the planet can cope with the energetic transformation already announced and which many of you are closely watching.

21. What will be a major tool the Reptilian force will use to dominate the humans and the planet?

Besides all the others mentioned earlier the Reptilian force's principal tool shall be the struggle for the total control of *The Internet*. Controlling the Internet vigilance shall be absolute. All of you who are awaking now and during the next 200 years have to thank the universe for the help received in the process. Those who will have to stay on the second phase, from 2347 until the year 2800, shall suffer great hardship.

It is of great importance for you to know how the thought-energy works. At present, the internet's structure is incomplete; thus, the information fed to the net is still moving in an uncontrolled manner across its system. You have not yet validated nor consolidated the thought-energies of the net. The Internet, ever since, has been expanding so fast, by storing millions and millions of data that it is starting to turn what you will call *Artificial Brain* intended to commanding the thought-energies of planet Tera in the near future. However, to develop the necessary faculties of thinking and discerning it has to continue accumulating even larger amounts of data.

The brain of planet Tera, so far, has functioned "naturally" with the thought-energies of all living beings on its surface. While you think, the electromagnetism of your brain creates thought-energies, which, to keep on existing, have to join up with the electromagnetism of the planetary brain. Thus, you still are free. In the time to come, but mostly during the second phase of the Cosmic Alignment, the souls (thought-energies) that have not transmuted shall be stuck with the planet revolving in a vicious circle of unreality and phantasy because they are not commanded by a "natural" brain but by Artificial Intelligence which also will control the planet's electromagnetism.

The Reptilian force shall manipulate and dominate them by taking total advantage of the millions and millions of thought-data stored in the monstrous artificial intelligence: The Internet. Today, nevertheless, you still are in a condition to free yourselves and leave, but if you fail, you definitely shall have to bear the oppression of the Reptilian force with all the suffering, pain and loss of freedom for some 500 years.

22. There will be then control by Machines as shown in some science-fiction movies?

Yes, in a way, this might happen. Nowadays, you are beginning to live on the verge of this reality; however, the machines have not yet taken over. Moreover, they will not unless humans let them. Technology is highly positive when humans use and control it with responsibility. All inventions, discoveries and technologies are beneficial when designed for the advance of the collectivity and the planet.

23. If after the 7 thousand years of Cosmic Alignment, only 600 million people will live on the planet, how will it function with such a drastically reduced population?

As mentioned before the Reptilian force shall have the dominion over the planet and its inhabitants until about 2800. Around that year an avatar by the name of Abigahel (Michael) arrives who will restore freedom and hope. It is the beginning of a new era. Millions of enslaved human beings will recover liberty, make progress and evolve. Unfortunately, a great many of them will be unable to elevate. Having suffered manipulation for generations, partial atrophy of their brains' right side impedes understanding of love, essential for elevation.

The number of inhabitants will decrease over the next one thousand years to about half of what it is today and totaling 600 million by the end of the Cosmic Alignment. Of the 600 million, half are positively evolved thought-energies who will disincarnate and enter the electromagnetism of the planet and later incarnate in the Yeti whom they will feed and help evolve.

When incarnating they get another chance to elevate and, overcoming a possible period of stagnation, continue their search for higher realities. The universal body of *EL SER UNO* (Being One) will absorb and recycle the disincarnated thought-energies that could not be saved. This reduced population with the help of such advanced technology will multiply its efficiency by 10. Humans will thus be able to concentrate on science and technology as a priority. As a further compensation to the reduced number of inhabitants, people will increase their life span up to 200 years.

24. When the creatures of Alfa Nova receive those recycled thought-energies (souls), we understand that they will start to evolve and eventually elevate. What will then be the destiny of Luzbel and Lucifer ¿ Will they continue to exist?

We have to realize that Luzbel and Lucifer are neither entities nor incarnations on the planet corrupting and striking humans with illness. Nor are they the fallen angels resembling ugly bats. They actually stand for distorted ill-negative emotions, which have proliferated and incarnated in humans in the form of thought-energies.

It is true that the planets Tera, Alfa Nova and Ebiares are going to transmute these sick energies. The effect of positive thinking will entirely heal them and Luzbel and Lucifer shall vanish from history, memory and reality.

What the Universe has ***created is forever***. It loses nothing and transforms everything. Therefore, when you and the beings of the other planets will have managed to change ill negative to sound positive energies, all your "demons" will have become "angels". Luzbel and Lucifer are the Reptilian force that has run the planet, enslaving and dominating it. Its thought-energy has partly disincarnated and incarnated in you. It had not arrived by interplanetary spacecraft to conquer Tera; it was here long before we all set foot on this planet.

It is the most ancient thought-energy (souls) that reached the planet and took possession of it and of yourselves while you were staying on the outside, with your thought-energies suffering distortion. This is why the Reptilian thought-energy is part of yourselves and only you will be able to transform and heal it. At this moment of your lives, you are part "demons" (Reptilians-left side of the brain) and part "angels" (Aya-planos- right side of the brain). These two antagonic forces are the essence of the reality you live in and as long as the ill negative energy of planet Satien occupies this left side, you will feel divided.

It is something similar to schizophrenia; you live in two realities at the same time and, unfortunately, neither force functions well. One is ill negative, the other positive, but full of phantasy and illusion. This is why you are living a serious dilemma: you have, by your own free will, to choose either one or the other.

25. We received 150.000 years ago thought-energies from planet Cyrius. However, which planets will send thought-energies (souls) to the Yeti to help him evolve and elevate?

The yeti as well as the gorilla, the chimpanzee, the kuturo ape and the Malaysian monkey will not need help from other realities of the universe the way you did since the Yeti can count on the support of those same thought-energies (souls) from Tera that will not succeed in elevating during the Cosmic Alignment. The lack of elevation did not affect their development and they are therefore apt to help the Yeti make progress. Consequently, the Yeti's advance will be much faster than yours, which had been slow and difficult, and even required the support of the Cosmic Confederation 150.000 years ago, since your species had been the first to be in recuperation.

If your willpower of creation is genuine and deep during the 200 years, it will **guarantee you the departure** from planet Tera. However, should you fail to reach this state you will have to work hard to develop your thought-energies all along the 7 thousand years of the

Cosmic Alignment to be able to leave the Internal City of Tera for the Internal City of Venus.

By the end of the 7 thousand years, the positive thought-energies (souls) start entering the Internal City of Tera through the Northern Cone to get ready for their definite cosmic journey. But all those thought-energies (souls) which at this point have not reached the nineth grade of vibration, necessary to leave the planet, shall inevitably incarnate in the Yeti.

Finally, the negative thought-energies (ill souls) which, despite all given opportunities, could not at all manage to elevate, will migrate to the Southern Cone to leave for Mars. After wandering from planet to planet of the Solar System, they will eventually depart for another reality of existence called Inferior Dimension where they will incarnate to encourage the evolution of the creatures of the planets Alfa Nova and Ebiares.

26. Will those who have not activated their desire of creation by 2014 fail to join the Cosmic Alignment?

Entry to the Cosmic Alignment will start July 7, 2014 and extend over a 200 years span. During this time, humans have the opportunity to activate their Desire of Creation and initiate their mental preparation. We feel sure that the changes on the planet along with your growing broad-mindedness will help you complete this process with success. Nevertheless, the ill negative force will be closely following the awakening of the humans of good and make enormous efforts to keep the level of control so far conquered. Through experience and great sacrifice on your part, good shall prevail, but changes will bring great hardship. You, therefore, have to develop another inherent capability of yours called *Renunciation*.

Summarizing what we said earlier, we have seen that you have to awake to prepare for the emergence of your spirit as of 2014 and over the next 200 years. Nevertheless, failing to do so does not necessarily mean that you do not qualify for the energetic transcendence because you will have all the necessary information and an extended 7 thousand years' time to become part of the Cosmic Alignment. Those who definitely lack the merits to earn this privilege will have to nurture the Yeti's brain with their thought-energies contributing to his evolution; otherwise, they will have to leave through the Vortex of the Southern Cone for Alfa Nova and Ebiarcs to help the creatures of these planets evolve and continue their cosmic journey. If you have the true desire of creation, you will have awaked your spirit that will make you resist satisfaction of superfluous and worthless requirements in the material world, which permanently emanate from the emotions of your ego. This is how your spirit will prevail.

27. What kind of love do we need to transcend this reality?

All that exists in the universe originates from the trilogy of the physical, psychical and mental bodies, that is, *EL SER UNO* (Being One). You cannot separate them since they are the inexhaustible source of feelings that faces, alters, transforms and conquers any possible obstacle in the way to cosmic perfection. LOVE is an eternal source of knowledge and cosmic feeling. This feeling is the spiritual inheritance engraved on the ancestral genes of *EL SER UNO*, which preserve the abundance and omnipotence of everything created by the Universal Mind.

You understand Love in many different ways; this is why there is so much confusion about it. Some praise it as being the purest feeling of all; others degrade it with emotional conflicts and passions. Why LOVE has always been the principal topic of innumerable controversies and interpretations? Why humans have been unable to grasp its plenitude? Can you speak of LOVE when humans, while creating magnificent public works and praising the magnanimity of the human spirit, wage war and are capable of assassination in the name of this sublime feeling?

To understand LOVE, you will have to make the following associations:

- I have a passion – physical body
- I am in love – psychical body
- I love – mental body

They will enable you to analyze what your feelings are when using the term LOVE. The One Origin has created humans in its image with three bodies that give existence and life to *EL SER UNO*.

PASSION – Physical Body – I Have a Passion

The term PASSION relates to the physical body, which the ancient Greek called: Nous or Soma. It serves as the shelter for the Psychical (soul) and Mental (spirit) Bodies. It protects the thought-energies to help them know and understand their existence. The physician and alchemist Paracelsus Limbus called it the material body, Christians named it the carnal body and in India, it is Sthula Sharira (Sanskrit) meaning dense physical body. It consists of dense structural units of living matter and is a marvelous compound of complex systems working in harmony and a vehicle, which allows you to live in what is your world, the third dimension.

With this body, you would not be able to exist in other realities. It perfectly adjusts to the dense environment you live in and is the vehicle to manifest your presence in the material world that is the third grade, third plane and third dimension and would not function in other more subtle grades. Pluto, Neptune and Uranus govern the physical body. Consequently, the first and second and a small part of the third zone of the brain are predominant since they have very defined characteristics such as Instinct and Sensation.

These characteristics command chakra one (elimination) and two (procreation). Both energetic centers automatically start to function after the brain transmits the orders implanted in the human genome at the outset of creation of the human species. When this apparent "Love" enters the centers of energy (chakras), you may not call love a physical attraction (passion, ego) which just aims toward the procreation of thoughts and the preservation of the species.

When dense thoughts or the relation between a woman and a man receive stimulus from these centers, the source of energy is not Love or the Mental Body but the passion sparked by the instinct firmly embedded in zone one and two of the brain and activated at the time the needs of the Ego produce the respective chemical attraction. These needs are also a reflex of sexual attraction triggered by a hormonal message, which signals readiness for procreation.

Passion very often fails when being created from the needs of the Ego because emotions such as envy, jealousy, vanity, arrogance, selfishness and indifference will not let it flourish. These emotions belong to very dense realities and are like a torrential flow of self-centered urges, which does not leave room for the *"Falling in Love"* and tends to make passion fade and eventually die. The relation between a man and a woman limited to this type of energetic conditions almost surely fails because the hormonal communication originates from instinct and sensation and the delight felt by the Ego.

This hormonal communication will gradually decrease owing to the lesser intensity of the hormones. Being chemical agents produced by the organism the hormones have numerous functions among which control of the Organs of Reproduction is one of the most important. The hormones travel to all parts of the physical body via the blood torrent. Humans activate their hormones to perpetuate the species. They have managed to introduce changes such as acceleration of the metabolism, the cardiac rhythm, the development of the reproductive organs and others.

Characteristics of Passion

Anxiety, nervousness, disorder, selfishness, materialism, ingratitude, indifference; a person who is extremely self-centered with little or no consideration and compassion for others, and indifferent to his environment. This person is always first and the *Ego* dominates actions, works and thinking. To father a child in this state of mind is risky, since the thought-energies the parents leave to this child are of low-quality vibration arising from a sexual act of pure pleasure and without the characteristics of the psychical or mental body.

We have to leave it to your discretion under which state you decide to give birth to a new life. How much the three states of mind differ from one another may be noted when you study the way your children feel and behave and when you try to remember what your sensations had been during the act of conception. We are not suggesting that you might have been under the effect of alcohol or drugs.

TO BE IN LOVE – Psychical Body (soul) – I am in Love

Here we can say that it is not any more a relation of pure instinct and sensation. However, the thought-energies (souls) are again seeking procreation to perpetuate the species they add to passion the feeling of sincere affection. Two human beings feel attracted to each other; two souls joined together in a cosmic interchange of thought-energies. Two souls needing each other, in a process of reciprocal learning and teaching. These are the truest relations between two people on planet Tera because they tie each other so strongly, that their souls and feelings often share each other's company during more than just one life.

What does being in love mean? You always think of a relation between a man and a woman in the first place. However, it actually means the comprehension of the thought-energies in a much wider context. You could be "in Love" with a vital experience you had, an extraordinary result of an action, a particular way of living, a revolutionary concept, an impressive work of art, all born from strong emotions. These same emotions will define and guide your "being in love".

Thought-energies in the third zone of the brain conceive the "being in love". They belong to Saturn, Jupiter and Mars and, thus, are adapted to the third and part of the fourth zone. The chacras, which command these zones and the planets, are those of Digestion and Respiration. These two energetic centers (chacras) determine that the act of "falling in love" has to be digested which means that the thought-energies have to go through serious thinking in order to flow with full conscience.

After the thought-energies have passed the process of digestion, thinking and understanding they make the "Being in Love" become stable and firmly embed it in the soul (emotions). There it starts to evolve turning a basic thought-energy that will foster its evolution and elevation and spur it to become a human of conscience rather than staying one of instinct and sensation. The "Being in Love" of a man and a woman expresses itself through the knowledge and understanding either one shows, that is, through mutual analysis, study, but above all, through the vivid exchange of thought-energies in the form of reflection, permanent dialog and action.

The words of this dialog are being absorbed through respiration and channeled towards the Solar Plexus, the center of emotions. These emotions will be the mediator of the relation and will guide the "Being in Love" (psychical body) toward the first two centers of energy (chacras) or to the center of the Solar Plexus and the intellect. All depends on the flow of sentiments and the Psychical Body's frequency of vibration. It functions as the intermediary of Passion and Love, that is, of Matter and Spirit.

The energetic union in the third dimension, your home, occurs between the two souls through the energy flow within the cells. The two souls have to merge their thought-energies to enhance and feed each other without the presence of the spirit. The two souls that must bring forth other souls so that these may head for their transmutation and develop their spirit to continue the infinite cycle of existence.

When two souls merge and feed each other, they grow to reach the plenitude of nutrition activating their energetic creativity, which will shape their concept and form forever. Occasionally, two souls "Being very much in Love" give each other all they need creating a cosmic symphony of frequency, vibration, rhythm and colors. They share company for some time and then quite inexplicably separate.

What went wrong? Did they stop "Being in Love? What happened is that, after they had helped each other fulfill their needs and fill the emptiness of their souls, chose to take separate ways for their infinite elevation. It also happens that one of the souls has met with its learning curve of "Being in Love" and conceived its spirit leaving the other soul behind. This shows that one soul grew and elevated while the other one has not yet completed its cycle.

Once conceived the spirit no longer needs the "Being in Love" of two souls. What it needs is LOVE and very often neither will it find love in just one other soul nor in its thought-energies. The spirit will find it in millions of thought-energies shaped in a thousand ways by: Philosophy, Literature, Studies of the Cosmos, Science, Technology and many others which will satisfy and give it the necessary energy for a correct development. The humans of planet Tera gather through their emotions of Passion and Falling in Love and not through their Feelings of Love. This is how they father children and raise them. This is how they live their lives. Being in Love is the mediator of time; it either grows or decreases during the course of life. Need attracts thought-energy which either grasps the energy of Passion or Love.

It is apparently LOVE you feel. In reality, it is passion. However, most people begin to understand that just passion leads to emptiness of the soul. Many of you are already discovering "Love", not only the one that arises from emotions but from a deep inner feeling; many are genuinely loving other persons, the environment, the planet, the cosmos and the universal creativity, a treasure that has always been the essence of your inner self.

LOVE – Mental Body (Spirit) – I Love

When the "Being in Love" occurs and the soul falls in love with the thought-energies, other people, the environment, the planet, the cosmos and the universal creativity you are actually beginning to understand the meaning of LOVE. The flow of feelings and thought-energies will become a Rainbow of frequency, vibration, rhythm and colors that will go beyond the frontiers of emotion and spark universal feelings. They will give love to all in need, and warmness and beauty.

The "Being in Love" will allow the conception of the spirit and develop it. Once conceived it will help you feel and understand genuine love. The "Being in Love" will undergo gradual transformation, thought-energies will no longer attach to emotions, but turn intimately merged souls providing the necessary energy for the spirit. When speaking of merged thought-energies (souls) we do not refer to people living physically as couples, but that each soul helps the other satisfy its needs and then be able to keep on by itself.

Religion (the church) and governments have shaped and institutionalized social and legal dependence at all times to exert control. Ignorance and irresponsibility have marked your planet and made you live in disorder and confusion. Getting together, separating. Fathering children, abandoning them. Lacking knowledge and understanding you look for inconstant relations born from passions and brief materialistic being in love.

A good relationship needs reasoning and analysis. More important is to enhance the energetic advance of the soul than to satisfy the needs of the ego and the pleasure of emotions. The flow of energy and genetic combinations make the thought-energies (souls) extract the very best from each reflection so that the crystals can merge forming large geometrical structures that will give birth to an Energetic Being you call Spirit.

This Energetic Being has special characteristics, since it does not originate from dense physical textures, emotions or external sensations, but from extremely light matter and deep inner feelings. The mental

50

body will be an intimate part of the electromagnetism of the physical body and both will live in the electromagnetism of the planet. It is the mental body that will help you understand what real love is like because it was born from Love and lives in the Love of the universal body of *EL SER UNO*.

As long as you do not conceive your Energetic Being (spirit), you will not know the Love of the Universe. However hard you try to feel, express and explain it, you will not succeed as all you have known, so far, is the "Being in Love" related to the Psychical Body (soul) and to the emotions that nurture it through its own Ego.

28. You must learn to love yourselves by falling in love with your souls. The Love you have to learn to feel implies a process that starts within yourselves.

What is happening to love? Why are many of you not finding your partner, better half, your soul mate? What effect the Awakening to Conscience is having on the humans of the planet? Are you feeling an emptiness you cannot explain? Are you feeling sad because among the people, you meet and like there seems to be nobody to make you happy; a lover, a friend, somebody to share your life with? Why is it that despite your trying so hard, things do not work out?

To all humans who are feeling this way we respond that the reason you cannot find this "special" person is that you are not "in Love with your soul". How is that? How can I be in love with myself? A mistake – No, it is not, because to find this soul you are so eagerly seeking you first have to discover who you are, and the moment this happens you will be captivated, enchanted, in love with whom you see before you... yourselves. When a soul craves love it is like looking into a mirror and noting of what it sees needs something equal or similar. Nevertheless, what has happened when two souls feel attracted and after a certain time realize that the relationship has no future?

I have a Passion

When a soul has a "passion for its physical body", it looks for a match via its Ego. The Ego resembles a mirror, which arouses attraction through the image it reflects. It works that way because the soul has not yet discovered its inner self and, thus, shows an external rather than an internal image. Consequently, it will be looking for an external match such as a delicately shaped face and a perfect body. If it is a man, he will look for a woman with the face and the body of the goddess Venus; if it is a woman, she will seek an Apollo to take her to heaven. If the physical body's Ego attracts both of them, the relationship will not last, as the bodies will age and passion no longer exist.

I am in Love

When the soul is in "Love with the Inner Self", it reflects a different image because it has discovered itself. Without giving importance to the Ego, that is, the physical body, it seeks now such important qualities as virtue, intelligence, talent, ability and others. If two humans feel attracted to each other and fall in love their relationship will have a better chance to last, because, being in love with their souls will have them perceive similar characteristics in the other person and caring for each other make their union grow, become stable, harmonious and mature.

Unfortunately, most humans still ascribe too great an importance to materialism, which often affects the development of true relations. *Therefore, being in love only occurs when you conquer the Ego and awake the Inner Self, your Conscience.* The first thing you will discover is your soul and it will be the greatest love you have ever known. Because your soul will reveal its splendor, you will know, cherish it and comprehend its yearnings. When you do, it will be easy for you to resist the temptations of the Ego and embrace the Inner Self's beauty.

Love for the soul will be so strong that you will control the Ego, resist the seductions of the material world and want to fall in love with a soul that feels the same love. The love you have to feel for yourself as a person means to care for your food, health and safety. Discovering yourselves denotes to study your emotions, analyzing, working, healing them. If you do not act this way, if you fail to discover your soul in the first place, you will never find your match. You would make the wrong choice because you would choose by habit, convenience, immaturity, without really knowing what you are doing.

Find your soul and love it!
It is the only way to find your match.

Loving your soul will help you seek and find this match, leading the way for it because your soul knows the path to this person from other lives, other worlds. The two of you will feel immediately attracted, recognize similarity, feel affinity and love their souls. When you start loving yourselves, you will feel wellness, pleasure and great joy and prepare for the love of this person. And when both of you finally meet, no doubt, you will realize that...

"This soul is you and you are this soul".

29. We understand that to transcend we have to deal with our ill negative emotions. How do we do this?

The cosmic inheritance of the universal family, this unique and transcendent legacy transmitted to all its loved ones, are the Mind (Father) and the Energy (Mother), which are synonyms of the soul. The very soul rules everything existent. It either densifies the thought-energies or has them transcend in a state of exquisite lightness. After you started suffering from distortion and contamination from a virus called ambition, you have lived for millions of years with two bodies only: the physical and the psychical one. It is these two bodies you have developed and used until now.

Consequently, you have to cure the soul to transcend and conceive your baby-spirit. Emotions and thought-energies live in the soul, which when malfunctioning, will strike you with illness and disorders by transmitting wrong orders to the physical body that has no command of its own. If the soul is sick and distorted, then it will not conceive the spirit.

There is an incredible number of places, techniques, messages, chants etc. on the planet ready to show you the path to "spirituality", but nothing about how and where to start the process of healing the soul to give transcendence and true spirituality a chance. *Genuine healing starts with the SOUL.* Before initiating meditation, chanting, spiritual exercises, looking for a retreat, attending conferences, reading books on metaphysics to find spirituality, you have to make great efforts to heal yourselves by analyzing and understanding important questions of your life to overcome the long-lasting process of mental stagnation you suffer.

Healing starts at home

To understand, enhance and fulfill energetic transcendence of the thought-energies you have to begin with the soul because the soul, that is, the thought-energies will either densify or lighten the energy depending on what your intentions are. If you do not secure the transparency of the soul's crystal-thought-energies, you will have trouble understanding the healing process and the thought-energies be unable to record the procedure. Consequently, they will be moving in a vicious circle, not knowing what is happening to them and why. Transcendence, purification and healing of the soul starts with profound understanding and the strong desire for the cure.

It is neither magic nor miracles, just plain, hard and conscious work and great willpower. However, many of you ignore where to begin the cure, are well meaning but lack the means to produce it. Please note that each one of you will have to do his part since every person is a universe of its own and as such has to be concerned with the activation of its spirituality. So, do not expect other people to come along taking you by the hand and guarantee you salvation and transcendence. Other persons might be able to exchange thought-energies with you and could possibly help, but the work to be done is essentially individual and all the merit therefore yours. There is no other way to gain it. Now, what occurs when you feel the strong desire to realize the cure?

- The first step is to awake your Desire of Creation, which means that you have the understanding and want to cure yourself.
- If so, your Pineal Gland will activate a frequency to prepare the spiritual womb for the conception of the baby-spirit.
- After having activated this cosmic frequency and vibration, you will begin to attract frequencies of other fluctuating harmonious thought-energies that will start nurturing the Pineal-Gland-Womb.

- As a result, you will automatically gather: experiences, friendship, literature, visual and audio infos, etc., that is, elevated thought-energies that your Pineal Gland will shelter for the conception of the baby-spirit.
- At this point of the process, two things might occur: you reject all information or you accept and make it part of yourself.

In the event of rejecting it, you show still lack of preparation to conceive your spirit and shall remain incarnated until you feel ready for it. If you do incorporate this knowledge, you will initiate a process of profound changes, transformation and transmutation that shall lead you on the path toward universal elevation. The above leaves little doubt that you might have expected too much from the Masters and Avatars who came to teach you about the Path of Return. You have to understand that it is not "they", who will accomplish this quest, but yourselves through the solid foundations, you are building according to their teachings. It is now your turn to make these teachings a part of you. Understanding and following them shall make you Masters and Avatars. When you stop thinking of magic, miracles and divinities descending on Tera, viewing a rose-colored world, hiding from reality, behaving like children who want the guiding hand of their father in heaven, when you have finally become responsible adults, you will realize that you have... *Awaked and Grown.*

30. Does the treatment with Reiki produce good results?

What you call Reiki, we consider *Transference of Energy*. It works provided the healer has the energy and knows how to proceed. Before initiating any treatment, the healer has to protect himself properly from the energy of the physical and/or the psychical body he is going to treat. This protection consists in activating his field of gravity (energetic defenses) on the highest level in order not to let through anything harmful to him. If the healer took all precautions he/she could begin the cure.

When detecting a degree of disorder (distortion) in his patient, the healer needs to take into account that it is the patient himself, who caused this distortion of energy. This means that the healer cannot just extract this ill energy from the patient, cure it and send it somewhere in the open. Having cured the energy, the healer must return it to its source, that is... *the one who gave it life and existence*. We are going to teach you how to do so: The healer therefore should proceed as follows: put his hands on the ailing area and use willpower separating the ill energy from the body; introduce it in a beam of radiant-white-light, transmute it into radiant energy and convey it back to the patient.

When healing through transference of energy, the healer is not to release extracted energy to the open, since he is dealing with sick and distorted energy that many human beings would breathe in. This would result in a vicious circle curing many but making sick others. Therefore, he has to be very careful when healing through transference of energy so as not to jeopardize himself and others.

The energetic healer is a doctor who cures souls and as such has to adopt the same measures of security a hospital does to protect his patients. The energy of an ailing soul is as contagious as a great deal of physical diseases. The healer has to isolate his patient, protect him with a beam of intense light, extract, cure his energy and send it back to him.

31. Does our "Awakening to Conscience" compare to concepts as treated in films?

The moment you "awake to conscience", a world you might never have wanted to see, defies you. It is a dark and unpleasant reality. You open your eyes once or twice, look around, listen and think to yourself – I do not want this for me – back off and return to the state of unconsciousness. The process of evolution and elevation of humanity is a gradual one and designed to make the species grow and mature. Nevertheless, the diverse phases of this gradualism entail such problems as illness, misfortune and lack of economic resources, painful separations and others.

Why does all this emerge from the soul? – Why the soul has to awake to a broader reality of life, needs to analyze and reflect on the meaning of its existence? Well, here is why. Your soul is the energy that spurs you to awake and ask elementary questions such as why are we on this planet, why do things happen to us, who am I, what is my mission in this life?

When humans start questioning themselves, they reflect the state of their souls, they make a retreat trying to mark a certain distance from the material world because they feel they need to be alone with their thoughts for some time. Meditation will help and reflection enlighten them. Their deliberations center on the important questions for which they so long have been seeking answers. Until they understand, that they cannot keep hiding in some quiet place just to reflect, but instead have to continue to live a normal material life, making a living, meet with their obligations and assume responsibilities.

This continuous process of reflection-action in life makes you advance... and GROW. Moreover, it will make you feel different, more stable, comprehensive, mature and more human. You will perceive that this strong urge from your soul claiming for ever more profound and solid solutions to your problems is the primary condition to be able to lead a dependable earthly life. Nevertheless, you come across the overwhelming realities of planet Tera.

It is this truth, your souls refuse to see, feel and accept because they have become fragile and vulnerable under the effect of extremely traumatic experiences. You, therefore, try to block adverse sensations. You hide sorrows and deceptions; you do not want them to interfere with the process of your awakening to conscience. Instead, you resort to Spirituality believing it to be the key to easing all your pain and hardship.

You want heaven on earth, living the fantasy of emotions of the Ego. By starting to walk the path of spirituality, you embark on enjoying the tastes and pleasures you erroneously believe the "Spirit" concedes you. You seem to feel sure that the Spirit not only will prevent you from having painful experiences, but also grant you intense and delightful excitements you supposedly deserve for being "good and dedicated persons". Meaning "good and dedicated" that you are happily married, have a good job, excellent medical attention and, above all, are in perfect peace with heaven.

Unfortunately, reality is somewhat different... Instead of facing situations, which require valiant decisions many of you prefer to go on living in a dream world created by the emotions of the Ego where peace and harmony are reigning while the real planet Tera is one of growing disease, misery, injustice, manipulation and indifference. The emotions of the

Ego do not allow you to find the solution to a problem; they give you the sensation of pleasure, attraction, fascination and seduction making you feel special and believe that the Spirit will protect you against any possible ill.

However, it is a trap, a delusion, an unreal vision, the Ego projects and which keep you from gaining independence, holding you prisoners of delight and fantasy. It is of great importance that you learn to distinguish sensations and emotions from true feelings that only the Spirit can produce. The Spirit works in a very different way: not only does it discard magic, illusions and superstitions, it feels free and capable of facing the real and endless challenges, obstacles and dangers that mark the life on this planet. The Spirit is brave, tenacious, decided, looks firmly ahead, perceives, questions, analyses, is outspoken, objective, clear, just and impartial.

It wants to discover, face and solve the real troubles of your lives, your environment and the planet. Its task is to establish order, balance and harmony and encourage peace and love. Accomplishing this, it feels it is fulfilling its mission. Enjoying the fleeting pleasures of life is not among its objectives but making this life forever a deep satisfaction of existence, is. The Spirit does not consider adversity a PROBLEM, but a CHALLENGE, an opportunity to keep growing and turning a genuine WARRIOR OF THE LIGHT.

Acting like that the Spirit will keep you "awake" and truly perceptive of this world of fantasy; you then will not only better understand your emotions but also be capable to correct and transmute what is unreal in them. In few words: you will transform yourselves, the environment and the planet. Everything else, all that drives you through the ego and fanciful beliefs are... dreams, theory, unreality and fantasy.

In this moment, it is the awakening, when you discover that fairies and Santa Claus do not exist. Do you feel pain, grief, anguish? These emotions can be felt by children but not by adults. When you awake and grow up, stories, fables, myths, legends, fantasies and more cannot be part of your life anymore. We cannot deny that the awakening to conscience is painful because it means facing the TRUTH. Nevertheless, accept the challenge; awake and look ahead and do not fear these emotions, which, as you work and understand them, will turn valuable experience, the key to the eternal truth called: SPIRIT. Say NO to the Emotions of the Ego and let... the TRUTH of the SPIRIT into your hearts.

32. What does activating the quality of Renunciation mean to us?

The One Origin has created all existing through its Desire of Creation. Its thought-offspring inherited this capability having realized an infinite number of beneficial creations on behalf of its Creator and of all the Creation. This positive, balanced, impartial, just and functional desire is what has maintained the Universe, that is, *EL SER UNO* (Being One), in perfect order. Order and balance of the One Origin and all existing is what keeps *EL SER UNO* always redoubled, active and dynamic.

The universe shelters an infinity of thought-energies. Through them, we are in perfect harmony with the creator and rejuvenating with the energy we receive. Since we connect with the center (creator), we benefit from carrying the desire of creation and have become creators as well.

In your case, the distortion triggered a "disconnection" from the center of creation of the universe. This separation forced you to build a center of creation of your own that has been commanding your lives ever since. The name of this center is the *Ego*. You have planned your lives around the ego. The *Desire of Creation* turned *Desire of Procreation*. You started to reprogram the requirements of your holograms by inventing imaginary conditions and demands for the continuous satisfaction of the ego, thus feeling alive and important. Many of you do not yet have the knowledge, understanding and love of the universe nor the desire of creation. Moreover, you no longer connect with the center of the universe and are therefore circling your center, the Ego. Instead of living according to *Grade*, *Extension and Profoundness*, you rather think of satisfying the needs of *Weight and Volume*.

We could compare these needs to the ill negative emotions you call selfishness, negligence, insensibility, passivity and indifference. By just listening to the ego, you will become indifferent to real life and to your fellow humans. Satisfying cumbrous and selfish desires of weight and volume, which is materialism, makes you lose the capability of seeing and feeling the needs of others. Awakening to conscience means to have a broader view of your life, your environment and your fellow humans.

When you awake your triad of conscience (physical, psychical and mental body), your vision of life will change because it is no longer the ego that will determine your attitude but the desire of creation. Instead of "Me", it will be "Us". To live in full conscience and truth you must wake your inherent capability of renunciation. This means that the desire of creation must conquer the ego and that you do not just center on your lives but on the lives of all living beings of the planet and the universe. I only then will you have restored the connection with your genuine center, your creator: The Universal Mind.

33. How can you predict future events?

Today the Reptilian force has infiltrated and is commanding several of your governments that have initiated the process of domination along with the most powerful corporations running the planet. However, they know that more and more thought-energies are freeing themselves from the yoke of oppression. These governments are getting inside information through mediums who communicate with the ill Negative Reptilian Antimatter Reality, disincarnated Human-Reptilians who are in permanent dialog with their incarnated counterparts.

This sinister power is providing the advanced technology to build the machines and equipment that one day shall dominate the planet. The process of domination is inevitable and will occur during the second phase of the Cosmic Alignment. Until now controls seem to have been discreet, and since most of you are still dormant, have not been truly aware of the extent of domination. This is why the Reptilian has limited acts of force to reach its goals, so far.

However, there is more and more evidence that humans are awaking, leaving the Reptilian force with the concern of gradually losing the immense human workforce, who so diligently had served it throughout millennials. Which leaves no doubt that the Volunteers-Ayaplianos' and Seramitas' hard and dedicated work for more than a 150 thousand years is helping you gradually rid yourselves of the ties of domination. It has been extremely difficult for them to awake you for your being so much behind in evolution and your minds with little response to stimulation.

We have been intending to show and teach you everything about the electromagnetic phenomena (Orbs) in order to make you react and wake up. We have come before you in holographic spacecraft and been trying to engrave on your thought-energies a message of high vibrations using conscious telepathy. We have been sending you a vast number of communications full of symbols, signs, images and knowledge and managed indeed to awake many of you who themselves are awaking others. We are protecting those who have awaked against the harm any uncontrollable technology and related electromagnetic disturbance could cause. We are sending you Orbs (Nimeos) with elevated thought-energies, which, once dispersed in the atmosphere, you will inhale providing your brains with a very special energy.

So far, the Reptilian force has been rather unsuccessful in fighting our technology and expertise in benefit of you and the planet. We have taken advantage of its lesser power and knowledge concerning electromagnetism to awake a maximum of human beings and aid them to escape the unreal existence they live in. The Reptilian force's fundamental pursuit of developing this technology has been and is, to modify the electromagnetism of the planet and of all living beings and thus keep the Ayaplianos-Volunteers of the spacecraft, the Seramitas and Interanos from helping your thought-energies (souls) transcend the reality of the planet. We, therefore, encircle whoever awakes with a gravitational shield to help them cope with the adversities of this new and defying reality. We shall be always close brothers, while you are in the process of awaking during the next 200 years. You will free yourselves from the oppressive yoke and slavery.

34. How do we know that you are protecting us? Will it mean to have some special perception of it?

Yes, you will feel around yourselves a protecting mantle of radiant energy and love. Each one of you will feel it in a different way, but all will sense the presence of someone or something giving them shelter. Varying perceptions are:

- A gentle cool wind
- An intense heat
- Sleeping disorders
- Vivid dreams
- Mystical revelations
- Extreme sensibility at the top of the head
- Emanation of a minty energy in the center of the head, like a morning dew
- Marked changes in personality
- An urge for laughing, crying, singing, dancing etc.
- Clear past life experiences knowing how to handle them
- Divination with "flashes" of the future
- Reception of messages or elevated knowledge
- Vivid communication with disincarnated souls
- Flow of elevated energy through poetry, paintings, music
- Need to change eating habits for purification
- Intolerance of certain food and tendency to allergies
- Giving up addictions
- Need for reading and learning
- Extreme sensibility to sunlight
- Consciousness of paranormal perceptions
- Great urge to communicate with persons having similar perceptions

By keeping calm you will overcome the sensations of discomfort and uneasiness. What happens is that your physical and psychical bodies are adjusting to the solar energy which is preparing your transformation into beings of light (of energy). However, to turn beings of energy you have to undergo a chemical process. This process is already under way. The solar winds are eruptions of energy from the sun playing an important role in it because they help you understand the alchemical transmutation that is taking place in both your Physical and Psychical bodies.

This transmutation or metamorphosis will occur in many different modes; one of them is through Knowledge. Upon investigating and studying the legacy of ancient cultures, you will discover secrets the knowledge of which is still a privilege of a limited number of human beings. Much to our regret, the treasures of the planet's history are in the hands of unscrupulous governments and organizations that have used them to manipulate and dominate humankind. You all are part of that history, you are the ancient, always were, but you have sunk into darkness and ostracism in this life, have forgotten who you are and taken to the pleasures of the emotions; this is why we say that you are alive but do not exist.

You are the Lemurians, the reincarnated Atlantes, the Huns, Persians, Vikings, Franks, Celts, Byzantines, Incas, Aztecs, Mayas and Egyptians; you are the historical legacy of Tera. It is of great importance that you concern yourselves with the essential subjects in human life. Showing genuine concern is of great value in the universe, as it will have you gain vast knowledge and arrive at important conclusions. It will activate the circuits of your brains making them more dynamic and, thus, lighten dense thought-energies.

In many ancient cultures, you will find signs of extraterrestrial presence. We, your Elder Brothers-Ayaplianos, have guided you truthfully at all times by transmitting you Universal Knowledge throughout the planet's history. There is clear evidence of our existence and presence in your lives. This evidence is no longer to be manipulated or hidden. It is imperative that you discover, work, understand and reveal the ancestral secrets.

You are bound to awake and recall; there is not a single force to impede it. You will remove the blindfolds and begin to see and, thus, have deserved the Universal Knowledge as a renewed message in your lives. Knowledge and understanding of your Planet and its relation with the Cosmos have long marked the true history of your lives and souls in the past. Universal Knowledge is the belief in the essence of a cosmic reality based on the profound Comprehension of Love. This knowledge is at the nucleus of your crystal- nimeos; you received it at the beginning of creation and it contains the eternal universal wisdom of the creator. The act of awakening and recalling will allow you to move within higher frequencies and

63

vibrations giving you protection against the influence of harmful negative energies.

35. What can we do to break free from domination and manipulation?

You now have the chance to overcome. After having analyzed and understood the type of domination and manipulation you are facing what you need is determination to proceed. For instance, you can make changes in your private and professional life. You could check on your career aspirations to reduce your workload to spend more time with your family. You can cut back on the consumption of non-essential products and services rejecting aggressive and misleading propaganda; relax in a quiet place more frequently practicing your favorite sport or just doing nothing; read and study using always information from as many sources as possible; be curious, critical, sceptic and independent.

From 2300-2800, the population of the planet will see its free will of decision seriously limited. In many parts, already low birth rates will decrease further, though people would like to have more children, because governments will implement strict birth controls manipulating food, drugs and vaccines. Many women and men will be born sterile and those who are capable of procreating be registered on a state-planned demographic program. Owing to structure changes of the planet and population shrinkage, the total number of inhabitants will live and work in a few large cities across the planet. Dominating governments will control these large urban centers hiring young and well-trained people to administrate them.

To secure mental dependence of the population through an electromagnetism manipulated by machines and equipment, enormous, hermetically closed domes with an atmosphere containing elements that guarantee absolute mind control will cover all-important cities. While still capable of producing useful ideas, older people will stay on, however, no longer be part of the regular population. After they lose this capacity, they have to leave the cities to live in remote and likewise controlled places.

There may be people who escape control to live beyond reach of the matrix, but they will be refugees liable to suffer prosecution and punishment. Nevertheless, today you are still on time to choose and live by your own standards, unless you agree to trade your freedom for the apparent advantages the matrix offers you.

36. What do we have to do to AWAKE?

There is no need for great every day performances in your lives to make you feel that you are in search for spirituality. No one in your dimension can claim to hold all the truth. Esoteric schools and spiritual working groups, however well intended they may be in their teachings, have no key to that truth nor can they offer an exclusive way of transcendence. True spiritual guides are those who, instead of creating psychological dependence, show other persons how to advance by themselves and accept responsibilities.

Therefore, give reading and studying a chance to arrive at conclusions. The very process of awaking starts when you feel that with will and perseverance you are gaining more and more control of your lives advancing in quest of knowledge, understanding and love. The universal guidelines ban any kind of dependence since humans are born free and have the right to decide what is best for them. Psychological dependence compares to drug addiction.

The real energetic awakens occurs when you feel able to take control of you lives, with Responsibility, Culture, Discernment, Will, Effort, Perseverance, Knowing, Understanding and Love. By doing so, means read, assist to conferences, belong to a work group, being member of any spiritual, esoteric, metaphysic school and more. Above all, do treat yourself, the environment and the planet as a whole with great respect by gradually changing habits that are harmful to your physical and psychical bodies.

Nevertheless, be sure not to let these changes affect your self-esteem and personality. Therefore, do not allow to become victims of any kind of sociopathy. Always keep an open mind but beware of opportunists and charlatans. The journey toward the awakening of the spirit requires a good deal of common sense, equilibrium and good judgement of situations that will arise on the way. Do not let yourselves be deluded and use discernment and reasoning. Consider, whenever possible, the benefit of the doubt analyzing events with a clear and positive vision. *Confusion comes when you believe that there is no such thing as one single criterion for this procedure.*

Do not cling to factors like places, dates and names; the significance of a message or teaching lies in its **essence**, which is fraternity, love and energetic transcendence in times to come. You have to assimilate the message making it an intimate part of your lives. The details that come with it, will add to your knowledge for spiritual growth. Read, instruct yourselves, investigate, be curious with a free and open mind because this freedom will make you mature and masters of your lives. *This way of thinking and acting is what we call: Maturity and spiritual evolution, this form of living and being: "The Awakening of the Spirit".*

37. Awaking is not that difficult, but staying awake is!!

BELOVED CHILDREN, BROTHERS AND SISTERS!!

This message is for all who have already awaked or are on the verge of it but feel that there are innumerous obstacles on the path to spirituality. What you have to understand is that the more conscience you gain, the greater are the challenges. Most of you are prepared for the awakening because they are aware of the spiritual part of their existence, know that extraordinary changes are lying ahead and are conscious that the cosmic transcendence of this reality will occur inside themselves.

With all the knowledge, understanding and love you are putting into your daily lives there is always something holding you back, yet difficult to detect. Staying awake is the most difficult thing to do. Why? Because when you are awake, you realize that the dense material world around never stops courting you with temptations of all kinds hard to resist. Do you really believe that the ill negative Force, the Matrix, holding you prisoners for so long, will let you go all so easily? We know that many of you will listen in disbelief when receiving this message. This is because of the codes the Reptilian force engraved on the human DNA to

66

safeguard the control it exerts by blocking your endeavors to persevere in the process of awakening and FREEING yourselves.

During an extensive time, incarnation after incarnation, the Reptilian force has settled in humans, being at the service of the Matrix to keep as many of you dependent as possible. This force has created and implanted codes and formulas in the brain of Tera it will activate by the time humans awake. The incarnated Reptilian force of each generation has passed these codes and formulas down to the next. Therefore, there are human-Reptilians who collaborate with governments and religious institutions receiving generous rewards. The thought-energies of the Tera-Brain are hiding the dark reality that you have trouble to detect but perceive in your lives.

When humans awake, they activate an intermittent light source at a certain frequency and vibration, which will attract the like. In this way, humans start nurturing themselves with new energetic frequencies preparing their Pineal Gland to host the baby-spirit. It is during this process that the human-Reptilians' codes and formulas strive to hinder the Baby-Spirit from being born, for once the spirit is conceived, these codes and formulas will no longer work.

38. How do these codes and formulas work?

As a rule, the awakening to spirituality is painful and those who do have to conquer many obstacles in their physical and psychical realities. Many have undergone serious privation while mastering difficult and often incomprehensible situations. They have been looking for possible explanations and understood that it is through the spirit that they will get them. However, awakening is suffering and this is when the codes and formulas created by the ill negative Force enter the scene, have humans turn their backs on spirituality and open the door to the temptations of the Matrix.

Nevertheless, like in an act of magic, awakening starts prompting positive changes in people's lives, work and career opportunities arise, social life prospers, finance improves etc. but always implies the risk of overvaluation and people's relapse into the vortex of the Matrix. These material benefits are so overwhelming that humans consider them as having been granted by just "Awakening their Spirit" failing to notice the almost imperceptible trap set up by the Matrix to send them back into the most complete material dependence. *The benefits you may draw from the act of Spiritual Awakening are never physical.*

The spirit will not mix with ambition, personal success, fame, money or property. It will give you joyfulness, simplicity, harmony, peace, knowledge, understanding and love. When people start to court you offering favors, do pay attention to what they are like, what you have to give in return or to sacrifice to get them, should you sell your soul to the devil? Caution!! If they mean the denial of your spiritual awakening, you had better keep your distance. The codes and formulas of the ill negative Force are subtle and some people believe that they are on their way to spirituality, as the codes seem to transmit the "knowledge of the spirit". Nevertheless, this is the most difficult part. These persons are making a serious mistake by considering the knowledge of the Matrix a spiritual message. Not having a clear vision and understanding, they proceed according to the ill negative force's concept: mistaking the message and subordinating it to the standards of the material world, becoming victims of its temptations once again.

The resources of the ill negative force to trap you are many: Fear, Guilt, Lack of self-esteem, Insecurity, Depression and others. Your brain changes spiritual reward for material compensation. The result is that, if you do not receive a material compensation, you feel you are not doing the right thing. Consequently, you wind up with a distorted vision that keeps you from freeing yourselves of the mental confinement you suffer.

So, be alert and keep awake!! There is no secret key to success. There are no schools, courses and books to teach you that by just thinking and desiring it success will materialize. Seeking, instead, illimited rewards in the material world (Matrix), has a high price: loss of free will and absolute submissiveness to ambition... forever.

Mistrust always things and advantages that appear to be at reach in no time and with little effort. Beware of those who believe in formulas for fast money, success and pleasures in life... they do not listen to their spirit, but cling to the dark energy of delusion and mirage from souls in distress. Their world looks real from the distance but fades when they get close proving to be a volatile fancy of materialism.

39. Shall we ask God to give us the strength to awake our spirituality?

When you pray to your god, does he listen? Could he possibly remember what each one of the more than seven billion people of this planet is asking for? You address him in so many languages, will he understand? Which way is he supposed to deal with your problems? Right after reception, in an alphabetical order, by degree of importance? How can he possibly manage to understand and solve billions of requests from all over the planet? Moreover, from other living beings in the universe?

Think of God as the general manager (CEO) of a large corporate enterprise. He receives a continuous flow of suggestions, requests and claims from areas such as labor, purchase, sales, finance, logistics and others which he turns over to the corresponding departments for handling giving personal attention to those of a more complex nature or vital importance or with no immediate chance of solution.

The universe has nine dimensions, each dimension nine planes and each plane nine grades of existence. Incarnated and disincarnated human souls incessantly travel these realities. Thus, we are beginning to understand and look at the universe as a large organization where intelligent human beings work in many different ways. What is it you are doing when, contemplating the sky, you ask God for help in a prayer? Well, you are asking him to assist you in a problem as if he were the CEO of the company and the only authority to turn to.

There is little doubt that the CEO is not in a position nor is it his duty to deal with each problem of his subordinates but to run the company to the best of his ability, generating the necessary returns to guarantee jobs and handling efficiently situations that could jeopardize its operation and future. Now, it would not occur to you to think that the CEO, by force of hierarchy and/or influence, should grant random salary raises and promotions. Let alone an infinite number of other similar requests. Since things do not work this way, humans learn that they can obtain almost anything from standard products to special services paying for them. This is how the economy works.

With this in mind, congregations, brotherhoods, sects, spiritual guides and others, offer their services and affirm that, transmitting the love and mercy of God, gives them the strength to guide those who trust them. Consequently, many people in an act of altruism but also hope donate to these organizations thus expecting God to spare them sickness and grief.

While you think that God mercifully protects you against all ill because they are serving Him, they will always charge you for what they say, do or give in the name of God. You so blindly trust them that, when things do not work out in the end you blame God for it.

As God seems not to be responding, you ask help from the "Son" who, having been among you, may listen and understand. When you see that neither he will answer to your earnest requests you think of the holy "Mother" as your last best chance because you believe her, being a woman, to be more comprehensive and, thus, capable of acting as an intermediary between the "Father" and the "Son". When you finally, after much begging and pleading remain without any response you decide calling upon the saints, especially those responsible for the impossible or lost causes. Again, there is no answer.

You then seek to make contact with more elevated incarnated or disincarnated beings or channels who are closer to or connect with higher realities and dimensions. You also see clairvoyants for the solution of your problems. You finally ask yourselves, who could possibly be of help? You are going to ask who it corresponds to, as long as the request is true, depending on the need and the place where you be. They will listen to you if is really necessary and a real trouble!! If we say that the universe works like a company, then they will go to the right person and to the specialist of the problem.

Let us continue with the explanation of the company and see how it works. First of all, the one who will be interested on your problem is the immediate boss, not the president and only if the situation is really serious and affect in a certain way your work and effort inside the enterprise. Other minor and unimportant problems, you will have to face them, since the company is not interested. Who will see the effort and work that you do, will be your closest boss and he/she will pass it on to the correct person, which will take the measures in favor of you and thus obtain the improvements you desire.

We want you to understand that problems must be channeled according to the need. If it is a physical disorder, you first will have to see a doctor for general medicine and perhaps later a specialist. If it is something that affects your psychical condition, the family, friends or a specialist may be helpful. If it comes to leading with deliberations that will determine the course of your lives, you will need the force of the spirit to decide which way to go. All this works by areas, grades, planes and dimensions. The above is advice to help you organize yourselves by establishing priorities, i.e., what is urgent, what can wait and what cannot be solved at the moment, among the many problems you are being confronted with at all times.

Too many humans believe that the solution of their problems lies in the hands of "God", when they actually can be solved using knowledge, readily available here and now. You have to investigate the how, when, why and where of the situation because when there is a real interest, answers and solutions come to you in many ways. Imagine if the employee of a company spends the time asking for something every single minute from the president and everybody as if he/she deserves all. Any enterprise will allow that kind of behavior, in fact, it will take some measures to avoid it. However, if the employee is a fearful, honest, compliant, hard-working, responsible, and more, the corporation will generally be helpful, and interested.

If you lead a life of conscience, you soon will realize that you should have spared "God" or an Enterprise called the Universe requests that are of no concern to them, since you have all the conditions to fulfil them as suggested. Now, if you are facing a situation of extreme gravity, you may call upon the enterprise-Universe in confidence because you are important and it will no doubt render you all the strength and support you need to make the right decision.

Here is what happens when you ask help from "God"... You live in the material world that is parallel to the world of Anti-matter. Depending on their frequency and vibration (high or low), your thought-energies form a combination in the respective zone of the brain. They are actually twin thought-energies of yourselves and, thus, subject to the universal axiom of attraction and rejection. These high-quality thought-energies allow you to communicate with other realities as they generally hold a mixture of high and low frequencies in accordance with the reality, they live in.

When you make a request to "God", which originates from the desire of the ego with low frequency and vibration it will remain in the third zone for being ambitious, superfluous, etc. and with no chance to transcend and attain the knowledge of the more elevated grades, planes and dimensions. However, requests presented in the presence of elevated thoughts with high frequency and vibration will receive treatment on a high level since they carry empathy, altruism, love etc. and readily traverse the superior zones until reaching the Pineal Gland, center of the most elevated thought-energies of the human universe. These elevated thought-energies will give you maximum support and have your request traverse grades, planes and dimensions of *EL SER UNO* (Being One) until reaching the most elevated reality, THE ONE ORIGIN or "God".

40. Does this mean that only requests with the most elevated thought-energies will reach "God"?

That is correct. What you have to understand is that you shelter a treasure of infinite possibilities the creator bestowed on you. Since many have not yet discovered this treasure, they keep on making requests. Others did find it, but do not know how to use it, ignore its value and continue with requests as well. There are finally those of you who have analyzed, comprehended and taken to love it because through its inheritance they have learned that existence is equal to eternity, and that assuming Responsibility for their lives is essential, as is Acceptance of the Universal Laws of Existence.

First, assuming responsibility for **yourselves** means that you are to develop the ability of solving problems by yourselves using all the will-power and intelligence the universe gave you. It means that you will extend this responsibility to all your thoughts and acts in life. The universe has bestowed intelligence on you, capacity of reasoning and understanding so that you may use these abilities instead of asking "God" to act on your behalf.

Second, responsibility is to **understand and accept that a negative Cause and Effect relationship** is liable for most of what happens in your lives. There are material procreations with negative effects, typical of an elementary dimension like yours that accumulate in the thought-energies affecting the quality of your lives. Third, responsibility is to **awake and grow**, which means that you are to refrain from asking for the solution of situations you are quite capable of handling by using your experience and initiative with conscience. *Stop being Children of "God" to become Adult Supporters to the Creation of "God".*

As adult supporters and outstanding staff members, the enterprise Universe will assign you tasks of relevance and responsibility. You will succeed not by begging but by giving. Upon acting with willpower, honesty, reliability, self-confidence, knowledge, understanding and love, the merit will be all yours. Again, quit soliciting. Concentrate on finding and analyzing the map of the treasure; it holds the answers to what you have been looking for so long. The answers are within yourselves.

Our creator has given you more than you could ever imagine that you be healthy and happy human beings. It all depends on your conscious and responsible search of that treasure which lies buried in the deep of your souls. Once you disincarnate and contemplate your image in the mirror of life, you may proudly say I did it on my own; I built my life using Knowledge, Understanding and Love... *this is when you will comprehend that you are adults who have grown in their universal existence.*

41. Then "God" will not listen if we ask for material things?

Definitely not. When you ask for things from the material world, you are addressing the ill negative Reptilian force. It will pass your requests on to the Matrix, which will see to it that you continue living your lives in slavery.

42. How long will the anticipated changes take to occur?

You might think that these extraordinary changes will come with spectacular apparitions in the skies and demonstrations that reveal the truth of the Universe... and that:

- Interplanetary alien spacecraft will take you to distant worlds
- Evil will cease to exist

- As of 2012, everything will be different, with times of joy and happiness
- All karmas will be overcome and nothing but LOVE reign in your hearts
- The financial system will abandon ambition
- Laboratories will wish everybody lasting health
- Congregations of faith will reveal the whole truth about religious belief
- Corruption will vanish from the face of the earth
- Drug addiction and alcoholism will no longer be a scourge of humanity
- Hunger, misery and extreme poverty will no longer exist

If so, what would you need then all the Knowledge, Understanding and Love for you are supposed to develop? How is it possible, even for an instant, to imagine that all this could come true with a touch of magic? Who is going to make these changes? The Ascended Masters, Extraterrestrials, Angels, God?... *Again, it is nobody else than you to bring about changes and y o u do have this enormous power to transform yourselves and the planet!!*

Nevertheless, there are human beings who insist to view the world through rose-colored glasses. They fail to show determination to face reality. Instead, they sit back waiting for "others" to do the job for them. They are not aware of themselves and their surroundings and seem to believe that life is a play of words of affection and feelings that flow from emotions. There are even those who have become spellbound with the expectation of reaching awareness by making great efforts to establish "contacts and channels" because they love thinking that they are the chosen, different and very special. However, all they do in the end is giving in to the temptations of their EGO and delaying understanding.

Yet others are truly aware of and extremely worried about the perpetration of all kind of abuses. Acts of severe corruption cause indignation and a sensation of impotence and there seems to be no real chance to fight them. They ask themselves: Will we someday be free of injustice, famine, misery and manipulation? Will the year 2012 bring the much hoped for turn-around? Is there a chance that the world will eventually start changing after so many hopeful predictions?

Brothers, true and consistent changes will be those of YOUR IN-NER SELVE!!... External changes on the planet shall materialize as you initiate the process of transformation of your inner self. Again, there is no magic, just hard work to transmute the thought-energies, which requires all your willpower, strength and determination. There will be a change in your way of living to correct patterns of behavior based on mistaken concepts and change your negative to positive emotions, which mean to transform 7ooo millions of human beings on the planet.

Brothers, these changes ... TAKE TIME!

When talking about changes we always refer to spiritual transformation, the essence of true life, different from yours that, so far, has traded reality for phantasy. As already said, changes will not come with big headlines, bombastic proclamations or fireworks, so very familiar to you from motion pictures and religious prophecies. They are subtle, with the thought-energy (soul) shaping your inner self and, little by little, you will let them become a reality in your lives, your environment and on the planet.

Brothers, these changes ... TAKE TIME!

Big corporations will have to admit unloyal business practices, since you will have the knowledge and means to make them change their policies. Followers who earlier failed to have the knowledge of themselves and the planet will start questioning religious institutions for having manipulated them with false messages and the history of the planet.

Brothers, these changes ... TAKE TIME!

The financial system will have to revise abusive procedures as people will cut down on overall spending and be more selective when it comes to decide on credit buys, thus, being less dependent on banking services.

There is more and more understanding that uncontrolled dependence on money and properties is an important part of modern slavery.

Brothers, these changes ... TAKE TIME!

You will come to understand that the medicines you take today, most of them are unnecessary and useless, they are drugs that induce them to dependence and drug addiction, keep you slaves and inert to the dangers that they cause and that many times lead them to a life miserable, joyless and unhappy or to the physical death.

Brothers, these changes ... TAKE TIME!

With a natural balanced diet, you will preserve a good health condition and prevent disease. You will pass this habit down to coming generations of strong and healthy individuals, eventually yourselves the moment you incarnate.

Brothers, these changes ... TAKE TIME!

Governments will have to be honest and truly concerned with the common good. VERITY will come to stay. Finally, they will reveal extraterrestrial presence in all its magnitude.

Brothers, these changes ... TAKE TIME!

After all, you are not entirely oblivious of your distant past, but prefer a life of convenience. There is no doubt. The density of a very different reality, however, led you to work with inexact or false information. Yet those who are gaining awareness have begun to adjust to the true reality of *EL SER UNO* (Being One). They have deeply reflected about the meaning of their lives and surroundings. They have AWAKED.

Our messengers are working very hard to make the Knowledge available to you. However, we are not sending you educational messages any more. You are now capable of facing the truth of the Universe because you are on the Path of Return. We are as ever by your side, but it is your turn now to act with profound belief and great willpower.

The beginning of the Alignment in 2014 will be subtle and easy going for you, with much love in your lives and in your hearts. For the first time, you will have this extraordinary vision to perceive... WHERE YOU HAVE COME FROM, WHO YOU ARE AND WHERE YOU ARE HEADING.

But all these changes, dear Brothers ... TAKE TIME!

43. What is the situation of people who are members of a religious institution or sect and pay for spiritual enlightenment?

People's search for spiritual knowledge has led to the formation of religious organizations and institutions, sects and other entities dedicated to the divulgence of spiritual messages. Why is it that these organizations have raised immense expectations in the name of the Creator and his cosmic wisdom making people believe that through them everybody will find the longed-for spiritual awareness, heaven and the end of suffering? Much to our regret, largely because of money, ambition and power.

At all times, mistaken or distorted concepts of spirituality have not only been a cause for passion, controversy and confrontation, but also the justification for atrocities committed by human beings in the name of "God". Notwithstanding, many people keep on with their lives pretending not to see and hear, ignoring the past and looking for excuses in the name of "God", firmly believing that they are on the right track. They hardly question things and prefer everything the easy way. As a result, they always turn to third parties for advice and help and become, thus, easily victims of manipulation.

Good "intentions" are plentiful in your lives, yet too often fail to materialize. Most are in the millions of thoughts or fantasies across the planet; there is much brain storming but little action and frequent indifference. That is why ill keeps moving and gaining ground. Ignorance, incapability, indolence and conformism are the ideal culture for the ill negative energy to extend control and manipulation. As long as humanity continues in the dark without noticing the state of unreality it lives, religion, sects, institutions and organizations will abuse of people's good will taking away their vitality and freedom of expression. People are incapable to develop their spirituality owing to lack of knowledge, understanding and universal love. Spirituality does not come with religion, sects and organizations. Spirituality is rooted in your inner self... *You do not pay for it... you earn it.*

You are developing your spirituality by using all your energy from knowledge and understanding, gained through hard work and dedication, all by your own, day-in, day-out, making progress and enriching your lives. These constant efforts rather than spectacular action will help you advance. You do not buy Spiritual Knowledge; it is within reach of everyone, in many ways: Friends, Books, Cinema, Concerts, Internet, Workshops, etc. It is all there, ready for you to grasp it.

Your contributions to religious organizations, institutions, sects will in no way free you from the task to develop and form your spirit. They will only increase the equities of those who affirm that you need them to know the truth. *Do you remember Joshua Emmanuel when he went into the temple and with the whip, he cast out the merchants who were doing business? It is the clear meaning of what he wanted to broadcast.* Spirituality is not a business affaire; spirituality is the way you live your lives, humanely, with compassion and intelligence, understanding and much love. Spirituality is the very center of your souls to bring about thought-energies of elevation, altruism, harmony and goodwill. You are to comprehend the greatness of and learn to live with the supreme importance of your spirit. This is all the truth you have.

We have to emphasize that only Knowledge and Understanding will conquer and preserve freedom. With ignorance, superstition, obscurantism and uncontrolled emotions humans will always suffer control and manipulation. "Others" will lead them on the way to dependence or total slavery to keep them from awaking.

Therefore, all of you need to have the Knowledge. Those who have awaked are to aid their brothers who have not. Do spread the message, do not hide your spirituality away and form the mental chain of knowledge, understanding and love... *Join to the ONE is what you need to fight ill...*

44. What will true awakening be like in 2012 and 2014?

Most of mystical human beings are not understanding the message. believe that gaining awareness is to have some kind of mystical revelation, to seek contact with extraterrestrials, become a channel for spiritual messages, belong to esoteric circles, reading on metaphysics or attend related conferences. Becoming aware is no other experience than the act of being truly conscious of yourselves as human beings and of everything around you on this planet in the first place.

The previously mentioned is part of the process. However, true awakening is to be conscious of the planet's history, to learn where you came from, who you are and what your destiny will be. This means +that you have to strive to enrich Knowledge, Understanding and Love. To do this, you will have to face an environment of misery, disease, injustice, corruption and, in whatever possible way, contribute to ease suffering. The ill negative force is reprograming you with holograms to keep you from critically assessing multimedia news and propaganda, trying to convince you that life in the Matrix is your only true reality.

It's teaching you that beauty is being anemic, emaciated and anorexic. Is infuse you with thought-energies, so that you see the rubbish of movies that they show on TV and make them believe that the villain, the murderer, the sinister and sadistic vampire is the most wonderful being on Earth, where the protagonist falls in love without caring if he is a murderer, but simply because he is beautiful and very interesting...

45. What kind of values are these?

Your thought-energies have suffered severe distortion affecting your capacity to prevent the new generations from becoming victims of false paradigms and harmful habits. Is it not because of manipulation, ambition and money that so many people fail to question to what extent the values transmitted and accepted for a peaceful and decent coexistence of the planet's inhabitants are actually the correct ones?

Most people believe that spiritual awareness means:

- Living a life of only love
- Praising the creator

- Belonging to a circle of spiritually advanced persons
- Circulating hearty and loving messages
- Omitting to think of negative things
- Believing that love has the power to change everything
- Considering, that their minds have no part in spirituality
- Believing in the great Avatars to be safe forever

People who live like that seem to have little doubt that they have found the path of elevation and that with their faith in God, they will gain a life in more advanced worlds. It is the delusion of those you call **Mystics**. Dormant, they do not have the courage to confront their personal crisis nor the adversities around them. They rarely ask themselves how they could help things change. They just do not want to get involved. They are victims of **dormancy**.

As long as there is ignorance, power, wash brain, ambition and manipulation will prevail. Nevertheless, you in good faith seem to have surrendered because "*you, the good people, have allowed it*" in order to live your fantasies and feel comfortable with mysticism. You do not want to awake and see the reality of your lives since this means: **work, reality, confrontation, and truth.**

Real changes on the planet as of 2012/2014 will depend on the transformation of yourselves in the first place. If you firmly decide to work on it, there will be no ill negative force in the universe big enough to come in the way. "Spiritual awareness will give you freedom". In a distant future, this planet will hold a population of some 600 million people only who will confront the ill negative energy with great determination and willpower. These humans shall be the true **Warriors of the Light** whose total spiritual awareness is going to banish the ill Reptilian energy from planet Tera.

46. What will happen to those humans who fail to awake?

Their somnolence will be such that they hardly notice the transformation the human species and the planet shall be undergoing during the next 7000 years. They will remain comfortably installed in their virtual world they built living in ignorance and fear under the apparent shelter of well-being. "Children and brothers", this is why we shall always be close. Together we shall return to the place we always belonged. You must understand that what you have experienced on planet Tera has greatly contributed to your evolution. However, you have to start preparing for the departure, for the reality of Tera is becoming ever denser and more dangerous with extensive periods of fantasy and darkness in your lives.

This book describes the various phases of the Cosmic Alignment over the next 7 thousand years. This alignment will not only occur throughout the cosmos, but also be felt in your minds as your thought-energies align with the energy of the universe. This makes you an important part of a process that will have an immense transcendence. It is a journey into yours and Tera's future. We have been gathering vast information to build this future, so that you may use it on your journey of transition to *EL SER UNO* (Being One), yours and the Tera-Cell's home.

We, the Ayaplianos-Volunteers of the Spacecraft, our Brothers Seramitas and Interanos shall provide you with all the details of this long trajectory. We all are involved in the process and will have to stand together to transcend during the alignment being participants of this extraordinary concept of cosmic evolution and elevation *EL SER UNO* is generating.

47. Many are very frightened by all these events. How should we react?

First, try to stay calm. Do not worry about predictions or prophecies made a long time ago. Extensive studies conclude that from today's viewpoint there seems to be much room for different readings with regard to possible consequences. To begin with, do not give rise to such emotions as anxiety, frustration, despair, fear or even terror. They must not be part of your life while you are initiating your spiritual awareness and elevating your thought-energies.

These are new times, with many incentives to wake a completely new Conscience in your life. Throughout history, humankind gained experience and learned that this experience can produce important impulses to help you grow and advance. Painful experiences from the past confirm that superficial, egocentrical, selfish and overly ambitious be-havior can have very negative consequences on persons and, in many cases, is the source of traumatic conflicts among communities and na-tions. Therefore, do not let sufferings affect understanding and turn you weak and instable.

From now on!! Concentrate on being cheerful, positive and dynamic individuals who feel and give love and do not forget that every human being deserves a chance to be happy. Sister Earth has always suffered such phenomena as earthquakes, tsunamis, hurricanes and volcanic ac-tivity considered "natural" geographical and meteorological accidents, however, at the same time, denoting planetary evolution. The losses of many human lives among relatives and friends that unfortunately occur are painful but you should not see them as a punishment from "God" for errors or wrongdoing.

Therefore, stay calm and composed and make sure that you have full understanding of your thoughts and ideas. If so, you will have no trouble to make feelings of quietness and harmony reign in your souls. Do not get desperate intending to stop what is bound to occur for the better... *"We have to die to be born again"*. Very often after adversity, forsaken-ness, disaster, tragedy and death, there are periods of great renovation. Sister Earth is going through all this making adjustment for a more sta-ble and secure future.

You therefore must handle the Maya prophecies with great caution. When they speak of yours and the planet's end, they refer to the death of an era of ambition, materialism and oppression and the advent of a new Human Being, mature, responsible, with outstanding knowledge, great un-derstanding and intense love. The Mayas gave much importance to the Star Sun as it stands for elevation, illumination and light of understanding.

You will object: "But there is death and destruction all over the planet".

In reality, the term "death" does not exist in the universe. When hu-man beings die, their souls disincarnate but preserve their energy, which is eternal and will incarnate again to continue in a new material body. The universe does not eliminate, exterminate, destroy, decompose or re-ject... it just recycles because everything continues alive within. The uni-verse is always thinking of a larger and more efficient project for itself and for all living beings.

82

That is why you have to have peace in your hearts and not anxiety or fear about the future. Keep on with your lives, work, family life, your spiritual evolution, have better days, gain more knowledge and understanding and, above all, learn to love. Living your life like that will make you feel always prepared to face any adversity, not necessarily disasters or tragedies, but current problems of daily life. Do you not have constantly earthquakes, hurricanes, and more inside you, because of your internal emotions that are not worked or understood?

Trust in the universe with love and endeavor that this love will lead you to elevating your thoughts and attitudes in life making, thus, come true the "miracle" of the planet's entire transformation. This is how you build the much sought-after Eden for you and future generations. You will end up with nothing while feeling fear or terror, for they will weaken your inner strength impeding any positive development. You are still not aware of what this tremendous energy can do which, henceforth, will start transforming the planet if you only decide to put it to work.

However, to achieve the transformation you first must understand the very nature of this dynamic force and learn to employ it consciously. This is why you need tranquility, maturity, judgement, responsibility, knowledge, understanding and much love. Once activated, it will take you to explore the infinity of the universe.

48. How can we make up for all the affection Tera bestows on us?

Unlike you, Sister Tera has all the experience that comes with age. You are her younger brothers and sisters. She has always protected you, so now it is your turn to make up for this dedication and love by becoming responsible adults who will begin *to protect, defend and preserve absolutely everything existing underneath and on her surface.*

To do this, you are to make important decisions like:

- Ceasing to extract oil and fighting the greenhouse effect
- Stopping massive arms tests
- Protecting water resources
- Increasing the production of healthier food
- Correcting errors in and misteaching of knowledge

- Taking all-over responsibility in public heal
- Increasing support to poor countries
- Securing appropriate distribution of food
- Making sure that humankind draws maximum benefit from inventions

Being conscious and taking responsibility is *for all* and nobody can turn away. You owe this to yourselves and the planet. Everything highlighted before each human being has to conceive as a global responsibility and take it on with awareness and conviction. This is the way to correct the errors that are committed time and again, many not against better knowledge but out of ignorance, and have been passed on from generation to generation.

49. How can we transform a world where people of conscience seem to be minority? How do we end injustice, control and manipulation?

Nowadays perhaps you are minority, but you will definitely not in the future... The awakening of conscience is global and the strength that lies within resurfaces like Phoenix rising from the ashes. There will be so many of you that the ill negative force will vanish from your lives and the planet. That is why no physical power on your part is necessary in this process of confrontation and transformation. Quite different from the ill negative force which depends on the use of physical force, the trademark of violence, ambition and power, thus aiming to perpetuate fear and terror.

Confrontation is not an act of physical power but of intellect. However, to succeed it needs the convergence of thoughts and ideas to form a compact intellectual union, and TIME to obtain tangible results. When we are saying that you have to stand united, we mean that the awakening of conscience must occur deep down in your hearts and become a way of *Living, Thinking and Being*. However, so far, you appear not to have dug into understanding; it is still superficial because you fail to realize how the Cause-and-Effect relationship actually influences your thoughts, actions and deeds.

Let us give you an example. If everyone were conscious that certain food sold on the market presents a serious health risk, they would *not buy* it anymore. What would be the producer's reaction? He would have to *discontinue* its production. However, needing to stay in the market he would have to decide on the production of *higher quality food* at a similar price.

Standing united, you successfully manage to block intentions of prejudice and corruption. This is how you will gradually transform your world because you will have different requirements and want them satisfied. *If people gave up drinking alcohol, it would disappear from drinks. If drug addicts quit drugs, drugs would vanish. Rejected as harmful, junk food would no longer be part of people's diet.*

Much of what you still not accept has changed the habits of many of you because they decided so. You are beginning to awake and that is why there is hope for the future. The humans of conscience will put things in order transforming the face of Tera. Start opening your minds forming the chain with your families, friends, acquaintances... and get together in true conscience. Leave your fantasies behind and wake up.

50. To what degree are we capable of interfering with planetary events?

Regarding "natural" phenomena, you do have to deal with aspects of evolution because you will have to cope with problems you may not be able to solve with your current knowledge and understanding of the planet. You however should take into account that the human being of the future can rely even more on science and technology to minimize negative consequences of the phenomena. You will be learning from painful experiences to advance and broaden your knowledge of the planet and the cosmos. This will favor your evolution as a whole by widening your understanding of what occurs around you. Consequently, you are fit to make the right decisions in the scientific and technological fields to give support to the very process of evolution.

You can only correct the causes that you created, with negative effects for you and the planet, when you fully understand and accept that those causes have their origin in you and that you are the ones to end the sufferings they brought. Failing to do so would condemn you to bearing the most severe consequences that come along with acts of irresponsibility. The only way to avoid this is to be conscious, humane and loving human beings. Nowadays people are already showing awareness on a planetary scale and the mentality to advance and secure peace, harmony, union, knowledge, understanding and love. You are on the verge of great initiatives that will be generating health and prosperity, because you are **consciously** working with a clear view for the future.

To have a proper understanding of the changes that are taking place you have to comprehend in depth the significance of a Cosmic Alignment. All of you belong to a mind called *EL SER UNO* (Being One), but despite being part of it you do not manage to sense it as such, do not perceive it like a mind but like some unidentified source that gives you life. You do not know for sure where you stand and imagine this mind as being something invisible and ethereal. You and all the thought-energies moving freely in the Universal Mind are suffering changes, which mark cycles of existence where recorded energy is moving from one frequency to another settling there to adjust its vibration. The energy does this for many reasons.

Brothers! Why would we have to enlighten you about the universal context, when you have experienced it millions of times? In the form of energy frequencies, you have moved in and out, ascended and descended over and again but seem not to recall any of it. The thought-energies are traveling the vastness of the Universal Mind. You have been, are and shall always be its loving offspring. Yet being on your own in this unfathomable density without knowing where exactly you stand you are desperate and suffering.

51. What does it mean to awake? Is it being a more responsible, conscious or spiritual person?

In a way, as the only manner to achieve it is by elevating your thought-energies. For if you do not, you will be unable to recover your **memory**. This requires great efforts, for you are desperately seeking to understand the messages of the universe but do not know how to cope with this enormous flow of information emanating from the various grades and dimensions.

The crystals of your thought-energies are being polished and ready to assimilate the teachings of the universe. However, you are feeling confused because of the disorderly manner your brains are processing these teachings, moving them back and forth between the left and right side. It is important that you understand that spiritual awareness is a very personal experience differing considerably from one individual to another in form, intensity and timing. People's reactions, opinions and perspectives differentiate after having read the same article and book or watched the same motion picture. It much depends on what they expect from their lives, what their needs and their beliefs are; in other words, it depends on their grade of evolution.

To believe or not what you read, hear or people tell you will take common sense and time. Nevertheless, to find genuine answers to realistic aspirations and conditions, distant from fantasies, miracles or magic, you have to look for these answers deep inside yourselves. It is very hard to give credit to each communication or image released by governments, institutions, multi-media and the public in general. You have to be alert showing intelligent judgment, lucidity, comprehension and responsibility to distinguish credible from doubtful or false information. It is relevant that you only assimilate the knowledge you really need at a given moment using good judgement.

Reading a book does not mean you have to agree with the author's concepts and ideas nor having to use it as some kind of spiritual guide. You should rather try to capture the spirit of its message and use it on yourselves if this makes you feel better persons who consciously live up to the challenges of every day's life. In the future, you will have the gift to communicate with parallel worlds. There will be no more secrets and everybody enjoy the knowledge of the universe. It is the result of the development of new neuronal circuits triggered by the enormous flow of information in science and technology you are receiving today.

It is the task of *EL SER UNO* to show you to be critical observers of yourselves and the world around you, and not to convince you that it is the one and only source of truth. When you come across channeling, messages or books be open-minded and get out of them whatever basic and universal teachings they may contain. When you receive information about the future, which seems too much ahead of today's scientific and technological standards, store them in your memory. Sometime in the future, there may be means to prove them correct; they will then add to better understanding.

You have to keep very alert to assimilate universal knowledge. Do not cling to just one way of looking at things as if there were no other choice. Nobody can claim to know all the truth in this grade, plane and dimension. For the time being, you perceive just part of it; nevertheless, this part is of great help for the Awakening of Conscience. Revelations of the cosmos come to you from various parts of the globe, through a great deal of channeling and other means of communication. Depending on the state of evolution of your thought-energies, you will adjust to new frequencies, rhythms and vibrations that will guide you on the way to...Knowledge, Understanding and Love.

According to the advance of your mental preparation and spiritual elevation throughout the 7 thousand years, the Cosmic Alignment will unveil the **Cosmic Truth**. Hence, we will describe, in a general way, the course of the 21 phases of 333 years each of the alignment. Each phase will mark an important part of yours and the planet's preparation and enable you to find the path that will help you transcend and merge your energies with those of the Universal Conscience.

The afore mentioned phases are particularly important as they will give you an insight of true cosmic realities and help you achieve what you have been seeking for so long...to Be One with the **Universal Conscience**. Many of you will join the Cosmic Alignment as of the year 2014 and during the subsequent 200 years enter the Internal City. Many others are still not ready and will have to stay on accepting great sacrifice to purify and transmute the thought-energies preparing the elevation of their frequency for the conception of the spirit.

Despite the immense flow of information from sources such as spiritual centers, channels, ascended masters, brotherhoods and others, **Spiritual Awakening** does not work the same way for each one of you leaving many with doubts and even confusion. Let us analyze, try to understand why people feel confused and do not know how to face the process of opening their minds to spiritual awareness. Analyzing the many schools and their spiritual messages could lead us to the conclusion that people feel uneasy because they seem to notice inconsistency in dates and contents as well as in the often-contradictory form of communication of many announcements and prophecies. In particular, we shall refer to the methods and techniques used by many spiritual circles, which consider these the only ones to make elevation possible.

Nowadays the flow of messages with spiritual content is such that people seem to be under siege receiving discharges from every angle. Consequently, they do not know whether to accept, reject or just wait and see what might happen. Those persons as a rule are members of esoteric schools or groups who hear from their spiritual **Guides** that only they know and teach the true way to spiritual conscience. When people make it a habit to attend spiritual centers and working groups for a long time, they generally find it difficult to open their minds to other types of spiritual criteria to guide their lives. They feel they are losing the ground under their feet when told that they have to take their lives in their own hands; they also have trouble to escape the influence of certain spiritual guides and gurus.

52. What do we need for a true Awakening of Conscience?

There is no need of anything special that you would have to realize in daily life. There is no request for extraordinary deeds to make you feel that you are on the path of spirituality. First, you have to remember that nobody knows everything in this dimension. However well intended they may be none of the centers of spiritual studies and teachings can claim to be the only one to show you how to transcend.

You must give yourselves a chance to train your minds through activities such as studying, reading, writing, painting etc.to develop your faculty of reason to arrive at conclusions. True spiritual advisers and communicators will always encourage people to stand on their own feet rather than talk them into psychological dependence. This way they fully comply with the principle of the universe that prohibits the creation of psychological dependence of human beings. Human beings have freewill to determine what suits them best. The effects of spiritual dependence compare to those of drugs.

True spiritual awareness occurs when you feel capable of living your life with: Responsibility, culture, discernment, willpower, dedication, perseverance, knowledge, understanding and love. To achieve it you should read, attend conferences, join groups or circles who study metaphysical and spiritual concepts but...always preserve your INDIVIDUALITY, PERSONALITY AND SPIRITUAL CHARACTER. In few words, do not allow to be abducted or vampirized by anything or anyone. This needs an open mind so as not to fall victim to mystification, deception or abuse.

While setting out on the extensive journey to spiritual awareness never lose your common sense, keep your wits, maintain equilibrium and preserve sound judgement. To awake means living an intelligent, positive and correct life. *Again, there is confusion when you choose to stay with a particular message hoping to be forever safe with it.*

Do not hang on to places, dates or names that might distract you from the main idea of a message or teaching. What counts is the **essence** of the message. When you compare messages, you will find that those important ones speak of fraternity, affection, energetic transcendence and positive changes in the near future. These are important guidelines you should capture and introduce to your lives. Read, be curious, investigate, but do all this broad-minded and with full FREEDOM, as being in free mind will make you advance and become masters of your destiny. When thinking and acting that way you will have gained Maturity and Spiritual Growth. You have completed the *"Spiritual Awakening"*.

53. Many people do not manage to awake. How can we help?

What does Spirituality do to make you more understanding, humane, delicate, gentle and loving persons? How does Spirituality get you ready to support your neighbor or induce you to embark on actions of charity? What actually happens in your minds seems to drive and transmute you, to make you engage in a process of considerable changes, almost characterizing a metamorphosis, a process that causes surprise and anxiety

90

but in the middle of strong emotions, you accept it without complaining and with happiness?

You call this process Maturity and Development of the human species. Nonetheless, there are many mature people who, having come of age, continue irresponsible, selfish and without understanding. Apparently, age is not of much help. The truth is that it does not depend on more or less years of life nor on the development of the species but on your innermost power of energy, which you automatically activate, once you show clear signs of preparedness.

Spirituality is not a matter of age, environment, education or social status, spirituality is a genetic condition engraved on humans' thought-crystals. Your scientists and investigators do not know yet where to locate it nor why it is part of Human Nature. The way you may have inherited your mother's character, your father's personality, your uncle's skills or your grandmother's generosity you have inherited the genes of spirituality or thought-energies, that is, the SOUL of the universal family. There is a moment in your lives when you activate and develop this genetic-spiritual inheritance. This explains why you start behaving differently. You begin to think and act as the true offspring of the Universal Mind and Universal Energy.

The process of awakening is the following: during the first 30 years of life, the biological DNA predominates. From 30 to 60 years, you activate your psychical inheritance. Finally, from 60 to 90 years you are vigorously awaking and developing your universal genetic inheritance. This is the path all of you, sooner or later, one way or another, have to follow to open your minds to spiritual awareness.as predetermined by your cosmic genes. Many people neglect activation during several of their lives, thus, turning the process slow. This occurs because their spiritual genes are hiding out but receiving pressure from the psychical genes. Reasons may be environment, lack of opportunities, social status, certain instilled and accepted ways of thinking etc. making it difficult for the spiritual genes to emerge. Also, the memory of strong own or inherited emotions tends to disguise people's true spiritual feelings.

Nevertheless, if they had not inherited the spiritual genes from their Universal Family, nowadays they would not know of nor understand the cycles of existence. They would be born, father children, live and die.

Their only home would be this planet with no chance to know and live other realities. The present one would be their only reality and consequently they would be unconscious of other parallel and infinite realities. You would be incapable of communicating through mediums or telepathy with higher entities. You would be just emotional, orderly, well-educated individuals, highly advanced in science and technology. There is, no doubt, in the middle of all the progress the most important thing of all is missing, the CONSCIENCE that you are more than that. You are to pursue higher goals, to follow a course of evolution way ahead of anything this planet can offer you. Without this conscience you just would be born to live, but would not be born to exist. *You are spiritual creatures of the cosmic family!!*

This is your inheritance. There is no use to deny or believe it a human invention. Name it as you please, progress, modernness, evolution. You will not escape the unavoidable truth...to accept that spirituality is part of you, of your genes and forever engraved on your thought-crystals, awake and conscious. You have to realize finally that this is your true nature and that you are eternal.

Notwithstanding there are moments in your lives when you refuse to believe, see, feel or listen because it appears to be a fantasy of your mind, your cosmic genes will emerge; when this happens there is no hiding since spirituality is much stronger than everything else. There is no other way but to accept and live it. Understanding that you are spiritual creatures means the end of orphanage, of feeling alone and unhappy, of suffering for not knowing your origin, identity and destiny. Knowing that you are spiritual individuals will make you go after your cosmic origin, make you feel certain of whose offspring you are. When you in the end know your origin, you will realize that it is the beginning of an existence of never-ending plenitude and happiness.

54. Many seem not to want this kind of awareness.

You must not deny nor hide your spiritual origin!!!... All you do is putting psychological pressure on yourselves. This will just leave you with the emotions; you are going to build an unreal life and give others a false impression of yourselves. You therefore should not at all deny your Spiritual Nature but let it be present in your daily life in a "balanced" way. Try to make it part of a natural way of acting without deliberately announcing nor exposing it. In this way, you will avoid making others feel uncomfortable with something they do not want to deal with. Spiritual Nature is the very essence of the spirit; you cannot hide it. It will arise when ready in its entire splendor. If you manage to understand and accept it with love, using all you know about the Cause-and-Effect relationship, you will know how to make it a part of yourselves without feeling ashamed or distant from current daily affairs. When you become aware of the spiritual nature of yours, you must quiet down, control your respiration and dearly accept what you are, Spiritual Human Beings.

You have to be conscious that your spirit needs to develop as an elevated BEING. You must comprehend that you have reached a point in your existence where you can no longer live the customary material human life and have to TRANSCEND the reality of this planet. The spirit we are speaking of is yours, only yours and the true universal expression of existence. If you want to elevate, you have to commit yourselves to joining your physical and psychical bodies. You thus will give your INNER SELF all it needs to have the spirit reach its cosmic culmination of creation.

Once you understand and accept your Spiritual Nature, you will have to develop traits and habits that will enable you to adjust your daily life to it. These qualities will help you be persons of conscience and, if you use them properly, make other people respect your spirituality and welcome you for what you are and transmit and not for what they might have suspected you to personify. An important quality on the spiritual path is *Common Sense*, in relation with a *SITUATION* that requires that you define the when, how, where and why. Showing Common Sense is the ability to position yourselves and know exactly when, with whom and why to start a conversation on spirituality.

Other traits such as Logic, Sensibility, Respect, Intuition and Humaneness will be essential to cope with situations on the Spiritual path. Let your Common Sense guide you while trying to communicate with people who do not take much interest in conversations on spirituality. Yet, if you feel the moment is right... DO NOT HESITATE TO SPEAK WITH AFFECTION OF THE NEEDS OF THE SPIRIT.

It is true that when having chosen the spiritual path you intuitively will be looking for good listeners and places where you spirit feels comfortable. There are topics of mutual interest and conversation will flow freely with people who identify themselves with the same way of thinking and living. You, no doubt, for the sake of your spirit will have to pay special attention to that kind of social environment where sociopathy, unhealthy food, alcohol and drugs have become serious threats to decent living.

Show the world that living a life of independent spiritual awareness without religion, mysticism or gurus can contribute to making this planet a much better place to live, with Harmony, Peace and Affection. There should be no doubt that spirituality is not only a religious concept, but one of cosmic origin, inherent to humans and all other beings of the universe... a legacy of THE ONE ORIGIN. *All of you are born spiritual creatures; many accept it whereas others are doubtful or just keep denying it for being still dormant...*

Nonetheless, you who do accept it are giving the example. You are using your Common Sense as told, that is, speaking and acting at the right moment, so other persons will believe and respect you for what you are, serious, trustworthy fellow humans. You are then the LIGHT of the SPIRIT for them we have been referring to so many times because you, more than speaking, are leading the way by your actions and coherent way of living your lives. So, let your ***Spirituality*** show. Straightforwardly, without paying attention to what some might think or say. You know that yours is the path all humans will have to choose eventually; so, keep on helping them through positive thinking and vigorous action whenever you feel that they are willing to pay attention. Simply be yourselves. Let your humble and courageous way of living do the work. They will see themselves reflected in the mirror of truth and realize that this world (reality) is birth, family, life and death, ***but looking at you***, will understand that... ***it is so much more...***

55. How will the Cosmic Alignment affect the planet and us?

Each time a Cosmic Alignment occurs we, wherever our place in the universe may be, are aware of the imminence of important changes. Our

Knowledge of the Universe has shown us that the frequency energies travel at a given rhythm to the confines of the bubble-sphere of *EL SER UNO*. To understand what really happens to the thought-energies of *EL SER UNO* we have to realize that, being part of the Universal Mind, the energy of these thoughts never stops diffusing new ideas. Instead of being worrisome, we are to value this as a sign of the magnificence of the Universe.

We, who have the knowledge of what is taking place, always welcome that diffusion with joyfulness after having witnessed it so many times. It helps us learn, grow and enjoy the experience of different realities of existence and living these new life forms has enriched our Knowledge, Understanding and Love.

So, to your question, how the Cosmic Alignment will affect us, we respond... in everything. Changes of frequency will make your thought-energies vibrate faster and more intensely. This will help you join other thought-energies by affinity. The very term Alignment means that you know what your place is and what the dominating factors are that spur you to merge with other thought-energies. You will define this during the next 200 years, which is the time you need to join the Cosmic Alignment.

Nowadays your thought-energies are a complex compound that has you look for messages from such different sources as channels, Ascended Masters, extraterrestrials or the Internal City. What should your choice depend on? Your way of thinking and inclination for one or the other source already may indicate where you stand and what your direction will be within the Cosmic Alignment.

56. What does it mean for the thought-energies to belong to other more elevated vibration frequencies, rhythms and colors?

A 150.000 years ago, the Cosmic Confederation of Orion sent myriads of thought-energies from Kryon, Antares, Aberon and Cyrius to Planet Tera. It appears natural that after their extended mission those thought-energies be eager to return to where they came from. At this point, there is confusion because you are thought-energies of planet Tera however, with teachings from different sources. All believe that they are bearers of the truth, which resulted in serious confrontations. Those of you, who feel close to Kryon, Antares, Aberon and Cyrius, shall use the magnetism of Tera, leave through the vortex of the Northern-Cone and join the magnetism of one of these planets by affinity. Your spiritual advance along with the teachings are the qualities to determine the planet that will shelter you.

On the other hand, those whose spirituality is in harmony with the Elder Brothers of the spacecraft or the Internal City will return to their planets of origin on the same spacecraft that had brought them here. All who, nowadays, recognize and join spiritually elevated extraterrestrials, are the thought-energies of the volunteers who arrived on the planet 600 million years ago. The universe is a place of order; this is why these thought-energies, replete with experience, will return to the origin of their ideas. Nothing is lost in the universe and there is no disharmony in the mind of *EL SER UNO*.

Your inclinations and qualities will not denote superiority nor inferiority regarding others. Therefore, all who set out on the path of spiritual elevation have to bear in mind that there is not just one single way to find the truth in this reality. To be part of higher frequencies depends on each one of you. This, however, does not only mean affinity of thinking and feeling. It requires, above all, thorough preparation. You need to have full conscience of your three bodies using chemistry and mathematics to control the possibilities and consequences of the energy.

57. How will our inner zones align with the solar system and the four universal dimensions?

Micro-Cosmos and Macro-Cosmos function the same way. You are a universe, a SER UNO (Being One) in the reality in which you live. Your brain has nine zones, five of which relate to the nine planets of the solar system. To take part in the Cosmic Alignment you have to study how your Micro-Cosmos works.

Brain Zone 1 – Represents Pluto – Hell – Instinct
When speaking of the Cosmic Alignment we refer to the knowledge you have to accumulate during the following 200 years so your thought-

energies (souls) can perfectly align and you may complete the preparation to take part in this outstanding event. Alignment means to know the correct position of the thought-energies to direct them to becoming part of a dynamic cosmic structure. It is, therefore, necessary to know how the brain zones work and why they relate to the cosmos.

Planet Pluto stands for the brain zone with the lowest frequency owing to its distance from the Sun (Pineal Gland). It is the zone of your subconsciousness where the most controversial and unstable emotions hide. In turn, its satellite Charon is lighter which means that both formed separately and joined afterwards. Its atmosphere consists of nitrogen, methane and carbon monoxide producing precipitation of frozen particles owing to great variations of distance and temperature.

This is where the "frozen" thought-energies (solidified thought-energies) dwell, which are unprocessed and waiting to turn fluid after unfreezing so you can develop, understand and transmute them. Considered the "Spiritual Planet" its symbol stands for improvement, transformation and perfection. Once you are prepared and willing to transmute your thoughts, Pluto will become the innermost part of your subconscious SELF, where your thought-energies will be undergoing a process of internal reversion and improvement.

Pluto symbolizes profound psychological changes with important impacts in the material world. It encourages you to give up obsolete ideas so that new thought-energies and beliefs can emerge. Each one of you must strive to realize these changes by his own free will using his inner strength, the key to all fundamental transformations. Clear your ways and get lighter heading for the brightness of understanding.

Knowing Pluto and understanding that it represents brain zone 1 will add to your knowledge. Nevertheless, Pluto also relates to materialism, the non-acceptance of a new reality of existence and the denial of a superior life of Knowledge, Understanding and Love. This means that, to be able to join the Cosmic Alignment, you must clear this zone from your lives.

Planet Pluto is a world of Methane:

Methane is a non-toxic gas that contributes to the warming of the Earth or greenhouse effect. Its main hazard is to cause burns when ignited. Being highly flammable, it can cause explosions in contact with the air and reacts violently with oxidizing agents, halogens and some halogens compounds. Methane can also produce asphyxia by displacing oxygen in closed environments. Asphyxia occurs when the oxygen contents is less than 19.5%. (Wikipedia)

Methane dominates Pluto and brain zone 1 likewise. The instinct controls the dense cinnabar thought-energies. Individuals who live according to zone 1 after disincarnating will have to leave for Pluto, a place of torment and punishment.

Pluto, however, marks a change in life by eliminating the instinct, the lowest grade of energy humankind holds, as well as the inclination to passion, fanatism and violence.

The Alignment consists in eliminating this zone by comprehending and consciously transmuting it. Once it is gone, Pluto will evaporate from the Solar System and dark holes absorb its methane particles to prepare them for new creations.

Brain Zone 1 and 2 – Neptune – Hell – Sensation

Neptune is one of the giant gaseous planets and the first discovered through mathematical calculations. Its core is a mixture of rock and liquid ammonia covered with layers of hydrogen, water vapor and methane, responsible for its blue color. Neptune is a dynamic planet covered with patches resembling the Jupiter tempests. The biggest one called Big Dark Patch had been the size of planet earth until it vanished in 1994 giving rise to the formation of another. The most powerful winds of any planet in the Solar System are those of Neptune. Many of them blow in the opposite direction of the planet's rotation. In the neighborhood of the Big Dark Patch, there are winds speeds of nearly 2000 km/h. (Wikipedia)

For the Universe, Neptune represents the roman God of the seas and the Greek Poseidon being the symbol of emotions, life and disease. It has great influence on the psychical body, the nerve system and subconsciousness, but above all, aggravates mental disorders owing to drug addiction. Neptune stands for passive receptivity characterized by madness, perversion and uncontrolled anxiety. Being an irrational and surrealistic world, it commands depression and manias.

A layer of toxic gases covers Neptune the energy of which has an impact on the human brain zone 2 where it causes confusion, disorder and even schizophrenia leading thought-energies to a state of subjectivism and changing humans' course of life to one of unreality and fantasy. Neptune, that is, brain zone 2 has a special attraction for alcohol, heavy drugs and games of chance, speculation and kleptomania developing symptoms of unsociability or sociopathy, sexual perversion and finally serious disorders of the nervous system.

Neptune aims at total control by transforming your thought-energies but fails because it is trying in vain to subdue spirituality through rudimentary emotions rising from subconsciousness. This is where it faces the unreal, platonic, virtual turning it witchcraft and miracle. However, it does nothing but flee the conscience of reality. Preposterous and vague situations you fail to understand and to which your psyche has no answers, intimately relate to Neptune. Because the very Neptune holds mysteries built from falseness and deception.

Neptune will always occupy the dark part of your thought-energies having no solid shape. Neptune means fog, darkness, remote, deserted and lugubrious places of your subconsciousness marked by alcoholism and drug addiction.

Brain Zone 2 – Uranus – Hell – Ill negative Emotions
Uranus relates to zone 2 and 3. It is a reality half way between hell and purgatory. You live in this reality. You have to learn to cope with the two zones and the dreadfully astrological-negative influence they have on you. Uranus is dualism: the divine and the human. It is electromagnetic energy by nature accumulated through understanding and mental perception. Uranus sparks your illumination and intuition. When weighing down on zone 2 Uranus is malevolent causing all your endeavors to fail. Ill negative Reptilian emotions are proliferating making you suffer as you sink into the ignorance and darkness of zone 2 and 1. Uranus has an overall influence on your nervous system since it commands electrical impulses that shape your thought-energies in these two zones.

Your today's world is under the influence of Uranus, infrastructure and systems running planet Tera are inspired in the concepts created by Uranus as it commands ambition and greed. Ruled by Geminis it is controversial and represents in reality and in dreams the X factor: Probability. Uranus, Neptune and Pluto govern the large corporations that rule the planet, while the energy of Luzbel and Lucifer commands these dense, low-grade, distorted and very ill zones. It is this world and the reality of negative emotions that seem to have sunk humanity into a huge bottomless pit.

Uranus worsens nervous disorders as it instils hatred, violence and chaos, the element fire affects thought-energies giving rise to rudimentary passions. At the same time, Uranus means reciprocity, symbolizes the capacity of the human mind to ponder all possible options of what the EGO has determined. Uranus sparks activation and dynamism of the thought-energy to encourage its evolution and elevation.

When Uranus works in favor of personal aspects of dynamism, it strongly stimulates reasoning and logics. You have to channel the dynamic force of Uranus your way to adjust your ability of reasoning through mental exercise using your creativity and immense willpower. Humans who want to transcend this reality have to show their creative genius. This suggests a new horizon of elevated and altruistic thinking in close relationship with the environment.

Brain Zone 2 – Saturn – Purgatory – Negative Emotion

Having studied and understood Pluto, Neptune and Uranus and the corresponding brain zones you are leaving hell for the purgatory of your lives. The Cosmic Alignment ranges over a wider context of knowledge and understanding. Thus, **whatever your desires, you always have to have knowledge**. You cannot hope to realize changes if you do not dispose of certain parameters to help you find the path of return. We compare the Solar System to your brains and the universal hemisphere. It is important that you put yourselves in the planetary and cosmic context. This will make you define the situation of your thought-energies. Alignment is synonymous of order.

When starting to work the elements of planet Saturn, home of Emotions, you will begin to change your Cronos-Time of hours, days, months and years to a Time-Rhythm commanded by Magnetism, which means that in the future what counts is no longer your life span but the quality of it.

The thought-energies will begin to find their place in the brain and no longer fluctuate between its left and right side. They will be in order and function fulfilling the tasks for which the One Principle had actually created them. This is when you align with the Planet, the Planet with the Solar System and finally with the Universe. **Saturn** is the sixth planet from the Sun and the second largest of the System. Much of what we know about the planet we owe to the mission of the Voyager spacecraft in 1980-81.

> **Saturn** has flattened poles owing to its high rotation. It completes one equatorial rotation in nearly 11 hours and orbital time is abt. 39 years. Its atmosphere is more than 90% hydrogen with small amounts of helium and methane. Its density is abt. 30% lower than water. Broad atmospheric bands similar to those of Jupiter show a sky of yellow clouds. (Wikipedia)

Saturn stands for **Conscience**. It reflects the stability of the thought-energies and intrinsic qualities such as prudence, concentration, responsibility, order and justice. Saturn, also identified as **Cronos**, represents the Roman god of agriculture, as does the Titan Cronos in Greek mythology. It marks the beginning and end of cycles, is restorative action, the power that shapes and marks times of change. It stands for deep reflections and endeavors over long periods implying loyalty, perseverance, renunciation and willpower on your part.

Despite all the will and action Saturn has evoked, its bright light, while still present, has become weak. Failing to understand this process, you suffer and have to confront innumerous challenges in life. Saturn is your purgatory and you will have to learn that only through **Renunciation** you will be able to free yourselves from its powerful grip. Suffering and renunciation will make you cut the umbilical cord that holds you prisoners of what is obsolete preparing the re-energizing of your cells and energy by freeing you of the passions of the Ego.

101

Nevertheless, Saturn's and brain zone two's reaction is to impede by all means your renouncing the ties of the material world, of ambition and greed, keeping you refugees of Cronos' (time) while he is devouring his children (your thoughts). On the other hand, you have to beware of excessive detachment from the material world and the Ego as this could lead you to stress, melancholy, pessimism and depression. Saturn is the Lord of Karma because it neither helps you find solutions nor understand your innermost problems, but makes you feel doubtful of yourselves, unprepared, insecure and without resolve.

Saturn symbolizes a time of sowing, growing and harvesting, yet a time that will devour you if you fail to do this without using your knowledge, understanding and affection. The material world always ruled over you, watching and holding you responsible for your thought-energy and every move you make. Saturn controls the time, is implacable, does not forgive nor measure consequences. You do have to pass the barriers of Cronos and show, that time is no longer important to you. You do not submit anymore to the limits of the material world since you are part of the universe where all that exists is electromagnetism. This will make you small compasses to help you travel the path of return by using your energy on quality rather than on quantity.

There are no maps of Saturn, nor is there time, it is just by experience that you will continue your existence under the process of evolution and elevation. However, this process will demand discipline and hard work, present great challenges and mean perhaps suffering. Suffering many times opens the door to awareness, when you become conscious of and start to develop the best of you. Suffering proves that you have the strength only energy can provide. This energy is your Spirit.

Brain Zone 2 and 3 – Jupiter – Purgatory – Emotions

Jupiter is the largest gas giant of the Solar System consisting of abt. 75% hydrogen and 24% helium and has no solid inner surface. Among its principal features is the ***Great Red Spot***, a persistent anticyclonic storm south of the equator. There are several cloud ovals surrounding the planet with winds speeds of up to 500 km/h. Despite the large volume of hydrogen and helium, it would need 75 times its mass to fuse hydrogen and become a star. The upper cloud layers mainly consist of ammonia crystals and the planet's red color seems to result from compounds of sulphur and phosphorus. (Wikipedia)

Jupiter stands for "Conscience of the Soul" having learned to deal with emotions turning them Feelings. Zone 2 and 3 therefore associate with the Greatness of the spirit, wisdom, generosity, order and joyfulness. It is where the human being turns humane and in an act of transmutation the masculine and feminine force become one. Jupiter is the supreme god of the Romans, Zeus in Greek mythology. It is the god of goodness and supreme deity of the universe; it stands for equilibrium, progress, plenitude, enhancement of the energy and transmutation. It rules over the other planets by putting them in order.

Jupiter commands blood and liver function in the human organism. With Jupiter, your thought-energies will develop altruism, generosity, peace, happiness and harmony. Working with Jupiter, you are preparing for outstanding events that will define your energy in the universe and confirm your very special conditions to set out for more advanced realities. You now have reached the point where you manage to treat your emotions turning them into Feelings. By doing so, your thought-energies start to align at first with themselves, then with their environment, the planet, the solar system and eventually join the universal thought-energies that will lead you to realizing the most brilliant ideas.

Brain Zone 3 – Mars – Purgatory – Emotions under treatment

Mars named after the Roman god of war is the fourth planet of the Solar System and often referred to as the *Red Planet* because the iron oxide prevalent on its surface gives it a reddish appearance. Mars is a terrestrial planet with a thin atmosphere having surface features reminiscent of the impact craters of the moon and the volcanoes, valleys, deserts and polar ice caps of earth. (Wikipedia)

Mars stands for energy, willpower, eagerness, tension and aggressiveness. These characteristics have great influence on zone 3 located on the brain's left side. Mars commands the muscular, reproductive and part of the digestive system being its symbol the fire, which relates to great dynamic masculine force. In many aspects, the planet has always been associated with earth, which led people to believe in the existence of intelligent life there, however, inferior and malevolent.

Its reddish appearance is associated to desire, passion and violence. As Mars gets closer to earth it tends to influence the masculine force or left side of the brain, spurring competition, combativeness and hostility while inducing the feminine force to feel dejected, sad, non-conformist, depressed and without affection. The influence of the planet weighs heavy on you since there has always been an intense energetic interaction of thought-energies between Mars and Earth. You have been assimilating immense amounts of the corrosive cinnabar thought- energy the continual incarnation of which has impeded the multitudinous awakening you should have reached by now.

Brain Zone 3 – Tera – Heaven – Emotions treated

Tera is the planet where alchemical combinations mingle producing thought-energies either more elevated or degraded. This depends on how intimate they are with one another and what the main elements are that the human brain processes. *The Solar System is where you live, its brain where you exist.* Thought-energies that fluctuate among the planets and its moons are your thought-energies (souls) that are traveling the Solar System after having left the dense energy of your present incarnation.

When observing and comprehending the action of the planets you will understand how your brain works and recognize the image they project of yourselves. You know the Solar System as having nine planets, nevertheless with the beginning of the Cosmic Alignment in 2014 the energy of two of them, Pluto and Neptune, will no longer be part of your brain, as the corresponding thought-energies have no more place in the brain of the Solar System and will be destined for new creations.

There is life on the planets of the Solar System. Each one with a different life form. However, on all, the thought-energies (souls) incarnate in accordance with their particular frequency, rhythm, vibration and color. You are eager to find life forms identical to those on Tera in the rest of the Solar System or the universe, but you will not. Life is present in millions of forms; nonetheless, you ignore their existence for not having the necessary knowledge.

Life on Pluto, Neptune and Uranus manifests itself through thought-energies (souls) in elements that are scattered in the contaminating methane and ammonia atmosphere of these planets. Incarnation in the human life form there is impossible. Those elements represent the ill negative thought-energies, which still occupy the human brain zone 1 and 2. On Saturn, Jupiter and Mars thought-energies manifest themselves in the human form, live in communities similar to yours but in a parallel reality; you, therefore, can only perceive them with the force of your spirit. Tera is the only place where thought-energies incarnate in the physical form through alchemy and thus shape their desires.

Tera represents both the masculine and feminine force, the principle of action and passiveness, darkness and light. It also stands for the hexagram or six-pointed star of the universal substance that regenerates the process of evolution in the Cosmos. Tera carries the dualism consisting of Mars (masculine, left side of the brain, Pituitary gland) and Venus (feminine, right side of the brain, Pineal gland) and is the Rima gland, responsible for the visualization of the reality of the Universe.

The Solar System is a brain and the planets are its encephalic tissue. The elements are the brain (thought-energies-souls) of the planets they formed. The Star Sun is the Pineal Gland of the Solar System. Jupiter, Mars and Tera are its Pituitary Gland, Tera, Venus and Mercury its Rima Gland. As you see planet Tera represents the duality because is split between the Pituitary Gland (Left side of the brain) and the Rima Gland (Right Side of the brain)

Regarding the brain of the Solar System, Tera represents the definition. Tera is the place where thought-energies take shape, are refined, develop their skills and finally head for their cosmic adventure of wisdom and creativity. Planet Tera has a profound oneiric meaning to you as in the context of universal symbolism it augurs prosperity; but also stands for ambition, possession, avarice, and greed. If you fail to live up to the challenges of your existence you will be victims of the energetic disintegration of your personality and your thought-energies remain in absolute loneliness and disunity having to realize immense sacrifices to reach the supreme objective, which is to win the treasure of eternity.

While ascending from hell to the purgatory passing through the Solar System's Brain zones the thought-energies (souls) will have to strive for the concentration of their energy to continue alive and, after finally arriving on Tera, advance on the path to eternal cosmic existence. All of you, all of over 7 billion individuals have won a place on planet Tera. You are souls living in community who endeavor to understand what the energy of light means. It demands super human efforts, life after life, in a fierce struggle to overcome and exist.

You are on a pilgrimage and have to learn to detach yourselves from the matter, from fantasy and unreality so as to make the transition to Venus (Love) and be capable to enlighten your thoughts and restore your communication with the reality of the universe.

Brain Zone 4 – Venus – Heaven – Feelings

Venus is the second planet of the Solar System from the sun and named after the Roman goddess of LOVE. Most ancient civilizations have known and studied its movements in the skies and it ever since gained relevance for the astrological interpretation of planetary displacements. In particular, the Maya civilization set up a religious calendar based on astronomical observations that include the orbital cycles of Venus. The symbol of planet Venus is a styled representation of the goddess Venus' mirror: a circle with a cross beneath, nowadays denoting the female sex.
Venus' magnetic field is the weakest of all the planets likely because of its slow rotation. As a result, the solar winds hit the planet's atmosphere without any filtration causing evaporation of most
of its hydrogen and with this the largest greenhouse effect of all the planets of the Solar System. (Wikipedia)

Planet Venus is the Roman goddess of love, represents the mirror that reflects vanity. It associates with the female nature, power of harmony, beauty and refinement, grace of form and spirit. As it stands the feminine, it represents the vagina, the uterus, the breasts, the reproductive system and everything that contributes to the feminine functions. It is also attributed to this planet the transmission of sexual diseases.

Venus also relates to the Star Sun for its similar appearance in the skies during the day and both are intermediaries between God and Humanity. Some ancient civilizations venerated Venus and Jupiter as messengers of the gods. Venus will lead you to the stars, to divinity, and make you understand that through love your thought-energies (souls) will form their union with the Star Sun. Venus is the right side of your brain where thoughts elevate to produce the alchemy that will transmute Mars into Venus...

From Violence to Love... From Ambition to Renunciation... From Emotions to Feelings... The greatest force humans have is Love. Nevertheless, the spirit will recreate the beauty and meaning of this feeling to make it reign in your lives and hearts. Love will increase your creativeness and enhance the capacity of your elements to unite by completing the transmutation of their energy in harmony and conscience.

However, without Mars helping you affirm your energetic nature, Venus will not be strong enough to transmute your emotions into feelings of love. Nevertheless, once Venus is in your hearts, your individual energy with a feeling of true affection will enter a state of wholeness. In other words, each individual of a community will become the principle of wholeness, a cosmic reality, an Energetic Being.

During the past 28.000 years, the dominant, impulsive, violent masculine force of planet Mars has ruled over you. This made your brain's left side develop but impeding in a way Venus to intervene and mold your thought-energies to turn them lighter and more loving. The power, force and control arisen from the domination of Mars had made you furious and spiteful individuals. Therefore, Mars is the planet the still unbalanced, cold, aggressive and violent thought-energies (souls) from Tera are heading for after disincarnating.

The Entrance of the long expected 2012/2014, is the Cosmic Alignment in which will be the source of energy for your thought-energies to change so that Venus, the home of loving souls, can and will offer them shelter, joyfulness, sensibility, equilibrium, harmony and peace.

On the other hand, at large intervals many thought-energies have entered and left Venus to incarnate on Tera enriching humanity with the powerful feelings of love. All incarnations carry the transmission of the universal canons that make you gain knowledge, deepen understanding and develop spiritually. Thought-energies (souls) from the right side of the Solar System's brain that are now incarnating in large numbers of human beings have come to conquer chaos. They have waited for the right moment to do so and are ready to join the forthcoming Cosmic Alignment. Elevated thought-energies (souls) will have to complete their process and become the expression of their elevation...meaning Energetic Beings. Therefore, many reincarnations occur giving rise to an extraordinary advance of Knowledge, Understanding and Love all human beings will share. As of 2014, planet Venus will rule over Tera for the next 28.000 years and give rise to the flourishment of an Era of Light and great cellular transformations that will lead to positive changes of the interior and exterior of Tera. Your brain's right side will develop an outstanding activity, the feminine force be omnipresent in the vastness of creation and find the way to important energetic realizations of Universal Wisdom.

The thought-energies of Venus are becoming protagonists of this extraordinary energetic transformation of Light. In turn, the thought-energies (souls) of Mars, Jupiter, Saturn, Uranus, Neptune and Pluto are doomed to vanish. Since humans will interrupt the flow of ill negative energies that nurtured them, the thought-energies of these planets will return to their source and their elements serve for new creations of *EL SER UNO*.

Consequently, assimilation of these elevated-thought-energies (souls) will have the beings of Tera remove zones 1, 2 and 3 from their brains and work with zones 4, 5 and 6 changing their planetary energy 3 to elevated energy 6 of Tera. These are the true energetic changes, the beings of Tera will experience during the Cosmic Alignment when their zones and centers of energy will align with the Universal Brain's Southern Hemisphere, thus connecting with the conceptual reality of an unlimited existence.

Being the brain free from zones 1, 2 and 3, the thought-energies (souls) disincarnate and Venus readily receives them. There they nurture themselves with elevated energy free of harmful elements. After that, every new incarnation will help them with their purification and advance. In the 21 phases of the 7000 years, 333 years each one, the thought-energies (souls) are capable of incarnating 3 times at intervals of approx. 111 years totaling 63 incarnations during the 21 phases of 7000 years.

The thought-energies of Mars will have a last chance to incarnate during 1 phase of the Cosmic Alignment. If they fail to awake, they will definitely have to leave planet Venus. The thought-energies (souls) of Venus will hinder their incarnation, as human offspring will be born with the love only Venus can provide. If the thought-energies of Mars do not manage to elevate their vibration frequency during these three lives, they will not be participants of the Cosmic Alignment. They will return to Mars through the vortex of the Southern Cone, and from there, start wandering from planet to planet, until heading for Pluto.

Proximate to Pluto, a black hole will attract and take them to the Inferior Dimension of the planets Alfa Nova and Ebiares, where they will help with the evolution of these worlds and their simian like creatures that will shelter them. These thought-energies (souls), while wandering from planet to planet, will be losing the memory of their lives on Tera. All they take with them to Alfa Nova and Ebiares are the essence of their species and the necessary elements to restart the natural process of evolution. They will gradually remember by reliving experiences from the past, but fail to have the "Consciousness" of having belonged to a planet called Tera that had offered them the chance to EXIST forever. *The One Origin never removes anything it just transforms it.*

Nevertheless, Awakening of Conscience occurs in many of you and **Love** is leading the way. As you elevate your energy frequency, you allow the feminine force of Venus to reincarnate, which helps you even more with the elevation of your thought-energies' vibration. These incarnating souls are going to be part of the Internal City during the next 7 thousand Years. Once completed the remaining incarnations, you are prepared to continue the course of elevation. You are going to leave by the vortex of the Northern-Cone, passing Venus and Mercury, to merge with the Star Sun and rise to the realities of LIGHT, transformed into Energetic Beings, spirits...this very different form of living and existing.

The souls of Venus are higher souls. However, they descend to this plane to attain the condition of BEING. They join up forming the Energetic Beings who will govern Tera. They are energy of the Light that will take human form to redefine the energy that will eventually take them

109

back to Venus as a Light of intense luminosity. They are elevated souls who shall turn spirits. While the thought-energies of Mars, being Reptilian energies, ruled over Tera, the thought-energies (souls) of Venus had no chance to shelter in humans. They had to wait for you to awake to be able to do so. What we are saying is that your brain's right side has become very active and that is why the elevated souls of Venus can finally incarnate and transcend.

Mars, as stated earlier, represents your brain's left side and its energies are an inheritance of Satien. They are thought-energies without elevation that have maintained their satanic nature and occupied the Solar System's left side brain (Mars) from where they had been leaving and incarnating on Tera. Nowadays, being aware and with your brain's right side activated you admit much more elevated energy frequencies. Consequently, the energies of Satien, present on Mars, will be incapable of incarnating, as these high frequencies will block them. This is how you will vanquish ill. During conception, the fetus will receive the parents' elevated thought-energies of Venus. You call beings so born Crystal, Indigo, or Rainbow Children. As mentioned earlier, Planet Venus will rule over Tera for the next 7 thousand years. During this long period, the thought-energies of Mars (Reptilian-souls) will have no chance at all to become part of these new beings whose minds will shelter thought-energies of the highest elevation.

This is why changes as repeatedly announced shall occur. Evolution and elevation of all existing in the universe is no other thing than the recycling of energy that flows from one place to another, accumulating life experience and developing new skills that will allow further recycling. Therefore, *EL SER UNO* always remains young and updated. Nevertheless, many changes resulting from evolution and elevation can be painful; you have to make every effort to understand them to avoid unnecessary suffering.

Brain Zone 5 – Mercury – Heaven – Feelings

Mercury is associated with Mind and Intelligence. It spurs human evolution and progress and symbolizes equilibrium and wisdom. Mercury relates to alchemy, that is, to solution and understanding.

Represents the element water, meaning purification and liberation of the elements. Mercury is the mediator between God and humans.

While Venus stands for Love, Mercury is the messenger of the gods and conveyor of Knowledge and universal Understanding. It is the unifier of movements and master of adaptation and flexibility and, thus, the "Connector" of thought-energies. Connecting the thought-energies is essential to the free flow of thoughts and intelligence and means: to maintain things in order to avoid inappropriate relationships.

Mercury denotes ideas wrapped in words, ideas with innermost impulses that help thought-energies prepare for their cosmic journey, connecting with myriads of realities to keep elevating with Wisdom and Love. Mercury is the planet of the mind. Although it is the smallest of the Solar System, it is the biggest with respect to influencing the physical, psychical and mental body.

It governs the relationship of the three bodies. The planet is impartial and sometimes depends on the Ego for the use of its divine abilities to inspire humans in their spiritual evolution. His divine inspiration is symbolized by the elevated soul and represented by a circle, this soul will never bend over the mire of the vicissitudes of matter. The spirit that reached its divine elevation, can aspire to belong to the Astro Sun and become an Energetic Being of light.

Mercury is the smallest and closest to the sun of the nine planets in the Solar System with an orbital period of 88 Earth days. Mercury is gravitationally locked and rotates in a way that is unique, e.g., exactly three times for every 2 revolutions around the sun according to radar observations in 1965 or 58.7 days for one rotation. (Wikipedia)

A long time ago the Interstellar Cosmic Confederation knew of the disastrous results that the explosion from Satién had caused in the universe. The Confederation took the necessary measures, separating and joining all the polluted planets in order to form a new System. They placed around a very resistant mesh, so that Satién's disease does not escape or expand and step by step it has been transforming and preventing it from spreading.

We know from earlier explanations that the Satien fragments were highly virulent, they were contaminated and sick of negative-thought energies (souls), these invaded the crystal-planets and everything what was close to them became infected and seriously ill. The Cosmic Confederation created an artificial Sun Astro and brought these planets together patients by spinning them around him. Believe it or not, the Astro Sun of the Solar System was created and formed by the Confederation Interstellar Cosmic.

Brain Zone 6 – Star Sun – Heaven – Universal Feelings

The Cosmic Confederation created the Star Sun as well as the nine planets that orbit it. After having studied, comprehended and accepted the Love of Venus (Sixth Grade-Internal City) and the Knowledge and Understanding of Mercury (Seventh and eighth Grade-Internal City) you now are prepared to proceed to the Star Sun (Nineth Grade-Internal City) and to continue to advance to the dimensions of Universal Energy. Once there, you keep on studying and working to become part of its profound Feelings (Tenth Grade-Internal City), its most brilliant Light (Eleventh Grade-Internal City) and its intense Luminosity (Twelfth Grade-Internal City).

In the final phase of evolution and elevation, you will turn Beings of Energy and live in the Star Sun, although you might find this now hard to comprehend. You shall belong to the Pineal Gland of *EL SER UNO* and be the creative source of the most precious ideas ever conceived. You shall be both Mind and Thoughts. Once part of the Luminosity, you shall be capable of roaming wherever the Universal Light of *EL SER UNO* is shining. You are the ones to bring Knowledge, Understanding and Universal Love wherever you go.

The Sun represents the force and omnipresence of the spirit, which with great effort builds its innermost... BEING. It contains your great universal mission revealing the projections of every one of you. It envisages and creates knowledge, wisdom and feelings. It denotes authority and splendor. Human beings associate its intense luminosity with the heart and cosmic feelings that will take them to the very essence of the universe. The Sun relates to the spine where energy flows to sustain the force of the Kundalini that will lead to the creation of your Energetic Being.

United with the feelings of the cosmic heart of life and existence, the Sun will fill the universe with warmth and luminosity. Coming to feel the Star Sun with your inner self is adding to vitality, affection, will, the principle of masculine and feminine force, is being father and son at the same time, is the union of:

- The physical Body with the Star Sun
- The Soul with Warmth
- The Spirit with Luminosity

The Sun's rays are the source of life transmitting energizing energy. All living beings in the universe, at different grades, owe their lives to the Sun being the thought-energies always present in their existence and their One Origin.

The ancient worshipped the Star Sun since they had the knowledge of the transcendence of its splendor. The Persian, Inca, Aztec, the ancient Greek, Egyptian and the followers of Zoroaster venerated the Sun attributing to it the true meaning of Light and Existence. The Sun is vastness of Creativity, of Divine Conscience. It symbolizes the immense spiritual togetherness of all beings in the cosmos. Its force manifests the Desire of Creation.

58. What is the Star Sun really like?

Millions of years back in time, the Interstellar Cosmic Confederation perceived that a planet called Satien, of the Secondary Dimension, would enter a process of expansion and that not even they would be able to control the disease that had attacked it, however great their efforts. Satien was doomed to disintegrate into a number of major fragments. This made the Cosmic Confederation take measures. Based on mathematic calculations, the Confederation knew when this devastating event would occur, that there would be 7 fragments, and what their direction and final location would be. It started creating appropriate conditions to receive them. At this point, we have to recall that these contaminated fragments represented compact, dense and ill thought-energies (souls). Throughout the books *EL SER UNO*, we therefore have classified them as a Malignant Tumor.

Consequently, the Cosmic Confederation covered each of the fragments with a resistant protective shield to prevent the escape and expansion of Satien's disease. As we know from earlier explanations, the fragments forming each an integral part of seven planets carried the highly virulent disease of ill negative thought-energies that invaded the planet crystals.

To generate heat and light for the treatment of the planets' disease, the Cosmic Confederation created artificial suns for these planets to orbit them. This was the birth of the sun of your Solar System, created for the sole purpose of eliminating planet Tera's malignant cells.

How could you possibly imagine what this Sun is really like? You see it as a hub, a center that gives you warmth and life. However, to understand its real nature you have to explore your minds to learn where you stand and begin to visualize the true reality of your existence. All the Stars Sun throughout the Primary Dimension are Pineal Glands of small brains you call: Solar Systems. The Interstellar Cosmic Confederation installed these artificial brains (solar systems) to transmit energy to the inferior dimensions, realities that live in darkness and need the light to advance their elevation and turn higher thought-crystals.

When the One Origin exploded with its crystals scattered far beyond any measurable distance, the only way to recover them was to have them group and join to create minute brains that would function with their own Pineal Glands. The thought-energies that were extremely distant from their center needed to feed on chemical substances but also on Cosmic Light so that they would not become victims of oblivion nor be lost in the deep of subconsciousness.

Being a long way from the center, from their One Origin, the crystals of the inferior dimensions condensed, but the heat of the Pineal Glands (sun) in this reality kept them alive. Therefore, the Cosmic Confederation continues to install Suns (Pineal Glands) and to create small brains at the most inhospitable places of the universe. We could say that these Pineal Glands are small strategically placed lights in the subconsciousness of *EL SER UNO*. Every time the spirits of Light enter these realities, they keep track and continue to receive energy from the Pineal Gland of *EL SER UNO*. Spirits can never remain in the darkness. They would perish. They need the Light and Luminosity of their creator.

59. If the Sun is a Pineal Gland, how did it form?

We reaffirm here what we have frequently sustained already. Millions of thought-energies form souls, while millions of souls form Energetic Beings (spirits) that shelter in the Pineal Gland of the Sun. This means that the sun you observe is the millions of spirits or Energetic Beings that, in union with other millions of suns are *the heat, light and luminosity of the... Universe.*

You must begin to look at your reality as one that obeys universal parameters, that is, the canons of the cosmos and make it work accordingly. You have thousands of names for all existing; nevertheless, once you awake you realize that everything is quite different from the teachings you received. This is when you are facing a truth, so real and tough that it means a shock to both your inner self and external world. You feel confused and derailed to the point that you do not know which way to go.

You all exist within a gigantic reality, inside an incommensurable Mind. We are its thoughts and as such are the only ones to be conscious of where we stand and what our real existence is. When you study the Star Sun, you study its chemistry, using formulas and giving it many names. You put it in a mathematic, astronomic and astrological context. You define the Star Sun as the source of energy and life. There are, however, questions such as what is energy? what is the nature of the spirit? what is a Pineal Gland? what does all existing consist of? and what is your place in the cosmos?

You must awake to be able to see the reality of your existence. We all find ourselves living in a huge Mind where thought-energies communicate with one another, assimilate energy, move from one reality to another. Studying your minds closely you will begin to understand how the Universal Mind works and realize that this Mind is, just like yours, a Universe of chemistry and mathematics.

Seeing the truth means to **awake**. During the first 200 and the following years of the Cosmic Alignment, you will concentrate on opening yourselves to awareness, which is no other than getting a deeper understanding of the kind of the life you are living. Nevertheless, awakening will not be the same for everyone. Some will do it in a gentle manner. Others will take little interest in it. However, for most it will mean suffering. We, the Seramitas, are always close to help you advance in this long and difficult process.

What we have seen so far, is that many of you prefer to continue day-dreaming; they do not seem to understand the need to awake. They continue prisoners of emotions and sentimentality. On the other hand, there are those who did start the process of awakening and it is with them that we communicate.

Awaking means to advance on the path to Knowledge and Understanding of the universe, to study the soul, the energy, the emotions, the feelings and the superior self (spirit). Yet many of you take intellect for Knowledge, Intelligence for Understanding and Passion for Love. That is why you are incapable of creating the vibratory conditions needed to shelter the souls of Venus. Venus is a planet that represents Love, not Passion.

Passion as already referred to is the attraction between a man and a woman. Many of you consider this emotion as being love and that it will open the door to the universe. It will not. Many people will not go past this emotion in a relationship but creating with it often the wish for children. We are far from despising the emotions you feel but we want you to understand that when we talk of Universal or Cosmic Love we mean Love without passion. Remember *EL SER UNO III – The Seramitas – The Long Path of Return* – when you degraded the Feeling Love subordinating it to a Cause-and-Effect relationship. The moment you understand what Love really means you shall be capable of sheltering the souls of Venus, for they need an appropriate environment of frequency and vibration to enter your thought-energies and, thus, help you transcend and find the true path.

60. What is the origin of the souls of Venus?

The souls of Venus are a convergence of the many thought-energies in the Solar System that incarnated on Tera and through evolution and elevation entered the Internal City, that is, Venus. They all have converged by affinity. You know from the previous books *EL SER UNO* that a vast number of thought-energies (souls) arrived on the planet some 150.000 years ago by order of the Interstellar Cosmic Confederation.

Others have directly come from THE ONE ORIGIN; and there are those that are part of us, the Ayaplianos-Volunteers of the spacecraft, of our brothers Seramitas and Interanos and, at last, of yourselves.

All these thought-energies have been gathering and creating through evolution and elevation of the Solar System's Brain the planetary soul of the System. Once conceived this soul will transcend its planetary reality proceeding to Venus to continue on the path to elevation, pass Mercury and shelter in the Star Sun to turn a Solar Spirit. After this, it is ready to leave through the dimensional door of the Star-Sun's Pineal Gland heading for other dimensions of existence.

61. How will be our passage from Venus to Mercury to enter the Pineal Gland of the Star Sun?

Referring to the Awakening of the Spirit, we are dealing with a large spectrum of the development of the energy. With formulas engraved, the thought-energies gather momentum while their genetic-spiritual-code takes them to the end of a period. As they keep activating, they adapt to a way of expression (life) the energy needs to continue the process. Regarding the Macro and Micro Universe, we have to remember that the Sun of the Mind has its place in the *Anti-matter Pineal Gland* of the brain's right side. It is where the thought-energies' crystals gather brilliance through the light of Knowledge, Understanding and Love. The Pineal Gland is every one's Innermost Sun where alchemy occurs, the laboratory of transmutation that gestates the Energetic Being (spirit) of Light.

When a human being consciously activates the Anti-matter Pineal Gland, his crystals or prisms function like a rotary antenna facing the sun and absorbing its luminosity. The Star Sun in the Macrocosm is a reservoir of elevated thought-energies-souls, the source of Knowledge, Understanding and Love for the entire universe. During this process, elevated thoughts of the mind receive energy from their Inner Sun called Antimatter Pineal Gland, which, in turn, draws energy from its external Star Sun called primary dome. There is a permanent energy exchange between thought-energies and pineal glands. Nevertheless, elevated thought-energies always have to safeguard the connection with their center, *EL SER UNO*.

Thoughts do not just carry energy to drive the process of thinking; this energy, generated following universal formulas, is the very source of the everlasting existence of thoughts. However, thoughts are not just to fluctuate in the universe; they need to express their existence. To do this, they will have to adopt a diversity of expressions that will help them maintain the dynamism of their existence. When the awakening of your Spiritual Nature occurs, the recorded energy will start to develop. It will undergo metamorphosis and incarnate in accordance with specific requirements to continue the process as conceived by its creator, the Universal Mind.

While being gestated in the Pineal Gland of each individual, the spirit already starts molding its expressions. There are imminent striking changes to the extent that the human-species-form will not be satisfactory and the spirit begin to seek a more advanced form of manifestation. Consequently, the spirit gestated on planet Tera will seek the expression of the human-species of Venus, then of Mercury and eventually of the Star Sun and hence. All of the universal expressions strive to elevate and transcend in an everlasting cycle of existence. In this process, they will cause the thought-energies to turn ever more delicate, subtle, light and of high frequency vibration.

62. Are there human-form thought-energies on all planets of the Solar System?

Yes, there are. Nevertheless, each planet shows particular manifestations representing diverse frequencies of thought-energies (souls). Mars, Tera, Venus, Mercury and the Star Sun present the most advanced phase of thought-energies in the human-form. On the rest of the planets, they are also present however less defined and many times appear in even grotesque and monstrous manifestations.

You have to remember that the thought-energies (souls) form in the brain and are born as created. The humans of the universe think and the thoughts are taking shape. They leave the brain wandering in the atmosphere, traveling from system to system, crossing black holes or entering and leaving the Pineal Glands disseminated in the universe. You take them in with your respiration, assimilating them, after attracting them according to your state of vibration frequency. Everything is attraction in the universe and determines how you live your lives.

They are manifestations that cross the Brain-Solar-System and live in corresponding spaces, and since born from the cosmic-human-brain, have gradually been adjusting to resembling their creator, but also showing dreadful forms related to Pluto, escalating and approaching the LIGHT (the Sun), wandering from planet to planet until turning highly elevated manifestations. The thought-energies are the soul and life of *EL SER UNO*. Without them, nothing would exist.

To transcend you have to get the most from these thought-energies through the air, the atmosphere and the Tera-planet-brain. To elevate and form your spirit it is not just through positive thinking; it needs thought-energies (souls) of excellent quality.

63. How do we have to observe the Star Sun to know if we are undergoing an alchemical process of energetic transmutation?

The Star Sun produces a huge and constant stream of superheated and electrically charged particles (plasma) called solar winds that permeate the solar system. The effect of these magnetic energy waves on planet Tera has so far been moderate but will be more intense as of 2014. The solar energy crosses Mercury and Venus before reaching Tera. Every time this occurs, millions of souls (elevated thought-energies) disincarnate and incarnate again.

As of 2014, the solar winds will be gathering intensity and continue so during the first 333 years of the Cosmic Alignment. When they reach their maximum high, they will give rise to the following cycle: The electromagnetic waves carry myriads of elevated thought-energies (souls) from the spirits of the Sun that are heading for Mercury whose energetic beings assimilate and shelter them. After a process of adaptation, these beings send them to Venus where they undergo the same procedure in order to prepare for their transition to Tera. Consequently, along this process the beings of Tera gain elevated energies from the Sun, Mercury and Venus (souls) thus receiving their brains' right sided Knowledge (Sun), Understanding (Mercury) and Love (Venus). It is the first time after 600 million years of distortion that they assimilate high quality thought-energies (souls) from different realities.

This will make humans of Tera participants of the Alignment on July 7, 2014. By assimilating high quality thought-energies, they begin to feel that there will be true changes in theirs and the minds of those who have worked hard to elevate their vibration frequency. Consequently, children born after 2014 will come with the extraordinary gifts that characterize the *Age of Aquarius*.

The Star Sun will continue to produce explosions of Knowledge, Understanding and Love. Its energy will have the thought-energies move back and forward and repeat the same cycle over and again during the 7000 years. From Tera it will gather elevated souls (thought-energies) and leave them on Venus, take those from Venus to Mercury and finally the elevated souls from Mercury to the Star Sun's Pineal Gland. This is how the spirits of all souls will begin to form. It is the universal cycle of the elevated souls (thought-energies). It is the long-term process of 7000 years. During that time, the beings of Tera will shelter thought-energies (souls) from Venus on their brains' right side. A new era. You hardly can imagine what this *Golden Age* will be like. All newborn humans will carry the highest energy and have outstanding skills.

Alchemists, astrologers, ascended masters and the Maya prophecies announced the advent of the Golden Age. You call it the Age of Aquarius. It says that humans will discover and understand long kept secrets. Celestial and planetary enigmas shall unfold. Governments will open their confidential files on extraterrestrial phenomena along with scientific and technological advancements. The Age of Aquarius means to get to know, understand and love yourselves, the planet and the Universe. It will bring freedom to humanity, physically and spiritually. The humans of the future will feel the force of the feminine energy that shall bring them peace, equilibrium, harmony, prosperity, tolerance and fraternity.

This age will last 2000 years. Even so, the Reptilian force will reign for 500 years during the second phase of the Cosmic Alignment (500 years of darkness), the ill negative force shall be completely conquered during the third phase (as of 2800), sent to Mars and its thought-energies (souls) be prepared to leave for Alfa Nova and Ebiares. After that, the Cancer of Ambition will never again be a threat and the Tera-Cell be cured during this third phase; from that time on, it will continue to advance on evolution and elevation throughout all of the cosmic alignment. At the beginning of the third phase the long waited for ABIGAHEL (Michael) will be born. He is an Avatar from the Star Sun, Mercury and Venus who will come to finish the Tera-Cell's cure. Humans shall live the plenitude of the *Golden Age* disincarnating to head for Venus and returning to incarnate on Tera until the end of the 7000 years of the alignment.

Many souls will leave planet Tera for Venus to prepare for their stay on Mercury from where they will finally proceed to the Star Sun's Pineal Gland to complete the formation of their spirit. Yet other souls shall volunteer to become the next Guardians of Tera. They will continue the work of our brothers Seramitas and Interanos and guide the Yeti's evolution the way we did with yours. Beyond their task of volunteers as Guardians born on Tera, they will continue the process of elevation on Venus. This means that each time their souls disincarnate, they leave for the Internal City of Venus and return to Tera to incarnate again. Teaching and learning are to continue to fulfil the canons of the universe in perfect order.

64. While incarnated, will these thought-energies (souls) recall their experience on Venus?

The souls of Venus shelter in the Internal City-Sixth Grade. They are the Ascended Masters you already know from telepathic contacts. Nevertheless, in the future they shall be able to incarnate to continue their mission on the planet since there will be humans to offer them the elevated energy vibration they need to do so. As they incarnate, you will not recognize them as Ascended Masters but just see human beings fulfilling their obligations with great responsibility and humility. They are what you all will be in the future. This means that you will be free individuals of great integrity who no longer depend on "spiritual leaders" and thus turn masters of your lives.

Undoubtedly, many of you who worked hard to advance on the elevation of their thought-energies will be the ones to shelter the souls of these Masters and Brothers who have come to fulfil a very difficult mission. Therefore, some of you, at least during the first phase of 333 years will have to prepare for great sacrifice. These Brothers have a vivid memory of their existence on Venus and never forgot the mission, the One Origin entrusted to them. You sure remember Herod ordering the killing of the newborn because he feared the advent of a messiah (Avatar). This has happened many times and will happen again. The Reptilian-force is aware that there will be always special beings and will go after them. It knows that they proceed from other realities and come to free you from darkness and slavery. Avatars do not just bring the word but cure physical and mental illness. They will be the Brothers-Seramitas of the Golden Age, the sowers of new fields.

65. Is this what occurs in our brains?

It is indeed. When you shelter elevated thought-energies (souls) from Venus, they enter your Pineal Gland (the Star Sun of the Human Universe). These energies give you strength, as they will descend to brain zone 3 (Tera) to help you transcend following the same cycle as the Solar System.

66. Why are we incapable of visualizing human form beings of other planets in the Solar System? Can they see us?

The various human form expressions of each planet have a vision of their own depending on their vibration frequency. As long as you remain thought-energies-souls who have not yet formed their spirit, you will be incapable to "See". Only an entirely formed spirit shall have the dimension, magnitude and faculty to perceive itself and its environment in a panoramic vision. This is why only the spirits that live in the luminosity of the Star Sun have a clear vision of other realities of existence. The beings (souls) of Venus and Mercury have a growing capacity to visualize other realities as their souls are in the process of energetic formation.

67. How can we protect ourselves against ill negative energies that could interfere with the formation of our spirit?

To protect yourselves against all ill you must activate the **Defense System of your Souls**. The immune system of an organism is the natural protection against pathological agents. It fights and destroys invading microorganisms before they can cause any damage. Science has made great progress by understanding how your immune system works and produced extensive literature on malfunctioning and its consequences. The psychical body has its defense system, too. When learning via the multimedia bad news, you deeply worry because you feel that there is something terribly wrong with the planet and that its inhabitants in many parts seem to have turned extremely insensible. Your conclusion is that people are very ill. It is beyond your comprehension how human beings can commit such atrocities. To you as spiritual individuals they appear derailed and lost. Nevertheless, before making a radical judgment, it is necessary that you ponder over the fact that their psychical defense system could be failing. The soul can fall ill because the immune system is defective letting in the virus of ill negative thoughts that will contaminate it degrading a person's way of thinking and acting. More so, besieged by negative thought-energies the soul also loses its capacity of activating the defenses of the material body; this can somatize psychical disorders causing the organism to fall victim of bad health or even chronic disease.

You have many names for physical disorders and know that virus, bacteria and germs cause them. Likewise occurs with your soul when it has to take on all kinds of negative thoughts that seriously reduce your capacity of reasoning. How exactly the ill negative energies enter the soul? You may say, perhaps it is a thought-energy-virus that penetrates through your respiration or a thought-energy-bacteria via the blood of an injury.

No, it is not the respiration nor an injury nor the possible proximity of sick people. The ill negative thought-energies invade the soul when the energetic immune system is at a very low voltage and vibration frequency. Here is when and why: Positive Objectivity is the immune system of the soul. Its place is the Pituitary Gland that it shares with the emotions. Positive Objectivity is a sensor that registers physical phenomena. Its tools are the five physical senses: sight, hearing, smell, taste and touch that you must protect and strengthen to prevent disease.

By doing so, you will be activating inner senses that belong to the soul such as perceptiveness, intuition, sensibility, comprehension, insight, perspicacity and clairvoyance. Both the physical and psychical immune system have to use all the 12 senses in unison to secure their correct functioning. However, there is more to objectivity...

Objectivity

It is the act of looking at an object without the influence of personal feelings or prejudice. Objectivity of a person often relates to epistemological and moral considerations. Objectivity in general refers to neutrality or impartiality. This implies that the observer (subject) keeps a certain distance from the object in favor of a proper approach. An objective person concentrates on observing the circumstances (cause) rather than the problems (effect). To be objective is a challenge as it means to face problems keeping reason and emotion balanced.

A realistic approach will allow you to ponder yours and the reflections, action and deeds of others. This will help you assess the significance of an object or situation and decide whether to make it part of your concern. As positive-objective persons, you have to observe your environment from different angles using consciousness, common sense, ethics, justice and equanimity among others. These are qualities of your soul's immune system guiding and protecting you.

With an objective-positive-immune system, you will be capable of making more efficient and just decisions. Your personal relations will improve. Considering your objectiveness, people will respect and value your balanced, peaceful and affectionate behavior. The objective-positive-immune system is always alert to detect and block harmful thought-agents. Whatever the agent, the immune system clearly identifies it (perception) as an intruder and keeps it from invading the soul (intuition).

To fulfil this task, the system has concentrated anti-matter cell-crystals in the soul called Perceptive Sensors (Antibodies). These perceptive-crystals circulate in the brain and psychical body (soul) watching closely any possible contamination of the energy. When an ill negative thought-energy is about to invade the soul, the perceptive- sensor (Antibodies) spots it and makes it a prisoner of the anti-matter-crystal-cell not letting it enter the soul and turning it later on into a positive-thought-energy.

Sometimes this is sufficient (intuition) to block the intruder. However, in most cases additional recourses such as reasoning, analysis, logic and reflection (other antibodies) are necessary to make the objective-positive-immune-system function to satisfaction. These antibodies freely circulate in the energy of the soul to gather more perceptive-sensors that will block multiplication of intruders that might have escaped control. Finally, the system activates a sensor of particular importance called Understanding that imprisons and transmutes all ill negative energies (intruders). As a rule, the objective-positive-immune-system works satisfactorily. However, in case of a failure the system may not perceive a possible menace. This will occur if the immune system fails to receive positive-energy; it will not work correctly since its inner senses have not awaked. Consequently, it cannot tell its own thoughts from others and, instead of fighting the ill negative-energies, tends to absorb and mix up all of the thoughts of the soul without understanding them creating a chaotic state of Anguish, Unwellness, Sadness, Disharmony and Anger.

If we say that the immune system is the objectivity of the thought-energies, that is, the soul we have to conclude that if the system does not work correctly the soul will remain without protection and consequently produce a state of disorder and confusion. You will remember from previous explanations that it is in the soul where your emotions live and feel everything in this life. You also know if you do not protect yourselves against the ill negative emotions, you will suffer material and emotional chaos.

What could you do to secure proper functioning of your physical immune system? A doctor will suggest that you eat healthy food, exercise yourselves, avoid drugs, control your weight and strive to realize what you consider truly important in your life. What should be your attitude regarding the objective-positive immune system? A spiritual guide will recommend you a positive way of thinking and acting, to let moral and ethics guide your lives and to broaden your Knowledge, deepen your Understanding and believe in the immense force of Love.

Show a lucid mind and clear conscience. Value the life the one origin gave you and respect the lives of others. Control your emotions and learn from new experiences. Thank the universe for living this life but realize that the responsibility for it is all yours. Living by these standards guarantees you that the objective-positive-immune- system will function properly as the sensors will prevent any possible interference of ill negative-thought-virus. The correct functioning of the objective-positive-immune-system is indispensable for the well-being of the life and the elevation of existence.

The world is as it is because people have no real belief, have not activated their inner self, live lives in darkness and ignorance. They have not put to work their objective-positive-immune-system. Therefore, their souls are in torment without the notion nor the knowledge of an existence that is much more than the fulfilment of material needs. Too many people are striving for money and power but it is all fantasy, a passage with little or no meaning. Their souls are ill and their thought-energies corrosive virus that contaminate everything around them... Beware of them by activating your objective-positive immune system!! Protect your souls against contamination from ill negative thought-energies!! Take care of sickening the soul and infecting ill-negative-thought-energies.

Try to understand your inner self and strive to improve your living conditions. So, whenever an ill negative-thought-virus threatens you, your objective-positive-immune system will be prepared to protect you against any interference or illness that could jeopardize your elevation and return to the origin...The Universe. Do not doubt for an instant that every one of you has a Positive Objective Immune System. All you have to do is to activate it by using your Belief, Will, Knowledge, Understanding and Love!!

This system is the guardian of your souls and a protection against any physical and psychical disorder. You therefore will find Harmony, Peace, Order and Equanimity that are among the conditions you need to transcend the reality you live thus adding to the elevation of your thought-energies (souls). If you moreover proceed with Knowledge, Understanding and Love, you have every reason to feel healthy and dynamic living a life of plenitude and happiness.

Beloved Brothers!! We are always close to protect and help you transcend your reality. Trust in yourselves and let your conscience guide you. Yet, beware of the Reptilian force in camouflage that will no longer hide and show what it always has been: The Distortion of Ambition. The Love of the Universe is on your side, never doubt, because the one origin lives in every one of you. While it reigns in your hearts, you have nothing to fear!!

68. How does the spirit form?

Whille using your Positive-Immune System you have protected your Pineal Gland and prepared it for the conception and gestation of the Energetic Being (spirit) which is an elevated energetic projection of yourselves.

Your elevated soul that turns a Being of LIGHT y LOVE. To form their spirit the thought-energies (souls) have to gather, develop and mature. Why do we say that the thought-energies are souls? For a better understanding, we first have to explain the difference between Spirit and Soul.

Soul

Soul is vital energy containing the fundamental formulas of existence. It is everything in the universe that has life and as such the manifestation of all existing in millions of forms, grades, planes and dimensions.

Spirit

Spirit is vital energy bearing the thoughts of elevated and conscious souls. Thus, only the human species can form its spirit, as it is the one species to be conscious of and capable of comprehending its existence. This is how the One Origin created it.

The creator (the one origin) is the Universal Mind and the human species its thoughts. All other species just live but do not exist because they have no conscience and thus cannot form spirits. To form your spirit, you have to assimilate thought-energies of the highest elevation, created and developed for the human species. What we want to say is that the soul of an animal cannot belong to the human being and vice versa. This means that you all need to feed and nourish from special and elevated thought-energies in order to form and gestate the baby-spirit.

69. Can an animal soul incarnate in a human being and vice versa?

Never. The universe is a place of order and an energy based on specific mathematical and chemical formulas cannot adapt. Human and animal energy may have some common elements but will never be the same. Human energy will always be human; it might suffer changes, even genetic

127

metamorphosis, however, basic elements, the formula, will forever remain the same. Human energy may be of a higher and lower grade, but will never work in another species. The same holds true for animals.

70. What is the conception of the spirit like?

Conception of the spirit is the union of: The Mental-Semen from Elevated Thought Energy and the Matrix-Ovum-Pineal-Gland-Energy from the Anti-matter. Life after life, humans keep accumulating and engraving elevated thought-energies (souls). These are going to seek a matching Pineal Gland Energy for the conception of the spirit giving thus rise to the accumulation of great wisdom from many lives.

When the moment of conception arrives, the Semen-elevated-thought-energies gathered in the third brain zone, will transcend to the more elevated brain zones 4 and 5. When reaching zone 6 they join up with the Ovum-energy of Pineal Gland for the conception of the baby-spirit. What happens in the Microcosm of your brains occurs likewise in the Macrocosm. The third zone shelters the elevated thought-energies of planet Tera (you), the fourth zone is Venus, the fifth Mercury and the sixth zone where the conception will occur is the Star-Sun-Pineal-Gland.

The third brain zone (Tera) represents the Conception and the first three months of the Spirit's gestation, Venus six months and Mercury nine months. Once formed, the spirit shelters in the Pineal Gland-Matrix of the Star Sun. This evolving process of the spirit is the manifestation of your elevated thought-energies accumulated along your many past lives. Wherever they are, the thought-energies (souls) take a form of their own. When they gather it occurs by universal concepts and beliefs; this is how they prepare for the Conception of the Spirit. When the Conception completes in the Anti-matter Pineal Gland, you will create the most elevated thoughts and begin the formation and evolution of your Baby-Spirit.

As this Baby-Spirit is in formation, in its first three months in Tera, will prepare to energetically travel to Venus, where the gestation will advance towards six months, being completed when it reaches Mercury. The nine months will finish gestating in the Astro Sol. Then it will form the spirit, being able to go out and belong to the Universal Spirit of EL

SER UNO. In those realities you will be born in much more subtle and perfect bodies, these will offer you the appropriate conditions, so that the Baby-Spirit continue to grow and be nourished by thought-energies of much Knowledge, Understanding and Love. As long as you do not conceive your spirit, the reality in which you live is fantasy, because the thought-energies are not concrete, united and cannot form a being awake and aware of its reality.

71. What are the steps to the conception of our spirit?

- To awake and activate your Desire of Creation
- To trust in yourselves and be broad-minded
- To assimilate elevated thought-energies
- To show consistency between thinking and acting
- To live the life of a truly elevated soul
- To gain Universal Knowledge
- To deal with your ill negative emotions
- To meet the needs of both your physical and psychical body
- To comprehend what Love means and live up to it

The above leaves no doubt that, to conceive the Baby-Spirit, you must create proper conditions so that the elevated thought-energies (souls) may gather and strive for the fulfillment of your... ***Spiritual Being***.

72. How do we know that we have conceived our spirit, can we communicate with it?

The spirit has a language of its own and the appropriate manner to communicate with it is, how you are thinking, feeling and acting. *The language of the Spirit denotes* **Intention.** When people talk, it is the intention that will concentrate the word-energies of what they are thinking. These word-energies will produce the same vibration frequency that made them gather and, depending on the intention they express, will find attention.

It is of great importance how you think and speak because this will shape your character and personality. There is little doubt in "The way you think is the way you are". Over the years, from childhood, adolescence to adultness, humans are used to thinking and speaking in a particular manner. This way to express themselves has probably come to stay. More so, many words they use in their communication are an essential part of their vocabulary, which they retrieve from their memory giving it positive or negative connotations, whatever the case.

Those who awaked following their conscience have certainly noticed changes in their lives and environment. They are aware of objectivity, act less routinely analyzing situations and their circumstances with the intention that the efforts of their inner senses may render positive results.

It is therefore imperative that you respect, love and protect your physical, psychical and spiritual body. Nowadays the knowledge how to watch over your material body is readily available: Healthy balanced diet, fitness exercises, good resting, cleanliness and reliable medical service (preferably holistic medicine). Your psychical body needs positive thought-energies to understand, control and transmute ill negative emotions.

73. How do we protect the Spirit?

If you properly care for your material and psychical body, you do so at the same time for your spirit. Remember that the spirit works with the energy from Electromagnetism, Vibration Frequency, Rhythm and Colors. There are, however, other energy sources, among which one of the most important is:

The Intention behind Thoughts and Words
Any reality starts with a thought because you are thoughts. Words express thoughts that bear an intention. Consequently, the intention in your minds, expressed in words, will become a reality or a Cause that generates Effects.

Intention
You speak and write with the intention to transmit a message that can consist in a routine information or in teaching somebody how to realize a certain procedure. For the two situations, you will use an appropriate language. Nevertheless, there may be more than one intention

in a message. In this case, to determine the how, when, where and why is of great importance in order to show the true intention behind thought, action and deed in a human being's daily life.

While forming, the Spirit will be eliminating the expressions or words with no causal connection from the language of the inner senses. It will also be deleting from its memory vibration frequencies, rhythms and colors that could cause instability of its electromagnetism thus securing harmony and equilibrium.

For a long time, you have been living with only two bodies. The Material and the Psychical Body have been the manifestation of your entire needs. Now you are conceiving a third body: The Spirit. During conception in the Pineal Gland, your spirit shall become the maximum expression of wisdom. Since it is the most elevated of the three bodies, it will initiate a process of regrouping and relocating the thought-energies. The spirit is order and functions in accordance with the mathematical and chemical canons of the universe. It cannot exist and evolve without education and in an environment of lasting physical deterioration and emotional conflicts.

With the formation of your spirit in progress, your Physical and Psychical body no longer accept inappropriate diet, contamination, superficial entertainment, tendentious media, people's improper behavior and violence. Consequently, your Spiritual Language's thought-vocabulary will turn more sophisticated using a wording that reflects your true nature and spirituality.

Your active spirit is going to change thought-words that sound rigid, severe, insensible and vulgar to those that transmit empathy, comprehension and tolerance. This means that people will start to hold back on the use of coarse language when communicating with one another. The destiny of every Spiritual Being in the Universe is to turn a vibration frequency of stability, harmony, peace and love and thus be in unison with the vibration frequency and beat of the cosmos.

74. Is Tera the place where humans conceive their spirit?

For you to understand, we have to go back in time. We arrived on this planet 600 million years ago. How did we manage to enter the Solar

System? Way before we arrived, the Cosmic Confederation had made preparations forming this Solar System by aligning the neighboring planets contaminated by the ill energy from the fragment of Satien and having them orbit a Star Sun-Pineal Gland with calorific combustion, to secure life throughout the system. This Star Sun Pineal Gland was the system's soul. Nevertheless, there were no beings yet to shelter in it. The Astro Sun, the one you see and know, was created mentally by the highest spirits of the Cosmic Confederation.

75. How could they mentally create a Star Sun Pineal Gland?

The Cosmic Confederation created the Star Sun-Pineal Gland with the force of its Desire of Creation, its imagination and the gathering of myriads of elevated thought-energies (spirits). The Sun you are contemplating consists of millions of elevated thought-energies forming the Spirit of the Solar System. The planets you observe are the union of chemical elements shaping the material body of the universe. If you had a look at the microcosm of your physical body, you would realize that its chemical elements are the same as those of the planets, all of them orbiting one center, one hub of light. When we descended on Tera, we knew we would have to cure the planets of the system from a serious disease.

Over these 600 million years, we have been recuperating immense numbers of thought-energies (souls), so they could form their spiritual body on planet Tera and then leave the system heading for other realities of existence. Planet Tera is a very special reality of the Universal Mind. Its particular form of evolution and elevation is such that no other place in the universe compares to it.

76. What does it mean?

While we function following cosmic parameters, you still abide by planetary precepts. We Ayaplianos are capable of crossing the entire universe whereas you, so far, wander from planet to planet. For millions of years, you have been incarnating between Tera and Mars, Mars and Tera, Tera and Venus, Venus and Tera, that is, you have practically been oscillating between the left and right side of your brain. Many of you remember having been to marvelous places and felt to have even lived there. You are still dreaming with these splendid and advanced locations, viewing spacecraft, cities of the future where life is all harmony and peace. You are most certainly reminiscent of Venus and, no doubt, many of you have incarnated there, lived several lives and had outstanding experiences in this paradise.

Also, many of you recall past lives as having been terrible nightmares of war, great suffering with painful and traumatic deaths. These are certainly memories of Mars or similar places where your thought-energies (souls) had to incarnate because of their low vibration frequency. Those highs and lows of your existence, which we do not have to bear, are the consequence of the enormous fluctuation of unstable or undefined thought-energies. This is why Tera represents: the definition of the thought-energies (souls), the place where the energetic Conception occurs and where you learn about the *Enunciation of Thoughts*.

77. What does Enunciation of Thoughts mean?

Enunciation

Enunciation is the short and precise formulation of an idea or the statement of a problem including information for its solution. Enunciating thoughts means that through action, thoughts and deed you manage to produce a frequency that will enable you to clear up and use your thoughts in an orderly manner. The Enunciation of thoughts will enlighten your feelings so you may begin to unravel your emotions and your soul find an adequate vibration frequency to gather with other souls of equal conditions. Henceforth you will be heading for the matching frequency, that is, first for: the Internal City of Tera, then the Internal City of Venus, afterwards the Internal City of Mercury and finally the Star Sun.

78. What will the 200 years, we still have to conceive our spirit, be like?

As of 2014, the planet and you will have the chance to join the Cosmic Alignment. However, to qualify, it is necessary that, during this period, you conceive your Baby-Spirit through the Pineal-Gland-Matrix. We, your Elder-Brothers-Ayaplianos, have come to guide and show you how to complete your preparations for this extraordinary universal event. During 30 years, Ascended Masters have significantly advanced on preparing you for the conception of your spirit helping you increase your vibration frequency, indispensable for the transcendence to higher realities of existence.

79. Why do you keep emphasizing the importance of the Awakening of Conscience?

You all have the chance to join this Cosmic Alignment unless you fail to wake your conscience, that is, to conceive your Baby-Spirit and increase the frequency to connect with higher realities, during the 7000 years the alignment will last. If you, however, want to leave for superior realities now, you will only have the next 200 years to awake. This is the equivalent of two or three more incarnations as of 2014, the year of the beginning of the Cosmic Alignment.

Those who want to leave now, will only have 200 years for awakening. If you fail to do so, great hardship will be the consequence during the second phase of the Cosmic Alignment, as the Reptilian force will do the unthinkable to impede that you transcend and gain your freedom of conscience. This is why we insist on your awakening now. We are providing all the knowledge you need to succeed. Do diffuse it to the confines of the planet. You are still on time. The 7 thousand years of Cosmic Alignment divide into 21 phases of 333 years each. The first two phases shall be dreadful and highly controversial for those who have awaked, as they supposedly have to face 666, the number of the beast according to ancient prophecies that will dominate the planet. Acts of manipulation, loss of freedom and persecution will spread like wildfire. It is the disease of Distortion and Ambition.

The Reptilian force is preparing to take complete control of the planet. Brothers, that is why you must awake and conceive your spirit, for once you do, the Reptilian force will start to decline as your energetic being (spirit) protected by the Baby-Spirit's Immune System produces a vibration frequency that will block the evil forces' energy and thus end domination. Regretfully, those who are incapable of conceiving their spirit will fall victims of the disease.

The Reptilian force incarnated in the human-form is building machines to generate electromagnetic waves that will flood their brains lowering vibration frequency and blocking the development of their energy. Thus, leaving them without defense. *You had better listen to what we are saying. Evil is ready to strike and times will come when you shall witness the atrocities governments will commit driven by an uncontrollable ambition for power and domination!!* Concluded the 200 years, evil shall have sunk deeply into the souls of those humans who had had no belief. They will continue to live on Earth like the slaves they had always been, showing indifference, greed and ambition for power. After disincarnating, their souls will leave for Mars. The universe, nevertheless, will not abandon them and send young volunteers from Tera to teach and help them advance. Those of you, who awake prior to those dreadful events, will be free from the virus of ambition and the effects of the electromagnetic waves. They will have the protection from the special energy of the Baby-Spirit and the Pineal Gland.

Disincarnating and incarnating along the 200 years, they will be ready to head for the Internal City of Tera and Venus. Through enormous efforts, belief, will, knowledge, understanding and love, they will finally have gained the longed-for freedom. When we say that special beings will arrive from Venus to teach and rescue the souls of Tera, it is because they are much stronger spiritual conceptions, prepared to work with both sides of the brain.

80. What spiritual conceptions will exist on Tera to rescue the souls?

As of 2014, souls who have already awaked or will do so during the next 200 years, will prepare, protected by their Baby-Spirit, for their return to Tera to conquer the Reptilian force. As we already know your thought-energies fluctuate from the left to right side of your brain. The left side are humans who lean towards the Positive-Knowledge and through this, they are getting the Enunciation of their soul-thought-energy, which is the energetic elevation.

Others manage to join in by Definition, that is, they are humans who "believe" in the superiority of existence. Although they do not have the knowledge, they manage to compensate with Positive-Understanding of their reality. Finally, there are those who have awaked through Positive-Love and thus gained their access to the alignment. Humans of any of the three conditions in the end will awake and conceive their Baby-Spirit. After becoming a part of the Cosmic Alignment, they will soon be on their way to Venus where the beings of that reality will welcome them. Each of the three options includes the 200-year span, or two or three more incarnations, to help them complete the missing conditions.

All, whose thought-energies-souls are prisoners of Ambition and Distortion will continue to incarnate and shuttle between Tera and Mars Nevertheless, they will have assistance from Special-Positive-Souls that return on a volunteer task to Tera to help save and transmute whatever thought-energies (souls) they can. There are Special-Humans who currently present and work with the three conditions. They are entitled to transcend and leave for Venus. However, many offers to volunteer and keep on with their work of purification, transmutation and recuperation of thought-energies (souls) that were unable to elevate.

These Special-Humans are incarnating souls who are going to fluctuate among Mars, Tera and Venus. Every time they disincarnate, they go to Venus to continue their learning cycle. While incarnated on Tera, they work to recover and transmute Reptilian thought-energies with the use of their own energy. It is voluntary work done with Knowledge, Understanding and immense Love. When descending on Mars for incarnation, the beings of that reality call them Avatars or Ascended Masters of the superior realities who came to guide them on the path to elevation. Members of Light and Love of the White Brotherhood volunteered for this work, that the universe would never ask or oblige them to do.

81. Despite the help from these special-humans, will it be not too late for the participation of the thought-energies that failed to conceive their spirit, with the Cosmic Alignment already under way?

Although the Cosmic Alignment will already have started, the thought-energies-souls on Tera still have the 200 years to conceive their spirit.

If they fail, they will suffer a long period of hardship and domination however have another opportunity at the end of the second phase of the alignment. The advent of the Avatar Abigahel will bring these souls renovation and hope so that, using all their willpower and energy, they will be able to conceive their Baby-Spirit.

If they do not succeed during the 7 thousand years of the alignment, they will elevate as souls in evolution rather than energetic beings. Nevertheless, their thought-energy will not be lost since it did evolve and, as such, is prepared to work for the advance of the Yeti and his descendants, the species that will take the place of humans on Tera in a distant future.

82. Who are the Special-Humans and what their obligations?

We have worked on your preparation for the past 150.000 years. Volunteers Ayaplianos of the Spacecraft, Ayaplianos-Seramitas and Interanos engaged in a continual task to help you develop your physical body and soul (thought-energies). Our concern has always been to cure you from distorted Emotions and the virus of Ambition. We have kept you healthy and awake, guided you on the path to elevation of your spirit. In other words, we have prepared and sown the soil for the harvest.

Many humans have waked their conscience and conceived their Energetic Being (spirit). They now prepare to shelter on their brain's right hemisphere the souls of Venus that have waited a long time to transcend as spirits and become one with the Cosmic-Spirit. Innumerous souls sent by the Cosmic Confederation 150.000 years ago had been elevating during 600 million years yet been unable to form their spirit, because they had failed to develop the three necessary conditions as mentioned earlier. Consequently, they depended on the advance in evolution and elevation of your thought-energies (souls) to connect with the universal energy.

The special-humans at present are working with the two hemispheres of the brain. You can readily recognize them. Many already conceived their Baby-Spirit some time ago. After disincarnating, their spirits go to the Internal City to continue their preparation. After incarnating again on Tera, they are going to fulfill certain cosmic commitments on the planet. They may be Mediums, Channels, Sensitive persons, Writers dealing with universal topics, Inventors who work in benefit of humanity, Esoteric Painters, Crystal and Indigo Children. You will recognize them by the sincere, respectful, tolerant and often altruistic manner, with which they treat their fellow humans.

They are doctors truly concerned with their patients, investigative journalists, incorruptible judges, politicians and executives, philosophers and freethinkers. These Special-Humans have vanquished Ambition and already are hosting on their brain's right side thought-energies from the Internal City of Venus, as well as on the left side those of Mars, however, in process of transmutation. They truly love their fellow humans and do what they can to help their souls transcend this reality of existence.

During the first and second phase of the alignment, the planet's population of some 7 billion individuals will see a steady decline for a number of reasons. One of them is the patient work of the Special-Humans to free the planet from ill negative energies gradually, which will drastically reduce incarnations. As a result, the total population will come down to about 660 million individuals by the end of the Cosmic Alignment.

As they keep neutralizing harmful thought-energies sending them to Mars for recuperation and recycling, the Special-Humans will prepare the planet for the post-human species, the Yeti. What makes them "Special" is that they will intensely work with the two sides of their brain.

83. What other reasons are there to leave the planet with only about 10% of its population at the end of the Cosmic Alignment?

There will be numerous changes during the 7 thousand years of the Cosmic Alignment. Another glacial period is imminent triggered by thermal loss of the Star Sun. This will affect the planet's electromagnetism that depends on the action of magnetic waves from the Sun and the Cosmic Alignment. The glacial period is a long-term event but nowadays there are already signs of it. As mentioned earlier the four seasons will be only two and clearly marked as summer and winter. The main consequence of this drastic climate change are gigantic telluric movements that will cause the separation of continents and reshape large parts of the planet's surface.

The ill negative force's manipulation and domination through mind-control will affect the remaining population's desire or capacity of re-production, but most simply will not want to have children. To offset a massive demographic, decline the negative energy will force in-vitro conception and even resort to cloning, thus creating a horror scenario in a desperate intent to keep running the planet. To stop this monstrous-ness, the Ayaplianos-Seramitas need to return and incarnate in humans who are willing to risk their lives facing up to the ill negative force.

While these and other yet unpredictable events during the 7 thousand years will bring about profound alterations of life on Tera, the planet and its future inhabitants will draw benefits from this entirely new environmental situation. The new generations will be born with highly positive thought-energies (souls). They will develop great intelli-gence and memory and advance on spiritual elevation by using the two hemispheres of their brain in perfect harmony. All along the 7 thousand years, humans will have made enormous advancements in science, tech-nology, space travel etc. Nevertheless, during one of their many inter-stellar journeys they will reach Alfa Nova, a planet with a poorly devel-oped species, and become prisoners of this planet's electromagnetism. From that moment on, Tera's process of Cause and Effect that charac-terizes the evolution of thought-energies is going to repeat.

84. How will be the departure of those who have conceived their spirit?

Those, whose thought-energies have been concentrating on positive things in their lives, have already started to wake their Conscience. These souls, as mentioned earlier, need two or three more incarnations during the 200 years or after having suffered at the end of the second phase to complete the process. If currently the beings acquire knowledge, understanding and love and conceive the spirit, they will not need neither the 200 years nor the suffering of the second phase thus he/she will disincarnate after 2014 and will pass to the Internal City of the planet in order to continue the path towards the Internal City of Venus and from there embark on the Universal Journey. What we are trying to show you is that you can do it now. There is no need to wait any longer. We are referring to what you would call a Quantum Leap, a new era as announced in the Maya prophecies to transcend this reality now, if you only decide to. If they do not succeed, they will have 200 years to prepare and if they still fail to conceive the spirit, they will have 7 thousand years to get it. If people, through the Knowledge, Understanding and Love they show now, have conceived their spirit, they will disincarnate leaving the physical body through the Pineal Gland after 2014 and shelter in the Pineal Gland of an Ayapliano-Seramita of the Internal City of Tera. Here they start to prepare for the passage to Venus to incarnate in beings of that reality.

Those who use positive thoughts have actually taken a first step to awake. However, with the Positive-Knowledge and Positive-Understanding of their brain's left side alone, they will have to stay on until they complete these qualities with the one missing which is Love. Consequently, you are, no doubt, aware that the elevation of humanity presents three different phases.

First – Those humans who already conceived their Baby-Spirit. They have the condition and right to transcend and leave for the Internal City of Venus after 2014. Some will volunteer out of Love on Tera to continue to work on the transmutation of thought-energies (souls).

Second – Those who awaked but only work with the Positive Knowledge and Understanding of their brains' left side. They have not conceived their Baby-Spirit on their brain's right side and will need the 200 years and Love to do so. Failing during that period, they must keep trying during all of the 7 thousand years of the alignment.

Third – Those who have not awaked since they firmly hold on to their material lives and are prisoners of the negative thought-energies of ambition and power.

The souls of those under 'second' who fail to conceive their Baby-Spirit on Tera during all of the 7 thousand years will shelter in the Yeti to help him continue his evolution and elevation. He will be the future Human Species on Tera. This means that they will contribute their knowledge and understanding of evolution in order to help the Yeti continue and be rescued by his brothers.

The number of those under 'third,' will gradually decrease during the 7 thousand years. The remainder will go to Mars and afterwards wander from planet to planet until heading for Pluto. On their way to Pluto, a black hole will attract and take them to a very dense reality you call Inferior Dimension. There, the planets Alfa Nova and Ebiares will be their new homes where they will incarnate in our brothers-Ayaplianos who had suffered distortion and whose state of evolution is close to that of the Neanderthals.

85. By your calculations, can you give us an idea of how many spiritual conceptions will transcend and go to the Internal City of Venus?

Our calculations indicate that about 20% of Tera's inhabitants shall transcend during the next 200 years as of 2014. Our numbers base on the vibration frequency currently emanating from you and on the quality of the planet's electromagnetic waves. For that reason, we are guiding ourselves by mathematic and chemical indicators that determine the necessary vibration frequency for the conception of the spirit.

86. Can you give us an example?

A large orchestra of average talented musicians will probably not produce the quality music a smaller one of top professionals will.

87. Why does the spirit have a special, sharp and high frequency?

The spirit is the union of thought-energies (souls) that share a reciprocal attraction for their quality and weighed elevation of expression. There is logic in the fact that an alliance of such extraordinary thoughts would produce a mathematical and chemical correlation capable of generating an acute frequential tone of the highest vibration. Following the laws of chemistry, we could say that protons of both matter and soul produce a modulated frequency that will attract a sequence of equal thoughts to form the Universal-Concept of *ONE*. When protons of similar characteristics join, the modulated frequency turns a wave with the characteristics of the signal it transmits. This means the protons turn Hydrogen (Beings of Venus and Mercury) which, in turn, will suffer transformation (fusion) to Helium (Beings of the Star Sun).

The universe works by electromagnetism. So that electromagnetism work requires large amounts of energy (thoughts) and very high temperatures. We are not talking about heat or fire but chemical temperatures that produce light, not heat, and by doing so its components crystallize. We refer to the photon and its elements.

Referring to photons, we mean energy from all existing in the universe rather than from the Star Sun only. In other words, this energy is a source of light present in your positive-thought-energies as well as in your diet (matter energy). Properly assimilated, it will help you transmute into energetic beings. Like plants work by photosynthesis, the energy of your thought-crystals will turn your soul into spirit, that is, by assimilating Light (Understanding), you will be able to conceive and gestate your Baby-Spirit that will take the very best of your thought-energies (souls) to grow and evolve. The conception of your Baby-Spirit in the Pineal Gland compares to the process of *cold fusion*, a thermonuclear reaction at ambient temperature and low pressure.

88. What are the symptoms of Spiritual Conception?

Spiritual Awakening is the Conception of the Baby-Spirit. We use the term Conception because it is a process of 'energetic gestation'. You will wonder how it works. People live one life after another, from incarnation to incarnation, a process that will lead them to the transformation of their thought-energies. These thought-energies or souls are forming chemical and mathematic qualities, owing to the energetic evolution of vibration frequency, humans develop through life experience.

Humans are concentrating these qualities in their Pineal Gland, which through continual incarnations becomes the "womb" where the soul accumulates myriads of positive-energies. Gathering and forming them, the soul reaches a point where it has to realize a creative Big Bang of elevated thoughts that so turn a perfect energy source for the formation of the Baby-Spirit.

The conception of the Baby-Spirit occurs when the Universal Mind and the Cosmic Energy unite and create a thought-child of high vibration frequency, rhythm, and light colors. It is not any thought-child, because it has drawn energy of universal Knowledge, Understanding and Love from thoughts of the highest grades, planes and dimensions. When humans raise the quality of their thoughts by transcending the reality they live, their energy is ready to gestate the Baby-Spirit. This gestation will make their inner senses feel symptoms that resemble very much those of a pregnancy. Nevertheless, ignoring the symptoms" origin, they might consider them as being a physical or psychological consequence.

89. What are the symptoms of gestation of the spirit?

During the period of gestation, you will experiment a series of changes in your soul meaning in your emotions. Some of these changes will reflect on your physical body resulting in nausea and general unwellness. Some symptoms will look normal to you; others however evidence difficulties when it comes to leading with emotions.

Humans will feel physical and psychical discomfort during the first three months (Elementary Reality) of the spiritual gestation.

The Big Bang of your Awakening and the Conception of the Baby-Spirit in the Pineal Gland will indeed make you feel strange and uncomfortable. The first consequence of gestation in the physical reality is the suspension of the menstruation cycle. How would this compare to the process of gestation of the Baby-Spirit? Blood (menstruation) stands for material life and it is from the material life that the spirit will learn to **detach**. Awakening means to stir the stagnant waters of subconsciousness, the hiding place of those emotions whose intimate manifestations you hate to feel and recognize, and therefore find difficult to work and control.

Having to face explicit or dissimulated emotions will make you feel physical and psychological pain. The purification of your soul will cause muscle aches and headaches, tiredness, loss of appetite and at the same time anxiety, sadness etc. The symptoms of the spiritual gestation are unmistakable; what you have to do is to accept, understand and work them.

Since gestation of the Baby-Spirit occurs in the Pineal Gland, humans' most elevated thoughts enshroud the baby to prevent any interference. To this effect, the thought-energies will set up an energetic field around the Pineal Gland to nurture the baby. The way the progesterone hormone protects physical pregnancy, the Energy will inhibit any disturbance of the Pineal Gland.

It is necessary that during all of the gestation the Baby-Spirit assimilate high quality energy. Such as a mother feeds on the right diet for her baby's sake, the correct nourishment for your Baby-Spirit to develop sound and strong energetic growth are elevated thoughts of cosmic and universal knowledge.

Humans may suffer psychological stress.

Owing to their mental development and the concentrated energetic feeding of their thought-energies, humans may suffer from over-feeding resulting in uneasiness, unwellness, stress and confusion. They nevertheless will be able to overcome these symptoms by deepening their understanding. Moreover, YOGA techniques of Breathing and Meditation, Reading and Spiritual Group Work will be useful to relax their minds and quieten down their souls.

Humans must control the type and amount of energy they assimilate. If they fail, their Baby-Spirit will just be fed but not properly nurtured. They have to realize that from now on they must be attentive of quality and quantity according to the very needs of their baby-spirit. This means they must be selective of the knowledge they come across.

Humans will feel a strong urge to discuss spirituality.

Humans use to suffer from lack of self-restraint during the gestation of their spirit and tend to be overly talkative about it. They feel that, if they held back on their emotions, would mean that they did not make the right choice. They are extremely concerned that as many of their fellow humans as possible experiment the same Awakening. This leads them to try to convince others that the way to succeed is the one they chose.

They are anxious to make their friends and relatives understand them. They wish to be part of many studying circles, to attend a thousand conferences and to read absolutely everything published about spirituality. However, they must control this obsession, relax, meditate and try to understand that humans are on their way, only each one at a different pace, some faster, others slower

The desire to leave a particular mark wherever they go, characterizes many humans' lack of spiritual moderation.

Humans have psychical insomnia.

Humans should avoid overreacting striving for Peace and Harmony instead. The universe does not ask you to embark on great missions. However modest you feel your life is, what counts is that you do the best you can. Spiritual intemperance will cause insomnia, tiredness, unwellness, weakness, incapacity, impotence etc., all of which contributing to weaken the energetic protection of the baby-spirit. You also have to watch over your physical body by exercising yourselves and eating healthy food to keep your material and psychical life balanced.

Humans keep worrying if what they do is enough to add to their spiritual elevation.

The development of the Baby-Spirit differs from individual to individual. Many of you believe that the more you know of spirituality the faster you will elevate, supposedly prepare better than others and making superhuman efforts hoping that this will guarantee your reaching the goal. Not quite. Spirituality requires the intenseness of quality rather than the abundance of accumulated information and knowledge. Care for your Baby-Spirit the best you can, but do not overdo it; use your conscience, will, perseverance, understanding, affection and your Desire of Creation that transmutes all existing. Overfeeding your Baby-Spirit will leave it with mental excess weight, which is neither good for you nor for the Baby-Spirit.

You do not have to chase after whatever information, book, knowledge etc. you believe will turn you more "spiritual". What you need is to arrive at a state of innermost peace that will enable you to concentrate on the gestation and development of your baby.

Humans accumulate excess information.

If it is true that the baby-spirit needs to assimilate the most elevated thoughts, how do we do this? What is the most appropriate teaching? Should some Ascended Master or a Channel be its guides or some extra-terrestrial message? What would be the quality energy nourishment for the Baby-Spirit? The Baby-Spirit should not be dependent on a certain teaching or message, supposedly the correct one, thus denying it access to other options.

Like the fetus during pregnancy that feeds on nutrients such as proteins, vitamins, carbohydrates and minerals, the Baby-Spirit needs a variety of thought-energies. In consequence, humans have to provide their Baby-Spirit with cosmic knowledge such as messages from diverse planes and dimensions, selective reading and teaching from Ascended Masters, participation in spiritual work groups and discussions. Any positive thought-energy is welcome as it helps the Baby-Spirit assimilate universal thought-energies avoiding thus the stagnation of its cosmic development. Again, do avoid excess energy that may affect the process of thinking and cause your spiritual progress to slow down.

Humans feel an enormous weight on their soul.

The more you know the greater is your responsibility and the weight on your conscience. At this point of the Baby-Spirit's gestation, you have feelings of plenitude owing to the increasing flow of Knowledge, Understanding and Love. Your thought-energies have made your soul feel one with the universe, the wisdom of the cosmos. All this knowledge and innumerous thought-energies have nurtured the Baby-Spirit and humans feel deep inside the spiritual union with their Creator. The volume of information accumulated in humans' brain may cause them to show such symptoms as heaviness, uneasiness, discomfort and disorientation.

However, the right amount of useful knowledge may counteract these symptoms. Thus, the weight of unnecessary knowledge would drastically decrease and humans feel the Baby-Spirit's gestation to be lighter. Humans who are gestating their Baby-Spirit tend to feel superior to those who have not yet conceived their spirit. To have succeeded before others have, may leave their souls with a pang pride and arrogance of the ego can produce. This uneasiness is capable of causing energetic alterations (like spots) in the soul that might disappear through understanding and evolution or rather be permanent, thus marking an energetic setback in humans that could affect the gestation of the Baby-Spirit.

These alterations (spots or stains in the soul) are the ill negative emotions that keep you from correctly feeding your baby turning an uncomfortable weight that adds responsibilities and obligations to the gestation. Those humans develop their spirituality as if it were an obligation rather than a free decision with joyfulness. Under these circumstances, their walk on the path to spirituality is not a light and joyful but a heavy and rigid one.

Humans' external senses sharpen.

The material pregnancy causes the external senses to sharpen owing to an increasing flow of hormones. Gestation of the Baby-Spirit will make humans' internal senses become more acute in response to a major flow of positive thought-energies that will activate perception, intuition, sensibility, divination etc.

Humans' temperature goes up during gestation.

Like the corporal temperature that tends to go up because of progesterone hormones, the soul's temperature, that is, its vibration frequency will increase. This gives the thought-energies greater mobility allowing Knowledge, Understanding and Love to move freely in their electromagnetism and that of the environment with celerity. The larger the number of thought-energies having high frequency vibrations the higher will become the vibration frequency of your electromagnetism and that of the planet.

Humans might experience digestion disorders.

Frequently, digestive disorders occur during pregnancy triggered by progesterone, a hormone that interferes with the control of the digestive tract relaxing the intestine muscle, which slows down the evacuation of waste. Likewise occurs during the gestation of the Baby-Spirit. Humans are constantly working their ill negative emotions, which their brain tends to control resulting in states of physical unwellness.

Those are collateral effects of spiritual gestation. Every human being will have to feel and comprehend them so that the Conception of his Spirit may finally result in an extraordinary act of Peace, Harmony and Love. Therefore, acceptance of the symptoms' spiritual origin is of great importance for the process of gestation. When humans have a deep desire to conceive their sprit, gestation turns the most dazzling of feelings that will make them realize this particular state of elevated existence.

90. We always thought that leaving planet Tera via the Vortex of the Northern Cone would be for Cyrius and not for Venus. Which one is correct?

Actually, many of you are preparing for Cyrius, but before, they have to see the Internal City of Venus, Mercury and the Sun. When reaching the Sun your spirit will almost have formed. Completing the process there, you turn Energetic Beings of Helium, which is the condition, in which the beings of Cyrius, all with their spirits formed, can receive you. When arriving on Cyrius, your spirit will first shelter in a Cyrian's Pineal Gland. After it has adapted to the subtle body of the being, it (you) will be ready to incarnate and share their reality.

91. How do we prepare to leave for the Internal City of Venus?

After several incarnations, many of you will attain the necessary vibration frequency to escape the gravity of their present life's reality and feel attracted to the planet's elevated electromagnetism. After disincarnating, the energy of your spirit will produce a high frequency tone that, along with others of the same frequency, will make the spirit gather with many other spirits. When, after tuning up, they all produce the same universal sound they are going to leave through the Vortex-Northern-Cone, following the joint frequency of the Internal City of Tera and Venus.

92. Will we be conscious of that journey?

You all will be aware of it. Nevertheless, do not think of it as a displacement by physical means. Universal and cosmic journeys occur by desire and force of the mind. When you are well awake and conscious of what you are thinking and doing, you belong to the vastness of the universe, yet will always be responsible for yourselves as individuals.

93. Will we lose our individuality when entering the Pineal Gland of a Being of Venus?

We all are ONE, which means that we are *EL SER UNO* for being part of it. We will never lose our individuality since we are capable of recalling our past life experiences. Nonetheless, this cosmic memory always reminds us that, despite our intense individual journeys across the universe, we forever are ONE, because *we* are the universe.

94. As mentioned above, there are spirits that will leave via the Vortex-Northern-Cone. What about the spirits that leave via the spacecraft?

From what we outlined in the first three books *EL SER UNO*, you know that you will be feeling an attraction for teachings for which your energy shows affinity. In effect, when spirits prepare to leave the planetary reality for the Internal City, diverse energy concentrations will form and unite by a similar vibration frequency of their universal thought-energies (souls).

Consequently, there is a union of human souls, who deal with extraterrestrial phenomena or follow the teachings of certain Ascended Masters. Somehow, they gather through energetic attraction or affinity of vibration frequency. All souls will eventually depart via the Vortex-Northern-Cone and shelter with the Brothers Ayaplianos-Seramitas of the planet's Internal City. Later on, they will be heading for the Internal City of Venus, then for that of Mercury to continue their preparation and finally enter the Star Sun to set out for new realities of existence.

It is on the Star Sun, where grown and entirely defined spirits, following energetic inclinations, will initiate the long path of return to their origin. As for our direct descendants that is, the Ayaplianos-Volunteers, we shall host them in our brains and together we will return to *our* place of origin: The Pleiades.

95. What will happen to the Solar System and Venus and Mercury, and the rest of the planets after all souls have elevated, formed their spirits and sheltered in the Star Sun?

When the last thought-energies (souls) will have elevated and formed their spirit, that is, their Energetic Being and find themselves in the Star Sun, the planets will have fulfilled their mission of having sheltered the souls according to their evolution and elevation. This way they will be ready for the great cosmic journey and return to their origin. When this occurs, the Astro Sun will extinguish and will become a Giant Red. Nowadays you are receiving its warmth, light and luminosity but actually, what you really see in the sun are the millions of spirits that do this work in order to maintain the life and existence on this plane.

We know that to you the Star Sun is just a celestial body whose continual thermonuclear fusion of hydrogen to helium generates heat, light and luminosity. In reality, what you perceive as heat and light is the phenomenon that millions and millions of spirits have created and that you call Sun.

When the Astro Sun sheltered all the spirits of the Solar System, it will go extinct, because the hydrogen in its core will be much less abundant, it will contract and ignite the adjacent layer of hydrogen, but this will not be enough to stop the collapse, it will continue compacting raising its temperature to such a degree that it will fuse the helium in the core. this will cause the outer layers to expand little by little.

In consequence, the sun will expand to a Red Giant by fusing helium to carbon and oxygen in its core and its enormous reach absorb the planets Mercury, Venus and Tera. Nevertheless, after shedding its outer layers, it will leave behind an inert mass of carbon and oxygen in its center called a stellar remnant or White Dwarf. The billions of spirits sheltered in this core will then leave for a new reality of existence called The Fourth Plane of Dimension.

The Solar System, as you know it, will cease to exist as the rest of the planets will enter a black hole and become part of a denser reality of the Primary Dimension. Their thought-energies will be preserved and recycled, and help with the evolution of our brothers and sisters of the planets Alfa Nova and Ebiares.

The sequence of events as mentioned will occur when the Solar System be 18 billion years old, so far it is 5 million years old, there are still 13 billion years to go. Within this extensive period, the species to take humans' place will have the expected positive evolution and elevation.

However, way before the Star Sun's annihilation and with the appearance of the Yeti, all souls shall be safe, as this Cosmic Alignment will do away with the malignant disease of Ambition (Distortion) on Tera, which will become the chemotherapy of cancer that invaded you.

96. What will be of those religious humans who received planetary rather than universal teachings? Will they likewise form their spirit and leave the planet?

Whatever their religious beliefs, entering the Cosmic Alignment will depend on the quality of their Thoughts, Actions and Deeds. Universe is ruled by Frequency, Vibration, Rhythm, Colors, etc. Gender, color, language, education, age, none of this is relevant for the conception and elevation of the spirit. What really counts is your way of thinking and acting throughout your lives and your innermost belief in the values that are guiding both. Only this will help you walk the path of Truth and Freedom.

It therefore is essential not to depend in any way on religious institutions or Ascended Masters. When we say, "not to depend", we do not at all deny the importance of much of their teachings, which we your Elder Brothers thought indeed necessary to use to encourage your positive thinking and acting, and with which you have managed to prepare the Conception of your Spirit.

However, feeling that you have reached a higher grade does not necessarily mean that you are capable of communicating with your Inner Self, receive celestial messages, be channels or mediums. What you do need to enter the Cosmic Alignment and head for superior realities of existence are your trustworthy feelings, the re-education of your soul, the true knowledge of yourselves. Those are the conditions required for the Conception of the Spirit.

Do not feel bad because others seem to be able to communicate with their Inner Self, talk to angels and extraterrestrials, to be channels, mediums and the like. It does not mean that they are more spiritual than you are nor that everyone on the planet must have these characteristics to be spiritual. They just awaked like any other human being, conceived their Baby-Spirit and managed to activate particular abilities others do not have.

They might also have inherited these faculties or the conditions to develop them. This would suggest that they are much older souls who built them by intensely using Willpower, Studies, Work, Knowledge, Understanding and Love life after life. Nevertheless, whatever their evolution and elevation, humans who already awaked and conceived their spirit, eventually will all show the same characteristics.

Do not expect, however, impressive advances immediately. Just be yourselves, positive and true human beings. Pass on Knowledge, Understanding and Love, wake your dormant brothers and sisters, live your lives obeying your innermost feelings, give Love, show responsibility and cherish the Tera-Cell. Take a real good look at the universe, study the cosmos, search for your ancestral past, try to get answers and be truthful to yourselves and the universe.

97. Why is it that we will live two or three more lives during the first 200 years?

It all depends on your particular needs to elevate the vibration frequency of your thought-energies. Many of you have already attained the vibration, rhythm and colors necessary to leave the planet. The moment you disincarnate, your souls are ready to head for the Internal Cities of Tera and Venus. Yet others are halfway. They do need two to three more incarnations, that is, more or less 200 years, to reach the required frequency. On the other hand, many will not be ready by the end of the 200 years. They will definitely need the 7 thousand years or the 63 incarnations of the Cosmic Alignment to conceive and develop their spirit.

Last, there are those carrying ill negative thought-energies who will be unable to join the Cosmic Alignment. They will keep on incarnating until leaving Tera definitely for Mars and in the future – if healed – return and incarnate in the Yeti to continue the universal cycle of evolution and elevation. Now when the universe eventually recycles and uses thought-energies (souls) for new creations, it is because these energies are at such a low vibration frequency that they cannot elevate on their own accord. They will then mix with other elementary energies for a re-start.

98. What is the process to neutralize the ill negative thought-energies (souls) on the planet?

As of 7 July 2014, humans who conceived their Baby-Spirit disincarnate and head for the planet's Internal City where the Ayaplianos-Seramitas and souls that already shelter there are going to give them a brotherly welcome. Along the 200 years, the positive-sound souls in an orderly process will group according to the characteristics developed during their incarnations on Tera and depart for the Internal City of the planet. From there, they will proceed to Venus. This will mark the end of the Alignment's first collection.

Throughout the following phase of the Alignment, ill negative energies will dominate the planet and the souls that failed to form their Baby-Spirit. Nevertheless, all of them will continue their cycle of evolutionary and spiritual advance, until at the end of the 7 thousand years the Cosmic Alignment will end with the second and final collection and departure. After that, the human-species as you have known it, will abandon the planet and the Yeti species take its place. Meanwhile, the souls that did reach the Internal City of Tera will receive teachings about Universal Knowledge. Among them are those who had worked with both sides of their brain while incarnated. This has made them "Special" and it is they, who will offer to volunteer by incarnating again on Tera. Their mission is to teach the souls, who had to stay behind, the path of positive living and transcendence so that their thought-energies would impulse the evolution of the Yeti. Nevertheless, these Special souls, despite having conceived their Baby-Spirit will return to Venus for further spiritual growth, every time they disincarnate on Tera.

99. What will the life of these Special souls be like having to live among ill negative thought-energies?

It will not at all be easy. This is why they have to use always both sides of their brain. While the left side keeps on following up on the ill negative thought-energies' (Reptilian) way of thinking and acting, the right side will have to concentrate on the task they have come to fulfil. There will be ill negative energies between Tera and Mars still for a long time. During the consecutive phases of the Cosmic Alignment, those souls will have to determine whether to incarnate innumerous times as humans and maybe in a distant future in the Yeti, or to stay on Mars for not having reached the vibration frequency needed to do so.

On deciding for Mars, they will not be able to incarnate any more on Tera in humans nor in the Yeti, thus having to await the following Cosmic Alignment to shelter in individuals of the race that will emerge after the Yeti is gone. This new species will help them transform and transcend their current reality. Those who fall back rather than advance will be wandering from planet to planet. However, when approaching Pluto, they will come across a black hole and enter the denser reality of the planets Alpha Nova and Ebiares of the Inferior Dimension the human-like creatures of which will host them.

The Special souls will be making every effort to save whatever ill negative souls the can. They will have to transmit them universal Knowledge, Understanding and Love so they would become part of the electromagnetism of Tera enabling the Yeti to assimilate these thought-energies (souls) for the sake of his evolution and elevation. The Special souls will face immense problems and not enjoy the freedom of thinking and acting you do since free speech on universal topics will suffer severe control. Consequently, they will have to work silently, yet always running high risks and not infrequently sacrificing their lives, as did many martyrs in the past.

100. Why the universal topics will suffer prohibition?

Once the positive-sound energies leave Tera, the ill negative energies of the dark Reptilian force are going to dominate the planet. This will happen at the end of the 200 years span and prior to the beginning of the Cosmic Alignment. Concluded the 200 years, the Tera-Cell and the humans who are staying on will have to face hopelessness, hardship and terror in consequence of a state of ostracism and darkness the Reptilian force has been creating to give them a decisive edge in their struggle for survival. The Special souls thus will be incarnating in the middle of chaos, yet prepared to confront the Reptilian force. Their arms, however, will not be force but their superior intelligence.

101. How long will Tera be under the pernicious command of the Reptilian force?

You have 200 years to conceive your spirit and abandon a planet that held you prisoners for millions of years. Nevertheless, the positive forces of the Universe have vigorously been working to heal you and give you the strength to free yourselves from the virus of Ambition. You have received such amounts of defensive energy that many of you are convalescent and almost cured. However, others continue very ill or even run the risk to have to face the process of energetic recycling. So far, all persons, whether slightly or heavily ill, have been in quarantine in just one place: Planet Tera. Nonetheless, for the sake of evolution, we decided that thought-energies (souls) of healed persons must no longer be in contact with those of individuals still seriously ill. We therefore are separating them by forming groups in accordance with their state of evolution. Of the more than 7 billion individuals on the planet, about 20% are cured, ready for the Cosmic Alignment and their journey to the Internal City of Tera and Venus. Another 40% are convalescent souls, who will need the 200 or even the 7 thousand years for their complete cure and then be able to enter the Internal City of Tera. A total 30% after healing may either transcend or engage in evolution of the Yeti. The souls of the final 10% will have to enter the process of recycling and new creations in the universe. According to these calculations, the number of incarnations is bound to decrease considerably.

102. How many Special Beings (souls) will there be to assist these souls with the recuperation of their energy?

There will be very few of them. Just as you communicate with Ascended Masters, Messengers and Channels today, in the future it will be them to communicate with you. They will incarnate among the 40% of convalescent humans many of whom are going to offer the necessary vibration frequency to receive these Special Souls. While some will incarnate, others will remain at the Internal City of Tera o Venus. From there they will communicate with you through telepathy (they will be the Ascended Masters of the future) and fulfill their mission, which is to help the largest possible number of souls transcend this reality and also leave an extraordinary legacy for the Yeti so as to enable him to fulfil his cycle of evolution and elevation.

103. What will be your task as Ayaplianos-Volunteers of the spacecraft and that of the Seramitas and Interanos at the Internal City during this process?

Responsibilities of the Elder Brothers Seramitas and Interanos will not be any different in the future. Their homes have always been the Internal City of Tera, Venus, Mercury and the Star Sun. From there they developed a comprehensive work for your benefit at all times. We Ayaplianos-Volunteers, on staying at the spacecraft, have always remained in the Anti-matter reality of the planet and guided from there the activities of our brothers and sisters Seramitas and Interanos in their mission to heal and recuperate you. We shall stay with Tera as long as necessary to be of help to you. Once our mission is complete, that is, when the last individual of the current human species has left the planet, we are going to form a team out of Ayaplianos-Humans to watch over the Yeti's evolution and elevation and make this team the future Guardians of Tera. After that, we will leave for Venus, Mercury and the Star Sun where we shall be waiting for all the human spirits to complete their formation. Remember that the Star Sun is the place where the spirits gather and prepare their energies to take them back to their origin. This is how the spirits are going to rediscover the path of return to universal existence.

104. Why do we have to leave through the Star Sun, and what will be the departure like?

To make you understand the functioning of the universe and the process of energy recycling we have to consider the fact that you, so far, have "not" gone through the process in this reality. You experienced it many times in past lives but lost memory of it. You were very ill and with your cosmic memory terribly affected. An energy shield installed by the Interstellar Cosmic Federation has surrounded Planet Tera, you and the rest of the Solar System for millions of years. You and all that exists in the Solar System had been busy recycling thought-energies (souls) so many times that the procedure resembled a process of brainwashing. Recycling turned a firm and unique concept and as such, you recorded it on your brains.

This is why the projection of images is always the same and why you fail to remember where you came from, whom you are and where you are heading. When you are having a "déjà vu" experience, you have the sensation to see and feel something you experienced before. However, what actually occurs is that you do start to remember. It is your first step to Awaking to conscience. From now on, it will be much easier for you to recall, as there will be a gradual activation of your memory through energy transmutation. You will start to give this transmutation strong impulse on Tera, in the Internal City of Venus, Mercury and the Star Sun.

You must realize that if the universe works following chemical and mathematic precepts, energetic purification occurs under identical conditions. Therefore, elevation from grades through planes and on to dimensions requires energy that has to undergo transformation in order to adapt to higher frequencies and to electric power sources that produce plain electricity as well as high luminosity. The difference is that you have Electrostatic Power (atoms without movement) on one hand and electromagnetic waves (atoms in movement) on the other.

Thought-energy has many different levels of existence and thus needs to keep on adapting to be fit to exist in these varying realities. When leaving Tera, you will carry energy that compares to powerful electrical discharges produced by a conductive element called atom. When you are about to conceive your spirit through the Pineal Gland, the atom to form the Baby-Spirit is a **conductor** and will be attracted to the interacting electromagnetic waves of Venus, the **receptor**.

This is how you will keep on transforming your thought-energies' (souls') basic electricity into Light. When entering the Star Sun, you first will exist in its cold heat, then in its cold light and finally in Luminosity.

The only way that the spirit-thought-energy can travel for a different plane (reality) or dimension of existence is in the form of: *A Being of Light that we could compare the process to a laser beam that, once released, never ceases to advance, it is infinite*. Nevertheless, it is indispensable that beings of Venus and Mercury with identical characteristics shelter you before.

105. What are the beings of Venus like?

Venus is the second planet in the Solar System in order of distance from the Sun, and the third in terms of size, from smallest to largest. Its name is on honor Venus, the Roman goddess of Love. It is a rocky, terrestrial-type planet, often called the Earth's sister planet, as both are similar in size, mass and composition, although totally different in thermal matters and atmospheric. In particular, the Mayan civilization elaborated a religious calendar based on the astronomical cycles, including the cycles of Venus. the symbol of the planet Venus is a stylized representation of the mirror of the goddess Venus: a circle with a small cross below, used also today to denote sex feminine. Venus has a dense atmosphere, made up mostly of carbon dioxide and a small amount of nitrogen. The pressure at the level of surface is 90 times greater than the atmospheric pressure at the surface terrestrial (a pressure equivalent on Earth to the pressure that is submerged in water to a depth of one kilometer). The huge amount of CO_2 from the atmosphere causes a strong greenhouse effect that raises the temperature of the planet's surface up to about 464 °C in the lower elevation regions near the equator. (Wikipedia)

As you can see, due to this explanation we can assume that the beings from Venus are made of Carbon Dioxide. It means that their emotions already have been transmuted into feelings. Earthly passions have cooled and acquired characteristics closest to the element Ether and Helium. Carbon dioxide is essential to the life of the human species and is present in the process of photosynthesis on Venus.

There is no doubt that life on Venus is different from Tera's in many aspects. This reminds us that, even though every planet creates its particular human-expression, its overall chemical elements are the same as those of the rest. Nonetheless, despite having human-form, the chemical composition and thus the energy of the beings of Venus is different.

106. You say the Special-Beings (souls) are taking turns at proceeding to incarnate on Tera. What does this mean?

Notwithstanding that the elevated souls head for Venus to continue their preparation, they are bound to return every so often for alternating incarnations on Tera. These elevated souls either incarnate or find shelter on the right side of the Special-Beings' brain. However, those who incarnate will need and receive support from the elevated souls, now on Venus, to fulfill their task.

107. How can elevated souls of Venus incarnate via our Pineal Gland having a different chemical composition and mathematic formula?

We have to remember that, despite a certain difference in the chemical composition, there are common elements. We know that these thought-energies (souls) are going to shelter in the Special-Beings brain's right side because both have the same characteristics, chemical conditions and vibration frequency. These thought-energies (souls) will occupy the brain for a length of time for adaptation and then be able to incarnate in a physical human body with an advanced degree of purification. Nowadays, they are channels who are transmitting universal teachings, since their brain's right side is ready to receive high vibration frequencies from other realities.

108. Are there nowadays Seramitas incarnated in physical human bodies? If so, are we ready to know who they are?

Yes, some Seramitas of the Internal City and a number of souls from Venus, Mercury and the Star Sun live among you incarnated in a human body. Their identity is of minor importance. In fact, various are the motives for their presence: Studies, a mission, always with the aim to be of help to their Human Brothers and Sisters. Some of these incarnated souls know very well where they arrived from, others do not recall because of the density in which they live or because they are in a process of learning and elevation. Never mind who they might be. Important is the task they realize in silence.

109. What important signs will appear in 2014 indicating that we are about to enter the Cosmic Alignment?

Some of the signs are as follows:

- Our Ayapliana-Seramita-Interana presence and the knowledge of the Internal City we shall transmit to all beings of the planet.
- At the beginning of the Cosmic Alignment, that is, July 7, 2014, you will clearly perceive the presence of and spiritual help from the Star Sun's Pineal Gland.
- The governments of four countries will announce the disclosure of confidential information on extraterrestrial life.
- Sighting of extraterrestrial Spacecraft and the phenomenon of electromagnetic Orbs will occur in different parts of the planet. We encourage these events to make you feel sure of our presence.
- Appearance of the Crop Circles prior to 2014 will be intense in England but then decline and be more frequent in South America.
- Communication, so far via channels, can be direct with beings who have awaked, among them scientists and researchers.
- A great many rainbows will surge over cities that have hardly ever seen them before.
- Aurora Borealis and Australis will occur in cities of intense cold.
- There will be unusual temperature highs and lows marking a change of the seasons in the near future.
- Some religious institutions will accept the existence of extraterrestrial beings.
- Many beings will have their first contact with us and begin to understand who the Ayaplianos-Volunteers of the spacecraft, the Seramitas and Interanos are. We shall be very happy to maintain direct contact with them.

- The Knowledge we are trying to transmit will reach the Western and large part of the Eastern hemisphere of the planet.
- Our messages, so far, through telepathy in the future will be on a palpable-holographic (3-D) planetary level.
- The signs will be visible everywhere and you will no longer doubt of our existence and presence in the electromagnetism of the planet.
- You will feel confident that we are here to help you transcend by heading for the Vortex-Northern-Cone.
- Many of you will be looking forward to making direct contact with us.
- About 20% of humans will have communication with their Inner Self and clearly remember their existence as the beings of Light they are.

After the year 2014, one of the most relevant events of all times will be the ***Discovery of Atlantis, the first city founded by Seramitas and Interanos,*** located in the deep of the Gulf of Mexico. The moment you locate this large submersed urban center you will be facing transcendent revelations the past still hides from humanity. Seramitas and Interanos left a legacy in Atlantis in the form of documents and scripts covering the history of the planet and us. They are proof of what we are revealing to you in the books *EL SER UNO*.

Our messenger-channels are people like any fellow human without particular social standing and voice. Consequently, the knowledge they transmit seems to lack "veracity". The discovery of Atlantis will therefore corroborate the truth of everything we are revealing in these books.

110. What is the language used in those documents and scriptures?

In the scattered documents and scriptures, you will find construction designs as well as writings in hieroglyphics and symbols. It will come as a surprise to you to find that these symbols are a perfect match with those of the Crop Circles, whose meaning, in turn, only scientists and investigators through in-depth studies will be able to decipher.

The Atlantida documents describe in detail that you are of **Extraterrestrial Origin** and explain whom we are, where we are from and where we are heading. Consequently, the knowledge as detailed in *EL SER UNO* is authentic. Many governments already have clues on the existence of Atlantida yet, as always, are trying to hide the evidence. We, Ayaplianos-Seramitas of the Internal City, will not let them. The truth will surface and have an immense number of souls strive to join the Cosmic Alignment. Freedom's name, Brothers and Sisters, is **Truth** and the truth will guide you on... **The Long Path of Return**.

The Cosmic Alignment will bring light meaning that the truth shall emerge in its splendor and there will be no hiding and deceiving. The awakening shall be such that the Reptilian force, at least in the first 200 years, will not have the strength to oppose the Light of the positive-Force of Knowledge, Understanding and Universal Love.

111. Why did they found the City of Atlantis in that particular area?

As you know, the continents of the planet were closed to one another time ago. A continual cooling process along with huge tectonic movements over millions of years caused the continents to start drifting apart until reaching the position they have today. Nevertheless, the Tera-Cell will experience further transformation under the effects of the electromagnetism, gravity, climate etc. If you join the coastlines of South America and Africa, for example, almost match. The same holds true for Spain and Central America. The landmass of what is today the Gulf of Mexico, however, disappeared except for the remnants that turned islands called Puerto Rico, Cuba, Haiti, Jamaica and the Lesser Antilles. The circle of the Gulf of Mexico practically matches the foundations of the City of Atlantis. This circle fell off and sank completely, it is in the bottom of the sea and at the same height as the Gulf. Other parts of land dismembered and moved through the oceans, forming the islands of the Caribbean, the Philippines and the Sea of Japan. Although most of the City of Atlantis is located deep in the Atlantic Sea and has the diameter exactly the size of the circle of the Gulf of Mexico.

112. Why is it that you do not communicate with us in a more direct way?

So far, we have been unable to communicate with you more directly because ours is an Anti-matter reality. The only way to do it is via the Electromagnetism. We have however been sending you an infinite number of messages through telepathy, Orbs and in the form of symbols in Crop Circles, contact from the Third Kind and more. Furthermore, we tried to use palpable holographic communication but failed, as this technique requires a stable electromagnetic field, which is not yet your case.

On the other hand, we had been hopeful to establish contact through telepathy with scientists, yet did not succeed. They still seem too conservative relying in excess on limited and distorted planetary knowledge. However, a good number of them will awake in the near future and be our first direct interlocutors. In fact, "Contacts" through holograms will be a reality as of 2200 Tera time when an enormous number of individuals is going to have the experience of awakening. Their elevated thought-energies will feed the electromagnetism and give us a chance to not only provide clear evidence of our existence but also make our appearance before you. For the time being, we communicate with humans who have a stable individual electromagnetism, which means that their three bodies are in harmony and we can realize a projection of our image and establish communication through telepathy. Thus, they are able to collaborate and help us fulfil the task entrusted to us.

113. Is there a way for us to know if we already made "contact" with elevated realities?

To begin with, there is an important difference between what you call "Contact" or **Reception** via a medium and a spiritual **Bond**. Since you do not yet have reached true spiritual awareness, you tend to misunderstand the particular meaning of these terms.

Reception

Many of you start receiving messages from the innermost part of their souls. When an individual awakes, he/she establishes a first communication with his/her inner self, that is, with thought-energies that live in the soul. While awakening, the individual opens a channel activating the frequency that produces both a particularly sound and an intermittent light that attract many nearby thought-energies.

As a rule, those who awake are not conscious of it at first because they do not yet have the knowledge of how the energy works during the process. As a result, the channel remains wide open and its frequency and sound attract myriads of thought-energies eager for communication. It is like leaving the door of your house open inviting all kind of people in. This is what can happen to an open channel; all types of thought-energies, many of them unwanted or harmful and hard to get rid of, may invade it.

At this point, many of you feel attacked by unknown forces, hear strange sounds, see dark figures and have dreams full of violence, all without any reasonable explanation. If people go on failing to gain energetic spiritual knowledge nor strive to elevate their frequency through growing knowledge of cause and effect, they will run the risk to have their brains overrun by thought-energies of very low vibration frequency and often have to face such severe mental disorders as schizophrenia or dementia. Opening the channel to awake or communicate with mediums not only requires the awareness of cause and effect but also the knowledge of how to deal with parallel realities. Many of you are **Receptors**, but do not create **Bonds** with the spiritual reality.

Spiritual Bonds

We already referred to the importance of creating spiritual bonds. By the time people awake, they have to have recorded on their minds the knowledge of their spirituality's energy. In fact, many often bring it with them from past lives. Consequently, while awaking in their present life they do not feel puzzled or scared and take everything in a natural way. Besides, they can generally count on the help of others to advance on the path to universal knowledge.

These individuals have actually created spiritual bonds and when they awake sending out the vibration frequency of intermittent flashes of their inner light they instantly attract elevated thought-energies (souls) that communicate with them through mediums or rather by telepathy in the case of entities of elevated frequency. We must however warn you of the inconvenience to rely on "schools" that promise to show you how to open the channel to spirituality. You cannot open your channel by taking courses or studying special techniques for the communication with elevated beings of light. The channel to spirituality will "naturally" open up through your inner self's conscious and meritorious work, day after day, life after life.

We also want you to realize that when you feel certain of having awaked, the moment to start real serious work has come. You must stay awake by maintaining your thought-energies always on a high level thus creating protective energy to neutralize any possible interference with your process of awakening. You are in permanent pursuit of knowledge but often fail to do it the right way. It is not through courses or searching for "Masters" that you will succeed. You must do it on your own mobilizing your inner strength and comprehending, controlling and changing harmful negative emotions.

114. Do you suggest that we are not to open a channel until we feel spiritually elevated? How do we know when?

There is no exact timing for the activation of the channel. It will open in a natural way when you reach an appropriate frequency. Therefore, do not consider using anti-natural means like, for instance, hallucinogenic drugs to accelerate the process. They will never work. On the other hand, there is no problem attending courses, conferences and seminars by people who with their personal experience try to help you with your preparation. Nonetheless, you should not accept the promise and even pay for it that, following their teachings, you will be able to activate your channel in no time. ***Do not be fooled***. No one is going to awake from one moment to another. No one can do for you what you have to do by yourselves with constant Efforts, Knowledge, Understanding and Love in your every day's life.

Many of you have the strong wish to be mediums, channels and masters to show their spiritually. Regretfully, most are just ***Receptors*** avidly pursuing knowledge to feel it and gain the recognition, that they are following the path of light, but actually use it to satisfy themselves. As a result, they have to face many extra challenges, as the work done, so far, has not been authentic for not having established yet **Bonds** with their inner self and thus been incapable of communicating with other realities of existence.

Nowadays there is a wild and still unconscious search for spirituality. To be able to feel harmony and peace, it is therefore imperative that you quieten down. We want you to understand that those who strive to awake will have all the help from the universe to find the path to verity. Nevertheless, they will have to follow quietly without claiming to have made a superior statement on spirituality or written such and such a book...this would drag them into a competition with no winner and impede the channel to open.

Everyone has the chance to AWAKE; to be a medium or channel, however is not for all. You must humbly accept this. To recognize that you do not have the condition to be a medium or channel should not make you feel inferior. Both are particular characteristics of some individuals. The universe, in turn, assigns tasks in accordance with millions of diverse characteristics and the corresponding thought-energies (souls) to fulfil them. In a symphony orchestra, many different instruments play; to create a celestial symphony, many souls are going to vibrate in their diverse frequencies producing the music of the cosmos.

115. What about the relationship between Science and Spirituality. Will they join some day?

That union broke up when you lost the knowledge. Yet science is progressing and the day will come when science and spirituality will rejoin. We do not refer to the union of science and spirituality as defined by religious belief. As of 2800, religion will mean individuals' belief in their inner strength, that is, in their spirituality. Religious institutions, in turn, responsible for the slow advance of knowledge during centuries will no longer exist. Science and Technology will flourish to the exclusive benefit of the planet and its inhabitants in unison with Understanding and Love.

116. How will the negative Reptilian force react when you introduce yourselves through holography?

Nowadays there are governments, scientists and researchers who study paranormal and extraterrestrial phenomena at secret facilities across the planet. Our presence is no secret at all. Governments, the Military, Religious Institutions and Civilians are aware of our existence. First three ones do not disclose information because they fear that the official acceptance of extraterrestrial life would seriously affect general belief in many accepted standards of life on the planet.

Those who are particularly interested in withholding this information are numerous religious institutions that depend on followers, who do not question their teachings. These institutions are making every effort to keep it that way. So far, only private researchers, civilians, after comprehensive studies have had the courage to reveal the truth authorities and organizations deliberately hide from the public.

There are also human beings, whom we hold in high esteem for their integrity, whose thought-energies have attained the vibration frequency needed to establish communication with us. Via channeling, we are transmitting them our message of universal truth, which they readily diffuse to serve their fellow humans. It will not be long that the evidence of our existence on Tera shall thus see the light. In consequence, the public will claim their right for an official statement and force governments to release the so far confidential information. This will give rise to fundamental changes on Tera. Humans will face the very truth of the cosmos and no longer doubt their extraterrestrial origin.

The half-truths of religious teachings will have to be revised, scientific advancements and their conclusions be questioned and chemistry, physics and mathematics be based on different universal parameters. For the first time, humanity gets the chance to focus on the universe from an entirely different angle, to be certain of its origin and have a clear vision of its future. No doubt, in the middle of these stunning revelations the ill negative force, the 22 corporations and organizations that run the planet will be opposing fiercely humanity's liberation and transcendence to other realities.

Knowing that it has no chance to transcend the ill negative force will be more decided than ever not to lose control of the planet, exerted for millions of years. ***Evil do not want to die*** and use all of its technological knowledge to retain the power to rule. The knowledge to awake is at every one's reach. Those who willfully chose the ill negative force to continue dominating the planet will do so with full knowledge of the devastating consequences the cause-and-effect relationship will have for them.

117. What is going to happen when the Avatar Abigahel frees humanity from oppression at the end of the second phase?

We have to remember that the Avatar Abigahel will arrive during a very difficult phase of the alignment having to face power and domination of the ill negative force that has exerted severe mental control over humans for the past 500 years. He will make his appearance in the year 2800. Abigahel is a Solar Spirit and considered one of the six-winged angels or Sephirahs (Sephiroth). You already know as: Binah, then he will be called: Abinahel and over time his name will become Abigahel. In the Western Hemisphere, he will be Michael. Coming from the Star Sun, he will go past Mercury and Venus to bring humans of Tera Knowledge, Understanding and Love. Belonging to the hierarchy of the Sephiroth, he will arrive to Tera to be born as the child of man.

Sephiroth

They are divine ancestral emanations consisting of Ten Sephirahs with such names as Kether, Chokmah, Binah, Cesid, Gueburah, Tiphareth, Nethzas, Hod, Jesod and Malkuth. Each Sephrah stands for a number of ideas, titles and attributes that represent parts of the human body and the planet. While the people of Israel was awaiting the arrival of the Messiah, Joshua Emmanual made his appearance and they received him as the Sephirah Jesod who later changed to Joshua and finally to Jesus. The Sephiroth belong to the 24 Ancestors of the White Brotherhood at the Internal City. They are the oldest Seramita spirits to come to the Solar System to fulfil their mission but found they could not leave it any more. It has been long, however, that they transcended

Venus and Mercury, and are now great Spirits of Light living in the Luminosity of the Star Sun. Their hope is to gather the largest possible number of souls to be able to return finally to their origin.

From this caste, heritage and lineage: The White Brotherhood, Abigahel will be born (Michael, his earthly name) in order to help you transcend during the 7 thousand years of the Cosmic Alignment. The history repeats itself. This Spirit of Knowledge, Understanding and Love sent by the White Brotherhood will incarnate in Tera to rediscover the lost path of return. All of your great avatars have descended from elevated realities since they carry the light that illuminates the path, the souls are to travel and where the spirits find their reason of existence. He is to break up the soil and give to drink to the thirsty because when he arrives to the planet, he will find an arid earth with hard hearts and an almost petrified soul.

Abigahel's task is to bring life-saving water to a dry planet that has hardened your hearts and rendered your souls insensitive. The life of Abigahel resembles much that of Joshua Emmanuel holding with his sacrifice and light a place in Tera's history forever. We want you to understand that, when the White Brotherhood sends an avatar with an important mission, he is not alone in his struggle to accomplish it but receives help from thousands of elevated thought-energies (spirits); jointly they fulfil this task by helping elevate an immense number of souls. Here is how it works:

Elevated spirits need to shelter in a brain that holds elevated thought-energies (souls). This means that a person has worked life after life with universal knowledge and understanding and that love has been an innermost feeling throughout his existence, along with continuous efforts and great willpower to advance on the path of elevation.

The White Brotherhood chooses those humans life after life because they carry the universal genetic inheritance and lineage of the volunteers who live in a cryogenic state of existence in the perfect dimension. These volunteers have preserved the pureness of their cosmic inheritance the origin of which are The Superior Dimensions.

118. How will Abigahel proceed to free us from oppression?

Like Joshua Emmanuel, Abigahel has the gift to wake the conscience of humans who at this point, live immersed in darkness and ostracism.

You must realize that throughout the 600 million years on the planet we have confronted the Reptilian-force (virus of ambition). This force never ceased to attack you. Nevertheless, during the innumerous cyclic changes, we were always present and ready to help you transcend. In every change, every transcendence we have been close struggling to lift you from this bottomless abyss in which you had sunk, without hope, without love, not knowing the truth, to help you get a real vision of the universe. It is hard work and the only way to do it, is through love. It is love that gave us the strength to keep on. Nevertheless, it is only with love that you will advance, which means that you first have to love yourselves to be able to understand your environment, the planet and the essence of the cosmos.

It will not be the first or the last time. How many of you, failing to think of this, complain about the life they are living on this planet. You seem to have turned against life because you feel you are in the wrong place asking: "Why do we have to face a situation like that in a place we did not ask for?" Therefore, you blame God and the universe for the miserable life you live. You do not seem to remember that you came to this planet as SCIENTIST-VOLUNTEERS and had been aware of what could happen to you.

Well, we your Elder Brothers, the Seramitas and the Interanos have not forgotten, recall every detail, every moment of our existence, but all the same are here with you helping and feeling in our spirit every emotion of yours. You arrived on Tera of your own free will. Our creator does not act by force. He hopes that his children fulfil their assignments in this plane of existence in a dedicated and loving way. You do have to remember that you are volunteers, as such self-confident and brave fighters, qualities that many characters in your motion pictures show. Do not forget that films, one way or another, reflect the life human beings live or should live.

119. What events will occur until the year 9 thousand once Abigahel frees humans of oppression?

Liberation of humanity is a slow-moving process. Gradually individuals will more closely perceive and observe their lives and environment.

This is not an easy thing to do as the oppressor, the Reptilian force, has marked humans' psyche heavily. However, as always in history of the human species, among a growing number of dissenters, strong leaders will emerge to confront governments, religious institutions and organizations. These leaders, while gradually freeing humankind of slavery and oppression will become the mentors of a new movement called the Golden Age. The process of liberation, however, is complex as it denotes constant confrontation, suffering, violence and often death. Heavy confrontations will go on for a long time until those humans who had reached full awareness will start gaining influence to secure Freedom and Order banning oppression and slavery forever. This is when planet Tera will finally enter the Golden Age you nowadays are voicing so insistently.

120. What will The Golden Age be like?

Positive transformation of a species, planet, grade or plane occurs in innumerable ways. It is the change of the energy of existence at all levels. When speaking of the Golden Age, we refer to an extraordinary compendium of evolution and elevation. After the 7 thousand years of the Cosmic Alignment, Tera's cure will be complete meaning that there will be longer any trace of the disease of ambition. During the third phase of the Cosmic Alignment, the planet will be assimilating pure transforming energy emanating from the dimensions that are going to generate the very process of the alignment. As of the third phase, souls of Venus and Mercury as well as spirits of the Star Sun are exchanging thought-energies to further the planet's cosmic advancement. Humanity will experience a vast increase of cognitive abilities and the birth of highly intelligent individuals who will lead the Tera-Cell to its final destiny: The Universe.

Those of you who awake now are Tera's future as they are working on their vibration sequence to reconnect themselves with the Universal Conscience. They will eventually incarnate as energy of light. The transition to this reality of Light and Love will occur during the 7 thousand years of the alignment when codes and the conception of the spirit will make those human beings enter a multidimensional reality and take them to the celestial sphere of Venus. The beings who live there will shelter these new thought-energies (souls) to help them transmute any possible alteration they might be suffering.

Nowadays there is a small number of crystal, indigo and rainbow children being born. Nevertheless, during the Golden Age, their birth rate is going to increase considerably as more and more of you will re-turn as re-born children. We must be careful when using terminology that refers to spirituality and the anticipation of future events. Your expecta-tions will not have an immediate response but will in the future in the form of an opening of the dimensional vortex at the planet's poles, birth of crys-tal and indigo children, the very Golden Age. All of it is going to start in the year 2800. Meanwhile, as iterated, the Reptilian force will dominate the first two phases of the alignment totaling 666 years, number and symbol of the beast which begin in 2300 until 2800.

The awakening allows many of you to "perceive" the reality beyond their present lives. They clearly feel the presence of their thought-ener-gies and thus the perspective of future events, a process that however has to start now so that these events can materialize. You are living a period of great agitation as knowledge seems to be everywhere; the bombardment of information is so intense that you have trouble classi-fying and understanding it.

Not all you perceive, assimilate and understand belongs to the same reality. Knowledge is at hand but you should realize that it is timeless. It moves freely while being activated. The universe does not function in terms of time but by vibration frequency. For that reason, you have to proceed to the classification of possible events in accordance with their vibration frequency so that you can project and execute them during the 7 thousand years. One of the reasons you have trouble classifying what you perceive is that your spirit is still in the process of formation. Only the spirit is able to determine and establish a chronology for the thought-energies, and to organize the most relevant events of the past, present and future.

The Golden Age summarizes the entire evolution and elevation of the planet's inhabitants. Science and technology hence will be very different from what they are now. Interspace and interdimensional traveling, ho-lography, floating and submersed cities will mark this new reality. Life expectancy will significantly increase owing to much improved health conditions and the fact that humans will become fully conscious of true living. Besides, the benefits of great inventions are going to be at everyone's reach. Back on Tera to incarnate, you will bring with you the most advanced technologies from Venus and Mercury for your further evolution and elevation on the planet.

Beloved Brothers and Sisters!

Changes on planet Tera will be many. Prepare for them by elevating your thought-energies (souls) so that the process of joining the Cosmic Alignment be a harmonious and balanced one. You must conceive your Baby-Spirit to be among the humans who will leave the planet during the next 200 years starting 2014. The Baby-Spirit is your Passport to transcend this reality. To know that you have conceived it you have to be attentive to the typical symptoms of spiritual gestation.

Do not expect magic or miracles to attain the transcendence of your thought-energies nor the presence of Ascended Masters to take you with them. It is nothing of that kind. When disincarnating you will feel attracted to the electromagnetism of the planet through the vibration frequency of the electromagnetism emanating from your Baby-Spirit. You will gather with myriads of other thought-energies, leave through the Vortex-Northern-Cone for the Internal City of the planet and afterwards proceed to planet Venus.

This gathering will start July 7, 2014. We, your Elder Brothers at the Internal City, will assist you during the passage. It is, however, up to you to find the right frequency to traverse the grade and plane that will activate your conscience. You have 200 years to achieve it. To reach this frequency you must dominate your ill negative emotions. Do not let negative thoughts penetrate your soul. Reject them and have your Baby-Spirit assimilate the most elevated thought-energies only. This is how you keep the negative-Reptilian force forever from manipulating and dominating you. Remember that you vibrate with the frequency of the elevated force of Knowledge, Understanding and Love.

Get ready. We are awaiting you. Do not fear. You will leave this reality of existence for one where you will incarnate in healthier and lighter bodies with an advanced state of wisdom and love. Free yourselves of the negative emotional burden that blocks elevation of your vibration frequency. Do not be doubtful and work hard. No matter what your religion, belief, language or country all you need is to activate your Desire of Creation and work on yourselves. You are WARRIORS who will gain the LIGHT on their own accord... this is how you will transcend this reality.

CHAPTER II

THE AYAPLIANOS-ELOHIM (*INTERANOS*) AND THE REPTILIAN-GRAYS

Brothers and Sisters, we want you to turn an open mind to what we are going to explain to you now. The Elohim and Reptilian-Grays belong to your species and like Ayaplianos-Volunteers of the spacecraft, Ayaplianos-Seramitas and Ayaplianos-Humans their origin is the constellation of The Pleiades. We all are descendants of the volunteers who arrived on this planet 600 million years ago. Having suffered varying degrees of distortion owing to climate and energy conditions, we had to adapt by developing particular characteristics.

Although we had given you details of our arrival meaning the four races that expanded on the planet, we did not reveal the history of the Ayaplianos-Elohim, whom you call the Grays, as well as that of the Reptilian-Grays. We had left it for this fourth book because an earlier disclosure could have complicated the description of distortion and its consequences for the volunteers. After descending on Tera, we proceeded to the planet's poles. It was not until after a considerable time that we started sending out groups of volunteers to explore the environment and learn how to adapt to the severe conditions for colonization.

We knew we were running great risks in view of the circumstances we would face on the open. Nevertheless, we kept on because we had a mission: to free planet Tera's magnetism from the energetic interference the fragment of Satien would cause. How right had we been to use both knowledge and intuition. The electromagnetism of our holograms threatened to distort our inner senses. This forced us to take immediate steps for our protection. We proceeded to shelter the two anti-matter spacecraft that had remained on the outside, in large quartz caverns underneath the poles where they ever since have served as our homes. They are the two Internal Cities of Tera: Lemur (at the North pole) and Atlantis (at the South pole).

As we explained earlier, distortion attacked our brothers and sisters volunteers, who had decided to continue our mission in the exterior, with varying intensity. We who are speaking to you are those of this group of Ayaplianos-Volunteers who by majority vote were to remain on the spacecraft for reasons of communication with our planets of origin. We therefore were safe from distortion. You as descendants of those who had stayed on the outside are the Ayaplianos-Humans who have ever since struggled to find the cure and reunite with us. However, another group of Ayaplianos sought to escape distortion by sheltering in caverns deep inside the planet. They are those you know as the Reptilian-Grays and Grays.

121. Who are the Reptilian-Grays and Grays and what their physical characteristics?

We have to convey with great sorrow that the Gray Reptilian brothers were the most affected and distorted. We call them brothers despite the fact that they have become beings so different from us that they make it difficult to communicate with them. Among their specie, there are those who have evolved a little more than the others. The Reptilian-Gray species are slightly similar to us, but mentally there are enormous differences that classify and determine them. Let's see why...

The Elohim (Interanos)
When these brothers left the spacecrafts outside, they were confronted with distortion, to avoid it, they took drastic measures, thinking that with them, they would prevent the disease. By that they went to live

in deep caverns below the south pole, next to the quartz caverns where we the Volunteers-Ayaplianos and Seramitas are. In a way, we, the one who are telling you this story knew what happened to them, although they had no idea that we were close to them in another reality of existence. Most of them are distorted, forming three races: The Reptilian-Grays; The Grays and the Elohim.

The Reptilian-Grays are totally distorted. The Grays only work as a robotic and helpful species, and the last ones, the Elohim were able to conserve 40% of their healthy thought-energies (souls) and it is this part of the brain, which is allowing them to return to the elevation of their universal frequency and vibration. The Elohim, brothers-Ayaplianos, are **NOT** called *Grays*, they are known in the history of the planet as: *The Elohim* (Interanos) and for their 40% healthy are managing to enter the Cosmic Alignment, added to the effort and dedication they have had in all this time to get out of the distortion. You are helping them a lot. Through human example, they have managed to understand their problem and they are solving it.

The Elohim are medium-sized, they reach 1.80 meters size in height, his skin is very clear, perhaps a little out of the ordinary, because they always lived in the deep caverns and there they developed. They are slim, have oversize hairless arms and legs, hands with five thin oversize fingers, heads with prominent foreheads, pallid white skin and eyes of light color. A community of 144 individuals, incapable to procreate they have also survived through cloning. Like you, they are striving to return to their origin. We Volunteers of the spacecraft and the Seramitas of the Internal City are giving them the same support we are giving you.

The population of the Elohim-Ayaplianos is small, there are exactly 144 of them, who have preserved 40% of healthy understanding in their soul (right side of the brain). They were always the same since they arrived on the planet, they have incarnated over and over again in their clones, unlike beings from outside. When you procreated, you were dividing and the thought-energies of those first Ayaplianos who left their spacecrafts, are scattered in all of you, the 7 billion human beings from abroad. The 144 Elohim, have had to clone themselves, to preserve their subsistence. In the society of the Elohim, the Grays exist, these are only clones, formed from those who were totally distorted, they were reproduced through cloning, for the service and work in the City-Ship in which they live. The gray-servers do not perceive their environment, they are fully parameterized and robotized for repetitive service. They are deer and workers of the Elohim society.

It is important that you do not confuse the *Grays* with the *Elohim*. The Grays are clones that don't think, they just execute commanded services by the Elohim. They are small in stature, white skin, large and dark eyes, very thin bodies. These are the ones you know about the Roswell case, sometimes they come to the surface for investigations or to collect samples for scientific and technological investigations. These are the ones that many times you have seen confusing them with the Reptilian-Grays.

Today the electromagnetism of the planet is stabilizing, there will come a moment in which they will be able to receive and shelter the 144 Elohim. This could not achieve in years ago, because the electromagnetic force was not found stable. We can say that they had to wait for you to emanate the electromagnetic force of the elevated thought-energies, so that they could shelter in them. To lodge definitively in the electromagnetism of the planet, the Elohim would have to be willing to disincarnate, for the moment, they are doing the following:

Transfer from body to body

When the cloned body of an Elohim arrives to fulfill its mission and finds himself at the end of his life, they are transferred to a new clone-genetic, continuing his life for one more cycle. With this explanation we arrive at knowledge that the Elohim have never died or disembodied, they have just lived millions of years in new bodies.

If they had disincarnated, the planet's electromagnetism would not have been prepared to receive their souls, since electromagnetism is still of low frequency and vibration. For this reason, they were forced to clone themselves and live millions of years in their adults-clones. In this way they kept their lives and their existence intact. We, the Ayaplianos-Seramites of the Internal City, have worked together with them, we have exchanged knowledge in all fields and levels. Unlike you who absolutely forgot all the cosmic knowledge due to distortion, the 144 Elohim have kept the knowledge intact and have further increased it through evolution.

The Elohim continue to work with their brains' left side, that is, with a 100% concentration on *evolution* whereas their brains' right side has only a 40% capacity of intuition and creativity and thus still limited possibilities of *elevation* and conception of the spirit. So far, evolution seems to be more important to them than elevation.

Like you, the 144 Brothers-Elohim have all the conditions to recover. We have intensely worked with them so that they may join the forthcoming Cosmic Alignment and transcend along with us to enter the planet's Internal City. These brothers never interfered with the human species in any manner nor conducted experiments with animals. They are 100% vegetarian elaborating food in accordance with their own investigations.

We can affirm that the Elohim always kept their distance from the outside world and only occasionally acted upon our or the Seramitas' request, when your species or the planet were in danger. The truth is that they, above all, have concentrated on their evolution and cure from distortion. Governments, religions, corporations and more have instilled in you the fear, terror and distrust in them, but we must tell you not to let's confuse the Servitor-Gray (amorphous clones) to the Reptilian-Grays (Nephilims) with the ELOHIM-AYAPLIANOS (Interanos).

The Reptilian Grays

The Reptilian Grays are a group of 33 individuals who survived through continual cloning. They are about 1 meter high, have gray skin, wide slanted dark eyes and four finger hands with membranes. Unlike the Elohim who have kept intact 40% of their right side of the brain, the Grays are 100% sick and distorted, their thought-energies are completely infected of the Reptilian-thought-energies that came from Satien.

122. What had happened earlier?

When the Elohim were about to shelter in the caverns near the south pole some of them disagreed saying, they needed a more secure refuge, close to the planet's center. Consequently, the group split and those who favored this option headed for the deeper caverns. When arriving there they found themselves in the presence of the fragment of Satien and creatures living next to it, which made their distortion grow. They are the Reptilian-Grays who had already brought with them a degree of distortion as descendants of the union between Ayaplianos and the Reptilian species of Satien.

All this happened some 300 million years ago. The continents as you know them now did not exist. They formed when large landmasses broke off and started drifting apart. During this process, the Reptilian-Grays were trapped in their caverns underneath the continent you call Australia. On remaining separated from the rest, they founded an Internal City of their own where they ever since have lived. Like the Elohim, they preserved their cosmic knowledge but neglected the development of their brain's right side and therefore lost the capacity of elevating their souls. They are the beings' religion, many governments and corporations made you associate "extraterrestrial" with a serious threat to humanity thus trying to leave you without a chance to consider us, your Elder-Brothers-Ayaplianos the true exponents of positive and elevated extraterrestrial life with the mission to help and guide you on the long journey of return to cosmic existence.

To understand the meaning of these "Extraterrestrial Contacts" you have to realize that there is a difference of grades, planes and dimensions between the "contacts" and those with whom they communicate. You feel confused because those who are the "Contacted", that is, channels and ascended masters, speak of contacts with diverse planes. This, in fact, depends on the vibration frequency emanating from their thought-energies (souls) which will feel attracted to the frequency of the "contact". You must keep this in mind to avoid misinterpretations. Possible contacts are as follows:

- *Spiritual contacts (subtle Holograms)*
  with Ayaplianos-Volunteers of the spacecraft

- *Ethereal contacts (semi-palpable Holograms)*
  with Seramitas-Ayaplianos- Internal City and the Elohim

- *Physical contacts (palpable Holograms)*
  with the Reptilian-Grays

When we say, that the contacted feel attracted to the same frequency we do not judge them superior to other individuals. Attraction occurs because their thought-energies has accumulated knowledge and understanding through past life experience. The accumulation of energy (knowledge and understanding) will allow them to establish "contact" by either using denser thought-energies (knowledge/left side brain) or elevated thought-energies (understanding/right side brain) in both the incarnated and disincarnated condition.

It will be an active "contact" based on matching vibration frequencies. The contacted may lower their frequency to adapt to denser realities, an ability they will acquire during the anti-matter disincarnated condition, but cannot willfully go beyond their present frequency or level of electromagnetism. Therefore, elevating your energy frequency is the way to establish contact with higher thought-energies.

123. What is the Ayaplianos-Elohim's life like?

To begin with, you should not fear them. These 144 brothers will never mean harm to you. Like many of you, they have resisted the advance of distortion and are gradually correcting it. Their home is the Internal City at the south pole. Throughout history, the Internal City has received such names as Land of Mystery, Paradise, Nirvana, Eden, Crystal City and others. You know that it exists but never could localize it. The ancient say that those who have transcended are heading for a place deep inside the planet.

The Ayaplianos-Elohim are full-fledged scientists having accumulated a great deal of knowledge about this grade, plane and dimension. We Ayaplianos-Volunteers and the Seramitas are enjoying a perfect cooperation with them as we are elevated energy and they have advanced the evolution of their thought-energies. While they are gradually transmitting knowledge to you, we have you broaden this Knowledge and deepen Understanding of it to help you transcend this reality and comprehend the concept of cosmic science.

The Elohim have a 60% advance on their left side and a 40% on their right side brain. We Ayaplianos of the spacecraft and the Seramitas-Internal City are 100% right side. You, in turn, are the only to develop consistently both hemispheres of your brain and thus preparing to shelter elevated thought-energies of ours in the future. The laboratories mentioned in previous books are located at the Internal City of the Elohim. These labs contributed to your recovery as these brothers efficiently use the planet's electromagnetism relocating your thought-energies (souls) at the correct frequency. The appearance of Unidentified Flying Objects (UFO) and Orbs in the atmosphere are manifestations of these activities.

It is important for you to know that the Elohim, unable to procreate, do not live family lives with their cycle of birth, growth, evolution and elevation. As a group of 144 individuals only, without a chance to increase this number, they secured their survival through cloning and interact as specialists of advanced science and technology in a well-structured working team. Nevertheless, they have always been expectant of your advance on evolution and elevation that would eventually open the door for them to return to their origin.

124. Why are they waiting for our evolution and elevation?

While we Ayaplianos-Seramitas went to live in the Quartz caverns underneath the poles guided by our brothers Ayaplianos-Volunteers of the spacecraft...our brothers Elohim decided to stay on at the deeper caverns since they did not understand our message because of the degree of distortion they had suffered and despite having preserved traces of telepathy.

We intended to assist them but the reduction of their brain's right-side activity to 40% and the effect of intense infrared radiation from large amounts of crystals caused us to lose 60% of contact with them for a long time. Some 150.000 years ago, however, we managed to reestablish communication with them and with you and since then have jointly been working for your, their and the planet's energetic recovery.

Infrared radiation is present almost everywhere in modern daily life though we barely pay attention. For instance, remote controls for TV sets and stereos use the emission and reception of infrared rays. Infrared rays also make it possible to operate a PC with a wireless mouse, and open and shut doors. Military forces localize and control movements of enemy troops with them. Furthermore, they largely contribute to controlling the greenhouse effect responsible for global warming. (Wikipedia)

No sooner had they arrived at the caverns, the Elohim suffered exposure to electromagnetic infrared radiation. Infrared as well as Gamma and UV rays from the sun hit the planet's atmosphere and surface with the infrared radiation penetrating soil layers. Humans sense this radiation of varying temperature through their nervous system and that is why you perceive cold and hot on your skin.

Owing to constant exposure and millions of years, our brothers Elohim, acquired certain species characteristics. These characteristics determined in the species the following: Very light skin, medium-size, large light eyes, no hair, fine and elongated body, five long fingers etc. The main characteristic of infrared rays is being absorbed easily, giving the appearance of the so-called «greenhouse effect». This effect is based on the fact that once the solar infrared radiation has crossed the atmosphere, it is absorbed by the soil and by the vegetation, which they refer inside the Earth and accumulate it in greater degrees. It means that is trapped in the earth, affecting the minerals and substances in there.

The Elohim´s Skin is very light and has a particular characteristic: **Fluorescence** due to ultraviolet rays absorbed and lack of exposure to sunlight. The large eyes are protected by a very thin film, a kind of glasses, to protect from light although this is artificial, because his vision is infrared. They take great care with their eyes, so that sometimes wear a cover with a special black material, which has the function of a viewfinder to see in the dark, this allows them to get an image (in false colors) that reveals the thermal levels of a body and locate those areas that have abnormal thermal conditions.

Likewise, these special glasses allow them to obtain images with a higher resolution, since they are made of quartz or fluorite glass, this type of material protects them from light. They don't have the vision that you do, they see through the infrared rays, therefore, perception and uptake are perceived through heat that living beings emanate. On the other hand, infrared radiation has helped them preserve perfect health conditions and maintain their body temperature stable. This enables them to fight infection and restore internal and external tissues. In consequence, they can live thousands of years with the same body. When close to the end of their life cycle they create a new body through cloning.

The Elohim have discovered the therapeutic effects of infrared rays when they realized that it would be beneficial in keeping the temperature of their bodies stable, fighting infections, preserving and repairing external and internal tissues. For this explanation, we want you to comprehend that Elohim have been preserved for more than 300 million of years and thanks to this they were able to continue cloning themselves over and over again. That is why they considered elevation of the energy less important than evolution.

The Elohim have gradually developed their souls (thought-energies) engraving on them a great deal of scientific knowledge regarding their species, environment and reality of the primary dimension. No other species in the universe equals the knowledge of advanced science and technology of this dimension they accumulate. Through the close and permanent cooperation of Ayaplianos-Volunteers, Seramitas and Elohim over 300 million years, the Interstellar Cosmic Confederation has gotten the most comprehensive picture of what really happened to all of us and what this before unknown reality means to the universe. The Elohim made a decisive contribution to your recovery passing their DNA down to you so that you would advance on evolution in accordance with the precepts of the universe.

The process required their energetic intervention, which many of you perceive as abduction and therefore domination by an alien species. Such domination never occurred. All the brothers were trying to do was to recover your energy and cosmic holograms. The Elohim have fostered your evolution by gradually transmitting universal knowledge. This is how you have grown and advanced as a species. They designed and channeled many of your inventions.

We Ayaplianos-Volunteers and the Seramitas helped you develop the right side of your brain, elevate your thought-energies, your spirit understands the universe and be individuals of conscience and "good". The brothers Elohim following our wish, in turn, have been transmitting to the left side of your brain scientific and technological knowledge. With such a powerful impulse for the development and use of both hemispheres of your brain, you among all of us, have drawn the most benefit from this process, as you are the only to work equally with the two sides of the brain.

In the future, as of the third phase of the Cosmic Alignment, that is, in the year 2800, the planet will live the advent of the Golden Age. Ill negative thought-energy will undergo a process of transmutation ending an era of ignorance, ostracism, manipulation, domination and slavery. Individuals who continue to shelter this type of thought-energies in their souls will leave the planet, prisoners of darkness where their energies will be recycled for new creations.

From the year 2800 on, planet Tera will unquestionably be seeing the LIGHT of its true existence. Changes are overwhelming to the point that humans will be in direct communication with us, their elder brothers. We shall be close to assist you during the entire Cosmic Alignment. Those who are going to participate actively in the process of your evolution and elevation are the brothers Elohim.

We Ayaplianos-Volunteers of the spacecraft never ceased emphasizing that there is no greater force than LOVE to develop and strengthen your spirit. Nevertheless, only simultaneous deepening of UNDERSTANDING with help from the Seramitas-Internal City and broadening of your KNOWLEDGE through never ceasing teachings from the brothers Elohim will give you the chance to initiate The Golden Age of Knowledge, Understanding and Love.

From this moment on, you will be free and able to head for the elevated realities of all existing. Your Baby-Spirit will advance at leaps and bounds, and when reaching the Star Sun you will have turned Beings of Energy, that is, Spirits of Light. This is how you will eventually find the path of return to your origin.

125. How is it that our brothers Elohim will transcend this reality through us?

Those of us who found themselves prisoners of this reality have a right and chance to transcend it...We are All we are One. The forthcoming

Cosmic Alignment will be our vehicle to take us to a different reality of existence. While we Ayaplianos-Volunteers of the spacecraft and the Seramitas-Internal City are working to make you participants of this journey of the spirit, you have a compromise to aid our brothers Elohim by sheltering them in your brains' left side. Thus, they get the chance to join us on this extraordinary journey of energetic transcendence.

With the beginning of the Golden Age, in 2800, you will be making immense progress in Knowledge, Understanding and Love through our working closely together in great harmony. Our brothers Elohim will stop cloning and their souls after disincarnating become dispersed in millions of crystals with each crystal bearing an enormous compendium of knowledge and evolution.

Millions of brains on the outside are going to shelter myriads of these crystals thus making you highly knowledgeable and wise. Through this process, you are going to help them become part of your souls and transcend by letting them enter your spirit. It is give-and-take. While they convey to you transcendental knowledge of the cosmos you help them be part of the spirit. This is how you gain wisdom and further your evolution. The moment your brain receives one of the Elohim's' crystals, evolution will strikingly accelerate, you will actively participate in interplanetary science and technology, explore the cosmos, create inventions of great relevance and occupy the place in the universe for which you have always longed.

As evolution advances the emergent spirits of Venus, Mercury and the Star Sun will be free to incarnate in humans on Tera to continue their evolution and elevation. 7 thousand years will have gone by when all these spirits conclude their formation and unite in ONE to find the transcendental passage to other realities. However, many of you are going to act as volunteers, as either Guardians of Tera or travelers of the cosmos. Scientists will explore galaxies and establish new human settlements in other worlds, build cities and create social communities as a vigorous demonstration of your species' creative progeny taking life to the confines of the universal body of our creator: The One Origin.

126. Will sheltering one single Elohim crystal already influence our evolution?

Yes, it will because the abundant knowledge of one crystal is enough to trigger transcendental changes in your and the planet's evolutionary process. Humans' left hemisphere of the brain in the future will shelter an Elohim crystal (soul) and Energetic Beings (Spirits) of the Seramitas in the right hemisphere. It is of great importance to remember that the energy of the universe is in a permanent process of recycling, concentration and transformation. In this reality, you perceive yourselves as individuals who believe that this is their true existence. However, when disincarnating the first thing your energy will do, is to join the collectivity of thought-energies (souls) with the same vibration frequency.

Souls gather because of energetic affinity and gradually turn spiritual beings (spirits). This is how conscience expands. As long as souls fail to awake and conceive their Baby-Spirit, they continue part of this collectivity. Once they awake, they start turning individual spirits. Nevertheless, it is the union of souls to give rise to the conception of the Baby-Spirit. At this point, individuality emerges and the energetic being starts to have a different, more particular perception of existence where it accumulates the experience that will mark a new expression of living. Without that union, the souls are not conscious of their existence and their situation would compare to that of a fetus during the first three months of gestation. The baby in the mother´s womb starts to perceive the entourage in the sixth month of pregnancy, before that, he/she will live in the unreality of life.

127. Will our physical traits change after we receive crystals from the Elohim and Seramitas?

Yes. Because you will receive new genetic information from the Elohim and Seramitas' DNA, whose engraved crystals will introduce gradual changes in your physical appearance and, in the course of evolution have you develop the characteristics of Extraterrestrial Ayaplianos. You already have a draw about us, you will be like that in the future, an Ayapliano.

128. Who really are the Reptilian-Grays?

Do not confuse the Elohim, the Servitor-Grays and the Reptilian-Grays because the last one are very dangerous. Those distant brothers had been part of the Elohim's group that took shelter in deeper caverns of the planet believing that this would stop and eventually free them from distortion. Yet it was a delusion. While descending, their situation worsened as they ended up in the proximity of the fragment and creatures of Satien whose energy invaded and left them even more distorted. Conscious of being entirely on its own, this group of only 33 individuals realized that it was facing extinction and started cloning.

Nevertheless, their clones have ever since been weakening, which led them to conduct investigations and tests aiming at survival with human help. However, tests did not work out because of limited genetic compatibility. They have not been able to develop communication by telepathy either, as their mental genetic codes have different frequencies.

Some human Reptilian mediums whose thought-energies are of Satien origin manage to establish contact with them, but both sides actually are still far from understanding each other.

Unfortunately, the degree of distortion those brothers suffered, has kept them prisoners of ambition. They are excellent scientists but, unlike the Elohim, failed to develop the universal knowledge they brought with them 600 million years ago, using what they preserved of it, for their benefit only. It was the Reptilian-Grays, who in a distant past had been abducting humans to study them. Nowadays, they are exchanging selectively knowledge via Reptilian mediums with a number of governments that cooperate with their investigations and experiments on a strictly confidential basis for mutual benefits. This contact is completely on a mental and energetic level.

These communications between the governments and the Gray-Reptilians, are given through the Reptilian-mediums, since we, the Ayapliano-Volunteers, the Seramitas and the Elohim, do not allow the Reptilian- Gray being out of their habitats. They are small and very fine stature, they reach up to 1 meter in height, they have huge eyes, covered by a black membrane that protects them, skin is greenish, giving it a reptilian appearance, prominent forehead, four fingers on hands and joined by a membrane. Some 450.000 years ago, the Reptilian-Grays took a chance trying to adapt to the conditions of the exterior. Nevertheless, high temperatures, UV and gamma radiation forced them to abort the experiment and return to the caverns for good. Since then, you also know them as the **Nephilim**.

It is true that they do experiments with the human species, with plants and animals in agreement with certain governments and with the Reptilians incarnated in humans from the outside, who provide them with everything necessary to do their experiments. The purpose is to achieve eternal subsistence on planet Earth for their species and to achieve the maximum knowledge, which will always turn it to their own benefit. Seramitas and Elohim-Interanos cannot make direct contact with them because their minds work in a very different way. They are isotopes, that is, they have different physical properties, are extremely self-centered and only worry about their preservation.

129. If they are Isotopes, how do they manage then to communicate with human Reptilian mediums?

There´s no verbal communication, these mediums use an out-of-body condition to visit them and study how they work, it is like they were watching a nest of insects. We also have studied the Reptilian-Grays using holograms and thus have kept them away from the outside. Despite being isotopes, they are very intelligent and perceptive when somebody else is observing them. In that case, we use the same tactic when we are in front of a flock of insects. They can perceive if there is a stranger around but do not seem worried while they do not feel threatened or attacked and keeping on with their work. Theirs is a social collective with a uniform and well-defined way of thinking.

Without the necessary physical contact, the Reptilian mediums and administrations that work with them have actually been unable to obtain their scientific knowledge. The fact, that the Reptilian-Grays cannot establish a direct communication with the outside, has reassured us that the part of universal knowledge they preserved has not yet fallen into the wrong hands. All we know about the Reptilian-Grays we owe the mediums who have given testimony of how they live, investigate and develop their technology. Theirs is routine work. They lack creativity and incentives to develop new projects and create inventions, as their knowledge of the universe is the same they had when they came to the planet and suffered distortion. Unable to use the right side of their brains they lack the capacity to imagine a universe, a cosmos beyond their reality.

130. When they kidnap human beings or animals, what criteria do they do it?

We can say that the Reptilian-Grays (Nephilims) is a species formed by the mixture between the Reptilian- Ayapliana species and the creatures that inhabit the center of Tera. This species is a hybrid and was formed from a terrifying genetic union, which gave rise to this new species of mutant being, whose genes we cannot even classify as Ayaplianos, humans or the animal kingdom. The 33 Nephilims cannot go outside, although, they receive the help from the reptilian-thought-energies, who are embodied in the outside human. They are provided with what they need to continue their experiments. They have no notion in differentiating living elements because their vision is infrared. Therefore, for them animals, plants and humans are exactly the same, and only differ by color emission and frequencies. The difference is totally energetic. The only thing that interests them is the energy that they can extract, since they use it as food, allowing the continuity of their lives.

When we say that they use energy as food, it is because they extract it from living bodies and reuse it for their survival and for the continuity of their clones. The center of the Earth is full of unusual and unknown creatures to you. They are mutants that have been formed from humans, animals, reptilians etc. Satien's fragment brought an infinity of monstrous things, which have been proliferating and mixing genetically between them. These creatures live near the center of the Earth, conserving their habitat, but are totally watched over by the Elohim, who take care of the creatures and the Reptilian- Grays do not come to the surface. Some of them escape by the caverns or by the internal rivers that flow towards the outside. For the Elohim, the Reptilian-Grays are also creatures of darkness and they are kept imprisoned just like the other creatures.

For example, certain types of snakes such as rattlesnakes have sensory elements that are used to make images of infrared light. Therefore, the snake can detect warm-blooded animals by performing infrared images. In the case of snakes that have two of these elements, scientists think they have some depth perception in the infrared.

Even if it is dark, these animals can see their prey due to the heat that they emit. Commonly known as pit snakes, they have small sensors at the side of your head that are used to detect infrared radiation. When they move the head from side to side, they find the direction of the animal by determining from which point the most intense radiation comes. We want you to remember that such was the distortion these brothers suffered 600 million years ago that they lost all their chances of evolution. Despite our scientific and universal knowledge, we are unable to recover them, as their genes owing to the mutation in the DNA are no longer Ayaplianos or humans. They are an entirely new species.

Therefore, this species is doomed to extinction as a result as cloning for such an extended period leads to cellular deterioration fatally affecting the organism. Visible exterior signs are that they suffered gradual reduction of body height. They furthermore are losing brain functions, which will cause their formula of cloning to stop working eventually.

Reptilian-Grays are in custody of the Elohim, who are in charge of keeping them off the surface. Despite the Elohim's close watch to forestall their winning the surface via subterranean rivers, a number of Reptilian-Grays, in a distant past, had managed on several occasions to escape the controls. They proceeded to abduct people submitting them to painful experiments to learn as much as possible about the human organism. Reptilian-Grays are known in the history of Tera as Nephilim. Many humans, who bear incarnated Reptilian thought-energies (Reptilian-Humans) worshipped them and continue so. This explains why to some organizations the number 33, the symbol of Lucifer, that is, of the Reptilian-Grays, is of particular significance. Yet, the Reptilian-Grays know they will not survive and are desperately trying to procreate with the woman of the surface.

They want to continue living in the outside although if they fail in the procreation, they will initiate the process of incarnating their souls in humans in the exterior. This, however, is impossible owing to the dramatic changes in their energetic DNA, incompatible with yours and that of the Reptilian-Humans who genetically have the same elements inherited from Satien and still keep them pure. While they will disappear as a species from the genetics of the universe, their legacy of knowledge will live on in the Reptilian-Humans as their legitimate inheritors.

131. Who are the Reptilians that incarnated in Humans?

They are thought-energies the Satien fragment millions of years ago brought to the planet and that invaded the souls of humans of the exterior. Nowadays these energies continue incarnated, organized in hierarchies to control and dominate and conscious of their origin. Today's Reptilian-Humans are descendants from human relations of convenience where inheritance and lineage go together to guarantee the power of the Reptilian-force. Their children learn and prepare to reign as Reptilians over planet 3.3.3 (third grade, third plane, third dimension) There is a never-ending transmission of legacy and lineage. This is how Luzbel and Lucifer continue to control, manipulate and dominate the beings of planet Tera.

132. There is the story about a creature that bleeds dry animals named "El Chupa-Cabra". Do you have any clues about it?

Such accidents will never occur again we prevented it from becoming worst. This creature of darkness was a hybrid clone between a Reptilian-Gray and an animal. It was made in Reptilian-Grays' lab experiments that escaped the controls and gained the open. The Elohim captured it avoiding thus incidents with human beings. On the other hand, however advanced your science and technologies may appear today you still have a long way to go to discover the many strange and sometimes terrifying parallel realities inside and outside this living cell, which is planet Tera. You are not alone and you have never been.

Realities exist side by side, one below or above the other. One day they will discover it and know for sure the real existence of the universe. You live in cities and they only show you what you should see. It is the Mental Matrix that you have programmed, you live your lives in the realm you choose, but that is not the reality of existence. The planet is a living-Cell, outside and inside it, there are the strangest creatures that your eyes have ever seen. And let's not leave behind parallel realities, where everyone interconnects, lives and does not know what exist.

This is the "Awakening" to see and know that reality is not what you see, feel, experience etc. The reality is so different. Someday when you be fully awake will know what we are talking about and then you will live the real and not virtual reality, as you have constructed it. The Elo-him, the Reptilian-Grays, the Servitors-Grays and the Reptilians incar-nated from Satien (Nephilims) are part of what you are knowing as re-ality of the planet. And we say this because they have physical bodies like you, they are semi- palpable and semi-visual. It is a reality that com-bine the physical and real condition of human knowledge and under-standing. In a not-too-distant future, you will make the first physical contact with the Elohim-Interanos.

133. Was the Roswell case real?

Yes, it was real. We already know from previous explanation that the Elohim have never gone out into their inner city physically (only holo-graphically). This City is inside an immense dome. They have lived there for millions of years. They are scientists and their job is to collect every-thing specimen from inside and outside the planet. We could say that it is like the Ark of Noah.

The crew who commanded the spacecraft that fell in Roswell, were the Gray clones of service, which were created in the laboratory. They were made especially as an experiment in order to check if they would be fit to withstand the outside weather. It did not work, we know that the ship fell, crashing in Roswell. The crew members suffered burns, although one of them were in better condition, they all died and were kept by the US government. The bodies are frozen for studies in Arizona.

After the Roswell incident, the Elohim suspended further exploration activities and therefore had no practical way of knowing whether they themselves could physically survive in the exterior. However, based on current investigations they will not be able to take a chance for some time, as the structure of their physical bodies is not apt to resist solar radiation and gravity, let alone the instability of electromagnetism in the atmosphere. Only with the planet's electromagnetism more stable and the Star Sun increasing emission of photons, will they have the opportunity to surface and establish physical "Contact".

Instead, the Elohim will start regular communication with you, which we already have, by palpable holograms, when the Seramitas ask them to. Unlike the Reptilian-Grays, the Elohim are entirely conscious of their reality of existence owing to the 40% of their brain's right side they preserve and a normal functioning of the left side accumulating outstanding knowledge about their evolution. Unfortunately, the degree of distortion they suffered left their right side with insufficient elevation for the conception of their spirit, yet with a clear notion of what is correct and incorrect, a virtue firmly engraved on their thought-energies of Ayapliano nature.

A REQUEST FOR APPROACH

Today, October 20th, 2010, at 5 am, our Elder Brothers Ayaplianos made contact asking me to prepare a questionnaire of at least 30 items to meet the Brothers Elohim at the Internal City on the South pole via an out-of-body experience, accompanied by two brothers Volunteers of the Spacecraft and two Seramitas.

After having channeled three books and worked for 8 years with this message, the Elder Brothers' request for a close encounter with the Elohim came as a surprise to me, as so far, communication had been through telepathy.

Why would I have to interview our Brothers Elohim?

It is necessary that you meet them because until now humans feared a direct approach in consequence of a mistaken understanding of what "extraterrestrial" life is like. Time is running out and it is of utmost importance that you take a closer look at ours but above all, the Brothers Elohim's reality, because it is they who are going to be the first "extraterrestrials" to have direct contact with you over the next 200 years.

By the time governments disclose confidential information to the public on alien phenomena you have to be prepared to recognize whether that information refers to the Brothers Elohim or the Reptilian-Grays. We Ayaplianos of the Spacecraft and the Seramitas have the obligation to enlighten you about the TRUE policies and practices behind visible activities of organizations, institutions and governments that actually run the planet. Beware of the holograms you will see them send across Tera announcing their new universal religion. These power centers are under the Most severe influence of Reptilian-Humans who are acting behind the 22 organizations.

Why did you choose *EL SER UNO* for this approach instead of scientists who may understand you better?

We, in fact, are in communication with scientists. You, nevertheless, are among the human beings who are prepared to receive and understand the message we Ayaplianos-Volunteers of the spacecraft, the Seramitas and Elohim are transmitting. You stand for the channels who already communicate with Ascended Masters at the Internal City. You, however, are the first human being to meet the Elohim "face to face" and therefore capable of giving the people of the exterior a detailed description of their features and attitude. It takes broad-minded channels to do this who, thus, help initiate an era of entirely new teachings about the cosmos.

Before religions misleading holographs in different parts of the planet and say that it is God the Father who is coming to the planet to lead you to paradise and many of you fall for the lies told by them... We announce it here, in this knowledge EL SER UNO, so that you can be mentally alert and prepared to free yourselves from the chains of slavery and all evil.

This is a moment of decision. You can no longer hold on to dreams and phantasies about celestial beings coming for your rescue. The brothers Elohim are part of yours and the planet's reality, a truth you must no longer ignore.

The day will come when you will establish personal communication with them and accept, whether you like it or not, that they physically are not the celestial creatures you had imagined to meet, but also admit that your physical characteristics might be just as ugly and horrific to them and to many other realities of the universe.

The human species settled in many different places of the cosmos with its descendants having similar or rather different characteristics, but all with their particular parameters of esthetics. One major characteristic of cosmic wisdom is the ability and determination to turn an open mind to any possible event beyond the planetary context or just beyond your knowledge and understanding.

CHAPTER III

INTERVIEW
WITH THE ELOHIM-INTERANOS

November 10th, 2010

I shall relate this personal experience exactly the way I lived it. I know that I am having an out-of-body experience and traveling with my mind. It is not the first time and I feel calm and in peace. Two Ayaplianos-Volunteers and two Seramitas are with me. They have tall slim figures, very bright slanting eyes and gentle movements wearing light, tight-fitting suits that give the impression of being an integral part of their subtle bodies.

I feel somewhat strange for still being physical but intensely perceive great harmony and love between us. I am not fearful and thanking the universe for choosing me as a human interlocutor of our Elder Brothers. Two Brothers Elohim welcome us on our arrival. They very much resemble the Ayaplianos, with only slightly larger eyes of a gentle and profound look. We are in a very pleasant place full of light. On looking around, I realize that the white light does not resemble sunlight; there is just luminosity. In the distance, I can make out the skyline of a city shining like a crystal.

After greetings and presentations, they lead us to a large boardroom with a round table and chairs in its center. Like our Elder Brothers, the

Elohim move very gently and almost instantly establish communication by telepathy. While I am making a mental note that they all wear practically the same attire, they interrupt me indicating that they are not here physically but through holograms where they all show the same visual appearance. When they say that, I realized that I am also like them, my body is not the same, I feel it is light and weightless.

They say that we all have gathered in the form of holograms through the force of our thoughts; while they are speaking, I realize that I myself am just a white human figure who thinks and communicates. I feel like fluctuating and having no physical body anymore and am in great peace with myself. As communication is through telepathy, their mouths do not move but their eyes are firmly focusing mine. They explain that their Internal City has the form of a huge spacecraft normally stationed at the south pole, but designed for displacements whenever necessary.

This City-Spacecraft operates using the planet's electromagnetism. The Elohim run it with a crew whose members hold particular responsibilities in compliance with the type of work assigned. They go on explaining that their history begins when they leave the spacecraft more than 300 million years ago and start perceiving that Distortion and Ambition are contaminating their energy. The virus of Satien. I nod in agreement and they proceed to a short review on whom we are and how many of us having Ayapliano origin are there on planet Tera:

- There are at the planet's poles two immense anti-matter spacecrafts home of the Ayaplianos-Volunteers. They never left the spacecraft but stayed on the planet to help, one way or another, all who had suffered distortion.
- From the books, we know that a small number of them did go to try the outside. However, when they started to perceive what seemed to be the first signs of distortion, they decided to take shelter in quartz caverns deep underneath the poles. They are the Ayaplianos-Seramitas.
- Others remained in the exterior suffering contamination from the virus: Distortion and Ambition. They are you, the Ayaplianos-Humans.

200

- There are those who trying to stop distortion had also chosen deep caverns under the south pole for their protection. There they built a City-Spacecraft which has been their home ever since. They are the 144 Ayaplianos-Elohim.
- There are finally the 33 Reptilian-Grays (Nephilim) who had descended to even deeper caverns near the center of the planet.

The two brothers Elohim keep on relating that after the separation of the continents the Reptilian-Grays had chosen the deep caverns underneath the Australian continent as their permanent home where they live in a City-Spacecraft similar to ours using the electromagnetism for displacements. It is important to remember that we differ from the Reptilian-Grays regarding skin, eyes, hands, feet etc. but, most of all, by the way we present ourselves before you, Ayaplianos-Humans in the exterior. Nevertheless, evolution has not been the same for every one of us.

As they keep on speaking, I am trying to sum up everything they say...

Communication is telepathically and the Elohim say that between themselves there are few differences because the evolution is not the same for each one of them. They ask me to start the questionnaire and offer to show me their habitat, the City-Spacecraft, afterwards. I feel in peace and harmony and am most grateful for this opportunity. I feel love for all present and am aware that we are brothers of the same species. My memory is clear and bright. We are One. The Elohim are delicate, with a gentle look in their eyes. The day had come to start working together.

I ask The Seramitas – Why do we have to gather? Their answer is – It shall be like that from now on, because we all belong to the species that arrived here 600 million years ago. We suffered separation through distortion, but will stand together in the future to free ourselves and return to our origin. We look at each other, feeling one soul, one spirit, as if we had never separated and that I always belonged to them.

I also perceive that there is nothing to be afraid of, that we are a universal family, brothers of the same species despite physical dissimilarities. I feel deep inside that the day we will leave this planet, we are prepared to transmit this experience with the knowledge our spirit has accumulated, to other realities of existence. The Elohim say that this is not a one-time gathering, and that I may come back whenever necessary or also may communicate with them from where I live by telepathy and they will be happy to answer all my questions. With this, our gathering ended and I departed calmly and with a feeling of great happiness.

They agreed that I continue the interview from my laptop. I asked them the questions we all would ask if we had this opportunity. I want you to know that it will take two more books to fulfil my mission and that the interview with the Elohim will continue in the fifth book *EL SER UNO*.

Readers who wish to participate in this interview are welcome to send us their questions. We all need to know and the Elohim are here to enlighten us with their vast knowledge. I myself along with friends and collaborators have prepared new questions after having received comments on the first part of the interview. Here is how continued...

INTERVIEW TO THE AYAPLIANOS-ELOHIM-INTERANOS

134. Is "Grays" your true name?

No, it is not, but because of some misunderstanding, you have always taken us for the Servitor-Grays and the Reptilian-Grays (Nephilim). We are your Brother-Ayaplianos since we arrived together with you on this planet 600 million years ago. About 300 million years ago we went to the outside which, as was also your case, for known reasons resulted in our somewhat different physical characteristics. You formerly knew us as the **Elohim** but today we are the **Elohim-Interanos**.

We are the Interanos of the Internal City of planet Tera. The Grays are cloned servants we had to create to take care of the physical maintenance services the City-Spacecraft demands. They are palpable holograms having mass and weight necessary for the work they do.

Elohim

Elohim is Hebrew and refers to a **Being of Power**. Many dictionaries also associate the word with "God", "Deus" in Latin and "Theos" in Greek. In Greek mythology, Elohim refers to the god Zeus. The ancient Hebrews used the term Elohim when referring to persons to whom a

higher authority had conferred power to rule, someone who had authority and leadership qualities, and whom they therefore worshipped. An
extended meaning of Elohim is *Angel* and *Judge*.

"Elohim" was used anciently when referring to some deity or people
who had received powers delegated by others who were on top of it.
What did it mean? That he was someone who was regarded as a divine
being with qualities of a god. It was a title given to almighty beings who
reflected authority and the gift of command. The Scriptures call Joshua
Emmanuel *Son of Man* but also *Son of Elohim* because he was born
from a woman, but received his authority and virtues from the Supreme
Elohim, God. (Wikipedia)

There is abundant reference to the Elohim in the Bible. Consequently, when we, your Elder Brothers, presented ourselves before you
through holograms, you believed us to be angels, archangels, cherubs
and seraphs, messengers of god or ELOHIM. So, we stayed with the
name, for it made sense with what we were doing on the planet, namely,
helping preserve your species by transferring our physical DNA to stop
distortion and prepare the grounds for the advance of your evolution.

135. Most humans fear you believing that you are the Reptilian-Grays. Why did you not make contact to correct this misinterpretation?

In ancient times, you were conscious of our presence, since we and
our brothers Seramitas and Ayaplianos-Volunteers of the spacecraft had
been working with you in harmony, peace and love. In times of Lemur
and Atlantis, you still preserved the ancestral cosmic knowledge. Nevertheless, the separation of the continents had affected the planet's gravity,
rotation and electromagnetism triggering huge ecological disasters that
brought chaos and darkness to your minds.

We have been distant physically and mentally for an extended geo-
logical time but by elevating ever since your vibration frequency, you
gave us a chance to resume contact with you. However, your frequency
must be even more elevated to create the conditions in the planet's electromagnetism to allow both of us to reestablish the quality communication we had before. This situation explains why most of you fail to

recognize us. Nevertheless, the memory of that distant period is in your DNA and many of you are activating it and receiving us in their minds.

136. Since you are the Elohim as mentioned in the Bible, would you say that religions know the truth about angels, archangels, cherubim, seraphim and God?

Religious belief has led to the formation of institutions with hierarchies controlling access to confidential information. Only the leaders of these institutions actually know. There are exceptions but there is also evidence that power and control of many religious organizations lie in the hands of a few persons owing to the knowledge they have accumulated. The same holds true for many governments. Power is not about the amount of money you own; real power consists in the Knowledge you have. The more you know, the more power you have within an organization.

You have to understand that we could not introduce to you under our real form, until now you have not accepted our presence. Governments and religions have been responsible for discrediting us by presenting us as ugly, diabolical extraterrestrial beings. All of them have conveniently been preventing you from knowing the truth and to justifying control and manipulation for reasons of general security. We are the angels, archangels, cherubim, seraphim to you from the Bible and in the form of holographic human images so that you would accept our presence.

137. Why did you take so long to let us know you?

Our organism is very delicate and has never been able to adapt to the atmosphere, gravity and electromagnetism of the planet. We therefore have lived in our City-Spacecraft since we came here 600 million years ago. Nowadays things are changing as you are elevating the electromagnetic frequency of your thought-energies (souls). This energy is going to shelter in the planetary magnetism making us visible to you.

Many of you are already mentally prepared to establish contact with extraterrestrial life forms. Even your scientists consider the possible existence of an inter-dimensional universe and are ready for channeling as well as for a physical encounter. We are preparing to show you our true Ayapliana appearance to help you realize that we are brothers of origin. We have been, are and shall be responsible for the advance of your evolution and are going to provide the universal knowledge and technology for it. From 2014 on, there will be channeling about science, philosophy, psychology and spirituality. Last one will be in charge our brothers the Seramitas.

We Ayaplianos-Elohim will provide Cosmic Science and Technology; the Seramitas-Ayaplianos of the Internal City transmit universal Philosophy and Psychology and the Ayaplianos-Volunteers of the spacecraft the Spirituality of *EL SER UNO*. This concentration of energies will be a powerful impulse to help you advance on the path of freedom and transcendence to higher realities.

138. Will you provide Science and Technology with the help of governments?

We shall start giving our knowledge to humans who have elevated the vibration frequency of their spirit. We could not do so earlier because ambition and greed would have left science and technology at the entire service of political power and control. We shall be transmitting both to scientists who have awaked and are thus mentally apt to deal with Cosmic Knowledge.

Contacts will start soon because you need to know us. We will maintain telepathic communication over the next 200 years until the planet's electromagnetism reaches the frequency needed for our projection through palpable holograms. Nevertheless, physical contact will only be possible with humans who will have made extraordinary energetic, scientific and psychological progress and probably not occur until after the year 2800.

It is a process and as such takes time, even more so because of the dense reality in which you live. In the universe, the 7-thousand-year lapse of the Cosmic Alignment is irrelevant. To you it is an almost endless sequence of incarnations. Yet, however long it may appear, the process has already started and will develop and conclude in accordance with the laws of the universe.

139. Why does the City-Spacecraft shut away under a dome?

We built the City-Spacecraft, our home, that way 300 million years ago. This was necessary in order to balance the elements of the six-pointed star so it would turn faster and allow us to stabilize rotation and passage of the planet and turn its energy lighter. It was also for your benefit, since you started correlating your thought-energies reaching thus your today's advance of evolution. This city-ship is 18 km in diameter. We, the Elohim, are 144 and we all live in it. Since we were not enough to maintain this City-Spacecraft, we had to make gray-clones, to serve as assistants in the minor jobs.

140. You all seem alike. By what criteria do you define hierarchy in your society?

Among the 144 Elohim there are certain individual differences owing to the fact that the distortion did not affect each one of us in the same way. Nevertheless, we enjoy perfect understanding and work together in great harmony. We communicate through telepathy. Certain dissimilarities you may have observed are physical not mental. We all communicate telepathically and have designated and specialized jobs, which will always be the same. As we said before, we are energetic clones of ourselves. We have not reproduced, because the distortion affected us, our reproduction system no longer works, so we were forced to clone ourselves, to continue living and be able to wait for our departure from this planet.

141. How have you been able to maintain the process of cloning?

We have been able to maintain cloning intact because we managed to preserve our DNA. Technically, we could continue the process forever, which nevertheless would definitely confine us to the reality of planet Tera. Yet, what is more serious, it would be against the universal concept that life must follow the natural process of recycling and transformation of the energy from one grade, plane and dimension to another which is why we in a distant future hope to transcend this reality and leave the planet. Cloning means stagnation and degeneration of energy.

This is also the case with the Reptilian-Grays. Their energy is suffering from saturation, stagnation and lack of new basic elements. Being aware of this they are trying to introduce their energetic genes in female humans for procreation however without success because of the incompatibility of their and the human DNA.

142. How does your Community function?

Considered the small number of individuals, we are a communitarian society with an equal share of responsibilities for each member, which may explain the absence of disharmony. Everyone knows how to proceed and fulfills obligations to the best of his abilities. For maximum efficiency, we have to coordinate our activities. We have hierarchies between us but not by category as you have outside. Our hierarchy acts by energetic quality, which is based on the understanding and qualitative work, in the field of cosmic wisdom. Owing to distortion there are certain differences between us, very slight, but necessary for working together, so we had to place ourselves hierarchically in a mathematical and chemical position of our bodies and minds. That's why the two of us are here talking to you, because we are the best suited to do so, expressing ourselves on behalf of our Elohim society.

143. Have you been responsible for the abduction of humans?

No. We already mentioned that the Reptilian-Grays in the past abducted humans and conducted experiments with them. These criminal acts will never occur again. They were a consequence of the severe distortion that had had the Reptilian-Grays gradually lose their cosmic memory. Unable to recover it, they are doomed to a total loss of conscience. As they suffered most from the proximity of the Satien fragment and the creatures of the planet's center, they have had all our support just as you have, but did not respond to our efforts. The state of alteration of their DNA is such that there is no chance to reverse it and the erroneous use of what is left of their memory has turned them creatures of the dark.

In the remote past, during a less advanced state of distortion, they surfaced with their spacecraft and abducted humans leaving everyone on the outside in terror. You remember them as demons and creatures of evil. Some ancient cultures worshipped them as God Baal or Beelzebub. Until today, incarnated Reptilian thought-energies (souls) on the outside worship the Reptilians-Grays celebrating black mass, offering them animal sacrifices and in some cases human beings.

Nowadays, they live in the confinement of the caverns deep down at the center of the planet. Owing to the elevation of the electromagnetism's frequency they cannot go to the surface anymore.

God Baal: The name Baal (also spelled Beel or Bel) is part of combinations and modifications such as:
- Hannibal>Anibal
- Bael
- Baltasar
- Beltis<Baaltis
- Baal Zvuv or Belzebuth (see Beelzebub)
- Bel-Marduk

"God ordered Gedeon to Destroy the altar and statue of Baal" (V.25) because you cannot serve God with Baal in your hearts. You will remember that the people of Israel lived amidst pagan tribes such as the Canaanites who did not accept Moses's message; nevertheless, many pagans lived in Israeli communities according to the book of Joshua. The Canaanites' religion tended to affect the faith of the people of God. The most popular religious cult in Canaanite territory was that of Baal. Many communities had a "local" Baal or Master, which is the basic meaning of the word. Yet despite the large number of local Baals, most Canaanites and many neighboring tribes considered that they were manifestations of just one God Baal.

According to Canaanite mythology, Baal was the God of the storm and therefore both providers of sustenance. The cults dedicated to this deity were terrible orgies of sensual debauchery as of bloodshed virgin children and women. Today some satanic sects continue practicing these rites. That is why we see how God commands Gideon to destroy the statue of Baal because you cannot serve God with Baal in your heart. The Lord Jesus Christ says in the Sermon on the Mount that: No one can serve two lords; for either he will hate the one and love the other, or he will esteem the one and will despise the other. You cannot serve God and riches. (Matthew 6:24)

The most prominent of the Canaanite gods was Baal. Every locality in Canaan and in other countries where Baalism existed it had its own Baal or, as The name Baal means "His own Lord" "Master" or "Owner". An example of this is the "Baal of Peor". They gave this deity the name of Mount Peor. Although there were many of these local Baals, the Canaanites, and the neighboring peoples understood that all the local Baals were simply manifestations of the one god Baal.

They believed that the end of the rainy season and the death of vegetation marked the triumph of the god Mot over Baal, forcing Baal to retreat to the depths of the Earth. But when the rainy season began, Baal worshipers believed this meant that Baal lived again, that his sister Anat had defeated Mot. They thought that the mating of Baal with his wife Ashtoreth at this time it ensured fertility in crops. Baal worshipers believed that participating in rituals prescribed in their religious festivals would serve to encourage the gods to follow the same pattern. Therefore, to celebrate Baal's awakening to life, to mating with Ashtoreth, they indulged in sexual orgies of unrestrained dissolution. In a way this was interaction magic that was carried out in the hope that the gods would imitate their worshipers and thus guarantee a fertile and prosperous agricultural year.

Shrines to Baal could be found throughout Canaan, where male and female prostitutes served and priests officiated the mass. Near the altars outside the shrines were stone columns, sacred posts (which represented the goddess Asherat) and incense shelves. Both the sacred columns and the sacred poles were symbols sexual. References in Ras-Shamra texts and archaeological finds they show that Baalism was a most degrading form of worship. The goddesses Astoret, Anat and Asherat symbolized both sexual concupiscence as sadistic violence and war. (Wikipedia)

Beelzebub: According to philologists, the etymological origin of Beelzebub is Baal Zvuv, which means "Master of Flies". The Hebrews used to use the name Beelzebub to mock the worshippers of Baal who let the meat of sacrificed animals rot in their temples attracting

myriads of flies. Allegoric expressions show an enormous, longhaired and threatening Beelzebub, sometimes with a swollen face, crowned with a ribbon of fire, black horns and wings of a bat. In Christian literature, the name denotes the Prince of Demons following an ancient Hebrew habit to depict alien deities in a monstrous appearance.
In the Bible, Satan has diverse names in accordance with his specific manifestation of malevolence and never-ending temptations. However, in Jewish-Christian tradition there is a demon of money called Mammon or one of bad smell by the name of Belial. Beelzebub is also Satan or Lucifer. There are yet names for other kinds of evil the imagination of his followers has created. (Wikipedia)

Nowadays the Ayaplianos-Volunteers, we the Elohim, our brothers Seramitas-Internal City and you have control over the Reptilian-Grays who live in total reclusion in the deep-seated caverns of the planet, which they will not be able to abandon. The reason is that they would not tolerate the increasing frequency of the thought-energies and vibration of the planet's electromagnetism.
This means that as long as you manage to maintain the frequency of the electromagnetism stable you will not lose control over them at least during the next 200 years. In the universe, always more than one event occurs at a time. By elevating the frequency of the planet's electromagnetism, you confine the Reptilian-Grays, the demons of the planet, to their caverns. The same thing will occur in your psychical body (soul) and physical body. By elevating the frequency of your energies, you will keep the demons of your subconscious and thus physical and mental disorders from dominating your thought-energies with sinister consequences for everything in the way.

144. Is this the reason that the followers of the demons on the outside, that is, the incarnated Reptilians will do everything to oppose elevation of the planet's electromagnetic frequency and ours?

Absolutely. Progressive elevation of both frequencies will undermine their power and eventually vanquish them. It is what we have been struggling for at all times. It is the ancient yet always new confrontation of the forces of good and evil. This is not fiction; it is TRUE what we are saying. We Elohim are responsible for keeping the Reptilian-Grays in confinement. We have won many battles they forced us to fight. However, the moment has come that we need human help. We have survived through constant cloning but are unable to go on by ourselves as our energy is getting weaker and weaker. We need you to assist us by taking command of the planet.

Brothers, you accomplished what we were never capable of doing, that is, to procreate and strengthen your thought-energies (souls). You are all the hope there is to vanquish evil forever. You have the strength we are lacking because you have learned to use both hemispheres of your brain, indispensable to fight the final battle.

145. What will be the final battle like?

How do you conquer illness? You will say by using a strong antibiotic, plenty of rest but, above all, that you feel sure to find the cure. Nonetheless, it is hard to conquer physical illness while suffering psychological strain. Before starting the cure, you should procure: To be conscious of your illness, to learn everything about it, to look at it broad-mindedly, to start to cure it using knowledge, understanding and love.

We want you to realize that you are not going to overcome a situation, to correct a distorted reality by just using free will and love. You need to know and understand whom and what you are facing. We as ever are with you to provide the science and technology you need to succeed. Nevertheless, you must use the Knowledge we transmit to broaden the Understanding you receive from our brothers Seramitas, and the Love the brothers Ayaplianos-Volunteers of the spacecraft instill in you so you may feel your inner strength grow. This strength is your spirit. Without these three virtues, you will not stand a chance against evil. *"To conquer your enemy, you have to know him"*

146. Are yours the flying objects we observe in the atmosphere?

Yes. However, you will always perceive them as what you call Orbs' phenomena of different shapes and colors. They actually are palpable holograms we project using the electromagnetism just as we do with ourselves for being unable to abandon our habitat in a physical body. As you elevate the individual and planetary electromagnetism, you give us the chance to become visible to you. This is why we have proceeded to project larger numbers of sightings into the atmosphere. However, when projecting ourselves via palpable holograms we do so using human features. We have avoided showing our true appearance knowing that you are still fearful of us.

From the beginning, the Cosmic Alignment will greatly help establish contacts with humans who have opened their minds and are prepared to communicate with us. Together we will start reliving the past when we all were one, working in harmony as true brothers of Light and Love do. We produce any of the sightings you observe in the atmosphere, the mountains and the sea since we are able to create them at different locations of the planet at the same time. This is how we will present ourselves before you during the next 200 years encouraging you to turn an open mind to a palpable reality like ours.

147. Do governments know about your presence on the planet?

They do. Our presence on the planet dates far back in time. Formerly, we were able to visit the exterior, as the electromagnetism was more stable and not yet contaminated by the virus of ambition. Over the past 100 thousand years, however, such had been the contamination of your thought-energies that we had to wait for their elevation before starting to present ourselves again.

There was a time when you knew us and were conscious of your history. There were no secrets and holographic and telepathic communication was easy. It was during the era of the cities of Lemur and Atlantis whose inhabitants readily assimilated our teachings and strictly followed the cosmic knowledge. This ended when the virus of ambition attacked them and they made contact with the creatures of the dark. When this occurred to us all, the Ayaplianos-Volunteers, Seramitas and Elohim withdrew because your minds had blocked us and you fell victims of darkness. You started to worship those creatures who demanded rituals and human sacrifices.

The darkness of your minds severely affected the electromagnetism. Gravity made your elements become dense and we as well as our brothers were no longer part of your lives. Nevertheless, despite the drastic changes, you kept us in your memory. Many of you remember but are fearful, as they believe us to be the Reptilian- Grays and sometimes even the creatures of the center of the planet. We now are waiting for you to elevate your electromagnetism so that you may fully recover your memory and we therefore be able to reestablish this long lost "contact".

Governments and religious institutions know of our presence but always have manipulated this knowledge for their benefit. They have made you believe that aliens are creatures of the dark, even Satan himself and thus prepared the ground to use your fears, feelings of guilt and your errors, real or supposed, for the purpose of exerting control and power over you. They know that our task is to prevent them from creating critical situations by irresponsibly using new science and technology they do not yet control sufficiently. Notwithstanding, in several occasions they had been on the edge of putting you and the planet into very serious danger.

148. Why are governments and religions so reluctant to reveal the truth about you to us?

What would religious teachings of a God Creator of the Universe be based on? How would they explain the existence of other intelligent life forms in the universe whose innermost religion is to believe in the supreme forces of the cosmos to create life and who do not need the guidance of spiritual leaders to express their feelings and beliefs.

How would they admit that Joshua Emmanuel (Jesus) had been a channel and messenger who had had telepathic communication with us and whose masters were his brothers of a different reality of existence? How could they possibly explain the fact that the God who created the Universe with all its life forms has just one son when this same god has created all of us? What would be of the gospels and other religious beliefs whose messages base on unreality?

Revealing the truth would leave them totally exposed of which they are conscious and that is why they are trying to maintain you dormant.

We are working to curb this power of ambition, reducing it gradually, to break it eventually. This is why they worry and hide the knowledge that comes from the stars. The worst thing is not the concealment because at the end of all you will discover the truth, but the reason to artificially and purposefully keep you under ignorance and fantasy.

149. What kind of knowledge will we receive from you?

Our legacy will be science and technology, that is, help you expand your Knowledge. We therefore offer you Evolution. At the same time, our brothers Seramitas insist on reminding you of the need for Understanding and Love. The universe is a place of order. Understanding and Love alone will not work for you without Knowledge to transcend your reality. Therefore, Knowledge, Understanding and Love are inseparable qualities of the thought-energies of *EL SER UNO*.

Having reached the confines of the universe the human species realized repeatedly that without wisdom there is no possible advance from one grade, plane or dimension to another. The Universal Mind does not admit shortcuts. Your spirit must complete its learning phase and gain wisdom to become a thought-energy or an idea of this very Mind. We are going to provide knowledge beyond all you ever imagined. Planetary and cosmic science and technology will vigorously advance from the year 2800 with the advent of the avatar Abigahel who will rescue and lead you into the Golden Age. There is no stopping you anymore. You will explore distant galaxies and settle on new planets. The Ayapliana-Human species will expand throughout the third dimension, its natural and rightful habitat.

150. Are there other ill negative alien species beside the Reptilian-Grays that interfere with the planet?

All similar kinds of human species in the universe work for the well-being and advancement of *EL SER UNO*. Ill negative energy exists on this planet only as consequence of your never-ending conflicts and confrontations, an illness called: Ambition from Distortion.

151. Is your diet the same as ours?

The systems of our physical bodies are very different from yours. We therefore follow a special procedure extracting nutrients for our diet from plants and algae.

152. Do you need oxygen to breathe?

Despite the shelter of the Spacecraft-City where we use hydrogen and helium we extract from the planet's atmosphere, our respiratory system requires a certain amount of modified oxygen. We also introduce electromagnetism from the atmosphere necessary for our displacement inside the spacecraft. We also modify this electromagnetism to fulfill our needs. The environment we have reproduced inside the spacecraft is the same we found when we first came to this reality. Since it does not exist anymore, we had to create an artificial matter-antimatter reality to survive.

153. Are you then anti-matter with no real physical bodies?

We are both matter and anti-matter. Our physical bodies, however, are so light and delicate, that is, they are more antimatter than matter that they do not compare to yours. You are familiar with the story of our arrival. We came from an anti-matter reality but the moment we left the spacecraft, the planet's crushing matter gravity started to affect our light anti-matter bodies. For that reason, we took shelter at the planet's caverns. However, we soon realized that this was not enough and started to build the Spacecraft-City to protect our minds against the effects of density. We finally succeeded in neutralizing them and thus preserved our light physical bodies.

Nevertheless, not even with additional security measures we had adopted we lost a 40% of flexibility of our brain's right side, that is, its anti-matter part capable of elevated cosmic thinking. Your case was different. You had deactivated your brain's right side and thus kept it safe. By gradually reactivating it, you realized that it had just been dormant and not suffered any loss of capacity or memory. Nowadays you are awaking by accelerating this reactivation of your brain's right side with total recollection and energetic mobilization of both hemispheres of your brain.

154. What type of science and technology will you provide?

During the next 200 years, the "contact", above all, will familiarize you with our presence and create the conditions you need to advance. After all, to be able to assimilate the great universal knowledge, you spirit needs more preparation. From the year 2800, you will begin to live the Golden Age. This is when our holographic-palpable presence will be part of your lives.

In fact, it will not be just our presence but also that of our brothers Ayaplianos-Volunteers of the spacecraft and Seramitas-Internal City who have always been with both of us. We are going to relive the age of Lemur and Atlantis. Many of you will be channels for the rebirth of Atlanteans. The evolution of your species will make enormous progress and we all will prepare for the return to our origin after the cure of the Tera-Cell, which has been particularly hard and laborious for those of us who had suffered distortion.

155. Did you occasionally present yourselves before us as some known Ascended Master via palpable holograms with human features?

Yes, occasionally and with the Seramitas-Internal City's consent we have appeared before humans in holograms adopting the human figure. We actually did not plan to reestablish contact that way, but thought it necessary because we would not risk startling them from the beginning by showing our real features. This is why we invited you for this interview. *EL SER UNO* has been the first to accept and announce channeling with extraterrestrials thus revealing the true image of the Ayaplianos. This opportunity never existed before because Ascended Masters have always presented themselves in the human form.

They have often adopted the image of a supposedly tall, fair-haired and bright-eyed Joshua Emmanual, whom you so much venerate but who born in the Mediterranean Palestine would actually have been medium-sized, dark skinned, with dark eyes and hair. There are also channelings of extraterrestrials from Cyrius, Andromeda, The Pleiades and Orion using human features. You may ask why none ever showed its real appearance. It is because we always projected human images to prepare your awakening and show you our real appearance only when we were sure you were ready for it.

Nowadays only *EL SER UNO* has the courage to show the image of our brothers Ayaplianos and consequently ours, as we all are alike. As descendants of Ayaplianos, you one day will have again the same or very similar physical traits according to the teachings of *EL SER UNO*. The Ayapliano-Human species has developed on the seven planets that suffered from distortion. Nevertheless, since you have preserved the DNA of the Ayaplianos of the Pleiades, you will gradually take on their appearance in the course of evolution. When you are about to abandon the planet and head for Venus your physical bodies will have become light and delicate and be able to live in a helium atmosphere.

156. How did you keep the memory of your scientific and technological knowledge while suffering distortion?

In the beginning, distortion attacked us as severely as it attacked you. Many fell victims and only 144 of us managed to resist and keep their minds from being irreversibly altered. Notwithstanding we lost 60% of the capacity of our brain's right side. What kept us from getting worse was the Infrared Energy. It halted the process of deterioration by increasing the number of white blood cells, which gave our bodies' defense system the strength to eliminate heavy toxins and favored the formation of new red blood cells. As a result, we developed physical but above all great mental agility that turned out to be essential for the preservation of our bodies. A visible effect of this process is that we are... iridescent.

Iridescence: This phenomenon displays a shimmering shift of colors on certain surfaces such as oil stains, soap bubbles and butterfly wings according to the angle under which the light hits those surfaces. Iridescence is the effect of reflections of light on multiple semitransparent surfaces. Subsequent change of phases and interference of these reflections modulate the light intensity according to the highs and lows of frequency.

By etymology, the term iris stems from the Greek word *iris* meaning light, and is also the name of the goddess Iris in Greek mythology, messenger of the gods who was leaving a wake of luminous colors when crossing the firmament and therefore represents the rainbow (Wikipedia).

The source of our iridescence is both our inner electromagnetism and the electromagnetism inside the spacecraft-dome. Depending on electromagnetism to satisfy our anti-matter needs we diffract the magnetism thus triggering the emanation of light. In the exterior, the Sun causes the diffraction of the electromagnetism producing the colors of the rainbow. We just create a brilliant white as our bodies absorb infrared light and transform it into this single expression.

157. What can you tell us about the Rainbow?

The Rainbow: The Rainbow is both a meteorological and visual phenomenon of reflection, refraction and dispersion of light in water droplets resulting in a spectrum of light appearing in the sky. The spectrum has the form of a multicolor arc showing red on the outside and violet on the inside. Sometimes a double rainbow arc appears. A secondary arc forms outside the primary arc and has the order of its colors inverted with red on the inside of the arc. (Wikipedia)

However, what you perceive as a rainbow and understand to be a reflection of Sunrays when hitting droplets of water is actually the image of a small portion of the Electromagnetism. This image has a circular shape since it covers all of the Tera-Cell protecting it against any possible cosmic interference. In fact, what you call rainbow, aurora boreal (northern lights) and austral (southern lights) is electromagnetism visible to the naked eye.

It is the habitat of the disincarnated souls. They occupy one of the colors in accordance with their vibration frequency. Those who are on a lower frequency stay with the first three colors of the Rainbow: Red, Orange and Yellow. The souls with a higher frequency stay with the colors: Green, Blue and Violet. Yet those with an even more elevated frequency proceed to the Secondary Rainbow. Every color defines a grade and plane of existence of the thought-energies (souls).

158. What is the meaning of these colors?

Green – mathematical Value = 1. It has great healing power and the most relaxing effect on eyesight, which it can even improve. It represents resistance and stability but occasionally also lack of experience. Stands for growth and hope. "Light" green favors protection and emotional healing. Dark green is associated with social status, money, ambition but also with envy, avarice and greed. Yellowish green suggests illness, conflict and cowardice.

Blue – mathematical Value = 2. It is the color of the mind. It suggests tranquility, stability, thoroughness, intelligence, wisdom, trustworthiness, faith and truth. It also symbolizes sincerity and mercy. Contrary to the hot colors such as red, orange and yellow blue is a cold color associated with intelligence and conscience. In combination with yellow and orange it becomes striking bright and could produce impact and alteration. Light blue stands for tranquility, gentleness, health, cure and understanding. Dark blue is associated with knowledge, integrity, seriousness and power.

Yellow – mathematical Value = 3. It is the symbol of sun light and stimulates mental activity. It stands for joy, happiness and energy. Suggests honor and loyalty but sometimes also cowardice. Stands for safety and stability. Pale yellow suggests precaution, jealousy, envy and damage. Light yellow is associated with originality, joyfulness and intelligence.

Orange – mathematical Value = 4. Represents enthusiasm, attraction, determination, creativity, stimulus and success. It also stands for strength and resistance. Dark orange could suggest deception and distrust. In combination with red, it is associated with happiness and bright sunlight. Yet it also symbolizes desire, passion, sexual pleasure, action, aggressiveness as well as a feeling of prestige, wealth, clarity of ideas and wisdom. It frequently stands for excellence.

Violet – mathematical Value = 5. It combines the stability of blue and the energy of red symbolizing nobleness, luxury and power and associates with dignity, independence, creativity and wisdom. It furthermore stands for magic and mystery and may evoke feelings of romance and nostalgia.

Red – mathematical Value = 6. It is the color of fire and blood being associated with energy, determination, strength, danger and war as well as desire, passion and love. It symbolizes courage and may encourage people to make important decisions at the right time. Light red stands for sensibility, joyfulness, sensuality, passion and love. Rose suggests romance and friendship but also passiveness and yearning. Dark red is associated with willpower, vigor, leadership but also with rage and malice.

159. How differ Orbs from the Rainbow?

The difference lies in the number of electrons and protons of each. While the Rainbow contains a larger number of protons, Orbs accumulate more electrons. Both belong to the electromagnetism of the planet but present themselves differently. Not all of them shelter disincarnated souls or thought-energies and often are just electric and chemical charges of the planet's atmosphere.

160. Observing the Rainbow, we only see an arc of narrow lines in the sky. Why are we unable to perceive if it is wider or covers a larger area?

If it were much wider, you would not be able to see it because of the angle of your vision. The rainbow is a local phenomenon, that is, it appears in any location where sunrays hit water droplets, mist or even fog producing reflection, refraction and dispersion of light.

161. What are your spacecraft like?

They are not how you possibly imagine them. They are palpable holograms we create using Orbs. Why do we call them spacecraft? Because our holograms look very much like them. What we do is introducing images into the natural electromagnetism of the Orbs that then appear in the form of unidentified flying objects (UFO). We take advantage of the naturally circular shape of the Orbs and put in programs that project the image we want to show.

The "holographic" spacecraft technology will be available to you in the future and allow you to explore the cosmos without your physical presence. You will thus proceed to planes and dimensions whose conditions your physical bodies would not tolerate and initiate a journey that will eventually turn you part of the Interstellar Cosmic Confederation. To project holograms we extract the necessary energy from the planetary and cosmic magnetism. Appropriate programs help us to adjust the form of the holograms to environmental conditions.

This easily explains why we can be in different locations at the same time, even walk among you without your noticing us. We have always been close to you through palpable holograms, living and working with you and thus knowing and awaking you. We have also interfered with your governments' inadequate use of technology preventing the planet from suffering irreversible damage.

162. This sounds like something out of a Science Fiction movie. Can you then adopt also the features of humans, animals and things on your holograms?

Yes. This technology has allowed us to study you and the planet thoroughly in areas of difficult or even restricted access when necessary but never affected human or animal life. It was necessary that we proceeded that way to accompany the evolution of your science and technology. Otherwise, ambition and greed still so deeply rooted in you would long have destroyed humanity.

163. Why was your advanced technology not enough to stop warfare on this planet? Why has it failed to free us from hunger, misery, slavery and injustice?

We can interfere directly using this technology only when there is clear evidence that your species and the planet are in danger of annihilation. For any other of your innumerous problems regarding food, health, security, housing, etc., however complex they may be, we have to follow the rules as determined by the Interstellar Cosmic Confederation not to interfere with yours nor with any other of the planets that suffered distortion. Notwithstanding, for reasons already outlined, humans are a somewhat special case and therefore deserved and also received additional help, with the Confederation's consent and supervision, for the solution of their most pressing problem, the cure of theirs and the Tera-Cell's elements.

Not interfering directly in the solution of your most urgent current problems does not mean that we are indifferent to them. On the contrary. At all times, we have assisted you with the development of new projects in science, technology and space by inspiring you to track down the cause of these immense problems and confront them with knowledge, understanding and the force of love. Unavailability of or inaccessibility to sufficient quality food is still a serious problem in many parts of the planet. Yet, it is one among many others such as racism, discrimination, corruption, growing violence and warfare.

The existence of famine associates with a poorly developed spirit reflecting thought-energies without compassion and is therefore a consequence of selfishness, avarice and ambition so deeply rooted in the human species. Even though spiritual human beings are eager to take responsibilities for the planet, they still are not truly conscious of the world around them.

If we, your Elder Brothers Ayaplianos gave you a formula to end poverty powerful ill negative forces would certainly welcome it as a highly appropriate tool for further manipulation and domination. Proof of this mentality is the holding back of many inventions and advanced procedures that could solve innumerous shortcomings on the planet, for political or commercial reasons. On the other hand, we are aware that numerous governments and institutions do endeavor to improve living conditions by fighting inequality and injustice.

A major priority, no doubt, is the production and distribution of food. There has been much progress regarding the satisfaction of the needs of an ever-increasing world population. However, there are still many deficiencies, especially in the area of distribution. In many less developed countries, poor infrastructure increases transportation costs often making products inaccessible to consumers. There is, however, not the least doubt that to overcome any kind of problems you need to accelerate the process of waking CONSCIENCE. If you do not, you will never be able to make a fair distribution of material goods nor instill spiritual concepts. As long as ambition, manipulation, undiscriminated pursuit of personal interests, selfishness and materialism prevail, humans will not receive the fair treatment to which they are entitled.

It is essential that humans become HUMANE because only *Humaneness* will turn them beings of *Compassion* and *Love*. The day they succeed in taking this enormous step forward injustice will no longer reign on this planet. Even though you may consider our interference as being too infrequent, the number of our interventions that have impeded decisions and actions that would have sealed the fate of the planet's population and meant eventual destruction of the planet itself would overwhelm you. In all our interventions, we have full support from our brothers Seramitas who always give us a complete picture of Cause and Effect for each intervention thus making it absolutely clear when and where to proceed. Believe brothers, we are with you, we have always been there, we never abandoned you, both in the physical part (the Elohim), and in the psychic part (The Seramitas). Despite everything, we must let you grow, we cannot intervene in everything you do, you must learn by own experience, it is the only way you become adults.

164. Are you responsible for the malfunctioning of the LHC and HAARP projects?

Yes. We sent palpable holograms to correct the procedure because we concluded that these are high-risk operations. Please, note that our task is to help, supervise and eventually intervene but not to keep you from developing and testing new technologies and equipment necessary to continue the process of evolution. Only when realizing that you are losing control of a process and facing great imminent danger can we justify a direct interference.

Like our brothers Seramitas, we are "Guardians of Tera". Yet, while their task is to heal thought-energies (souls) and study your mind using Psychology and Philosophy to encourage elevation, we are responsible for the healing and functioning of your matter reality associated with evolution. At the same time, we procure to advance by approaching the human sphere and preparing for a future alliance of mutual benefit. Please understand that we, like all Ayaplianos, are preparing for our departure using science (matter), psychology (soul) and spirituality (spirit).

165. Do you have emotions?

No, we do not, but we know what they are like since we had to study them thoroughly to understand how they and your brain work. Having suffered distortion and almost exclusively used our brain's left side, our brain's right side, center of universal feelings, has lost more than half of its capacity through atrophy. We profusely use knowledge and understanding. Instead of emotions, we have a need for satisfaction, appreciation or consent regarding decisions of coexistence. We do not have neither emotions nor feelings. You may be wondering: how can we live without these elements? We exist based on: *Qualities*.

Qualities: Identity related values as essential character traits of individuals guarantee stability and trust within the collective while self-esteem denotes the appreciation an individual has for himself. Individuals of a community or society will thus develop a sense of identity and act by strictly following moral values. (Wikipedia)

In the Elohim society, we do not conceive a process of evolution as centered on accumulating knowledge. We realized that it is of utmost importance to concentrate on the concept of multi-subject studying at every level as the one way to form individuals capable of integrating our society as well as facing the exterior. Having suffered an important loss

224

of universal feelings, we guided our spiritual growth by following the Laws or Values of the Cosmos with the feelings we managed to preserve functioning in parallel.

We have experienced the Cosmic Values as very complex and demanding forcing us to engage deeply in the process of developing will, morale and mental strength, ever since then the foundation of the Elohim community's social structure. These qualities make us truthful beings of our species. The below mentioned values are firmly rooted in our character and determine how we think and interact with the world around us:

Industriousness, Austerity, Honesty, Independence, Responsibility, Tenacity, Modesty, Collectivism, Creativity, Ethics, Solidarity, Discipline, Critical and Self-Critical Analysis, Boldness, Tolerance, Patience, Perseverance, Agility of Thought and Action, Integrality, Firmness, Freedom, Order, Moral Conduct, Research etc. As you can see, these qualities are what allow us to continue forward and have protected us from any emotional interference, as in the case of you. Our actions, deeds and thoughts were devoted to the values instead of the sick-neg-ative-energy. By having only positive values, we were able to avoid diseases, which never attacked us lightly, but we were able to face them so that they never entered our brains again.

Not having suffered from distortion, our brain's left side preserved the ability to establish a relationship between **Fact** and **Value**. This actually saved us by defining the path of an ethical existence we had to follow. It confronted us with the two realities, with which we Elohim had to deal: the world as it **is** and the world how it should **be**. We never were doubtful that honesty is our supreme guide, that is, all the positive qualities to make us look past the facts and open our eyes to recognize the true course that is leading to a superior reality.

166. How could we humans learn to transform our Emotions into Qualities?

Along the process of evolution and elevation, you will learn to transform emotions into qualities and these eventually into Universal Feelings. When this happens, we shall have fulfilled our part of the immense universal task called *EL SER UNO*, for then Ayaplianos-Volunteers of the spacecraft, Seramitas (Feelings), Elohim (Qualities) and Aya-plianos-Humans (Emotions) will finally form one single spirit. The process behind this grandiose event is that positive-human-emotions (Understanding) turn positive-qualities-Elohim (Knowledge) and these transform into Cosmic-Feelings-Ayaplianos (Love)... this is when the brain's left and right hemisphere will unite and our spirits belong to the UNO with planetary elements being transformed into cosmic ones. We have been working to accomplish this for 300 million years and, as you know, are looking forward to joining the Cosmic Alignment that will help us start the journey of return to our origin.

167. Can you predict the future?

Yes, we can, based on a Cause-and-Effect relationship between thoughts and actions. Adding events of the past to those of the present allows us to predict future events in your reality. We are trying to answer your question using the terms past and future for the sake of understanding. In reality, there is no past nor future. Everything is present in the vastness of the universe.

You are living in a present shaped by the effects of many negative causes and no paranormal powers are necessary to visualize the vast number of negative effects these causes are still going to produce. We are closely observing you because you have formed causes that produce devastating effects and will continue so. Ambition for power and domination is so strong that there will be no end to suffering and pain in a long time. We your brothers are therefore trying everything to help increase the frequency of your thought-energies (souls) and thus prevent you from creating further negative and painful causes. The harvest, that is, the departure from this planet, will be collected in the following phases:

- First Phase: The next 200 years
- Second Phase: From the year 2347 to 2680
- Third Phase: From the year 2680 to 9000

168. What would be a planetary cause we created that will have negative effects?

The climate crisis. We have warned you innumerable times of the negative and harmful effects the use of oil has on you and the planet. You, however, continue using it. To our regret, the planet and many of you are going to face an extended period of suffering, manipulation and domination. During this phase, ill and confused humans will repeat mistakes with effects the magnitude of which will make them realize what distortion, ambition, ignorance and power can do. Some of the most serious effects are:

- Lasting warfare centered in several middle-east countries
- The Third World War will be inevitable and it will start in the east.
- Global financial collapse, responsible for a sharp population decrease
- Obligatory birth control
- Absolute control through palpable-holography
- Manipulation and control through drugs
- Idem through machines
- Demographical control of large cities favoring the predominant presence of young people

169. How did you manage to control the Reptilian-Grays and the creatures?

We did with your help. By elevating the planet's electromagnetic frequency, you left them without a chance to return to the outside. We therefore worry no longer about the Reptilian-Grays and the creatures. What we actually must do is to face and control the Reptilian force incarnated in humans, negative energy we have been fighting ever since we arrived here and suffered from distortion.

The greatest challenge for all the brothers Ayaplianos continues to be the control and transmutation of Reptilian thought energy present in every human being. All the same, you still worry too much about threatening aliens from outer space failing to realize that the ill negative force is among you, in many of your organizations, governments and religious institutions.

227

The real menace you are facing is right here and not surging from beyond earthly boundaries. The positive force is in all life forms of the universe since *EL SER UNO* will never surrender to the ill negative force. Humans of planet Tera carry the two forces. Confined to an energy bubble, either one is struggling to predominate.

170. Could you tell us how much sound and ill energy there is in humans and in the planet's electromagnetism?

We estimate that there is 60% ill and 40% sound energy in human beings. In the electromagnetism, the figures invert to 60% sound and 40% ill energy. Why? The sound-positive energy has a greater force because it carries the "Light" (White Blood Cells). It is in the electromagnetism where this energy, in its disincarnated state, manifests itself more vigorously.

171. Would you say then that you have fulfilled the entrusted mission?

We might say so since with the improvement of the electromagnetism humans will be able to heal. Nevertheless, it is in the year 2800 with the advent of the Avatar Abigahel that we can affirm Mission completed after we together helped save the Tera-Cell and thus the majority of thought-energies (souls).

172. Why does the healthy energy in the incarnated state not have the same force of the Light as disincarnated in the planetary electromagnetism?

The incarnated thought-energy (soul) fails the 60% of force because physical density impedes full manifestation of its Light. To equal the strength it has in the incorporeal state it would have to double its force. In other words, gravity is the reason that incarnated energy is incapable of developing its true potential. This, however, is not the case with ill negative energy as its natural habitat is the physical body, the vehicle to materialize its negative force. We all are therefore working to help you elevate your electromagnetism while incarnated. This, for a start, will finish off the cancer called: ambition. Why? Because emanation of high vibration thought-energies will have the effect of white blood cells that conquer a disease.

What does that mean? For the past 150.000 years, we your elder brothers Elohim have been working on the cure of your physical body while the brothers Seramitas have taken special care of your psychical body. We Elohim have been responsible for the evolution of your physical body by energetically transferring large amounts of our DNA to you. This has helped lighten your density and significantly advance the process of evolution.

Joint efforts enabled us to elevate your DNA's energetic vibration frequency and transmit knowledge on healthy nutrition ridding yourselves gradually of toxic cinnabar energies to produce light out of your physical body. Consequently, purifying matter energy means to elevate the frequency of the electromagnetism along with that of the thought-energies. This will make light (like white blood cells) expand, fight the cinnabar disease (ill negative energy) and have the holograms function properly.

173. Are you Holograms?

Yes, we are subtle palpable-holograms. Everything within *EL SER UNO* is holograms, subtle or dense. The existence of the universe meaning *EL SER UNO* depends on the electromagnetism. Electromagnetism is the SOUL of the universe and this soul is an immense hologram holding thousands of millions of programs that make it work. Holograms traverse grades, planes and dimension adapting by turning subtle or dense and always depending on the electromagnetism that makes them run faster or more slowly.

174. Are you, the Ayaplianos-Volunteers of the spacecraft and the Seramitas closely watching us then?

We would prefer to say that we care for you permanently. Planet Tera's case is unusual in the universal context, a cell that had been extremely ill and needed very extensive care. Nowadays we would say that it is convalescent but not healed yet. The current phase is the most critical one because the planet could relapse and suffer a more virulent attack of the disease. We all suffered collateral effects throughout this healing process but most of you often fail to feel responsible for their acts and we therefore cannot leave them unobserved. Until ambition is entirely rooted out, we shall not stop caring for you.

175. What are your conclusions from this interview?

This interview is a psychological preparation to create the conditions for the "Contact". To establish this contact, we are preparing to adapt our thought-energy to the Ayapliana-Human energy procuring a gradual integration with humans in the exterior. Adapting to an energy means that thought-energies (souls) will have to adjust in a way to accept a new reality and act on it. To do this, there has to be a mutual psychical approach to prepare our energies for an adjustment of concepts regarding knowledge and understanding.

176. Do you communicate with disincarnated souls or other species as you do with the Ayaplianos-Volunteers, Seramitas and us?

Realities are arranged in an orderly way throughout the universe and do not mingle. We do not have contacts with disincarnated souls as many human mediums do because we are not human and because the right hemisphere of our brain does not have the capacity to do this. Nevertheless, this does not keep us from being conscious of these realities. Different forms of realities may relate, but for this to occur certain qualities for an energetic correlation are necessary.

177. Does planet Tera coexist with extraterrestrials other than the Ayaplianos?

No. For the time being, planet Tera does not offer conditions for such a coexistence since it has suffered quarantine over a long period in a bubble-sphere of healing energy. This energy favored the healing process but also prevented the disease of ambition from expanding to other realities of existence.

178. If an energetic correlation is needed how you, the Elohim, and I, a human being, are communicating with each other?

That is why we emphasize the need of qualities. Both of us have these qualities allowing communication by the Transmission of thoughts. Communication between you and us does not require the use of words as there is a mind-to-mind connection. This is possible because the left hemisphere of your and our brain managed to adjust their vibration frequency thus creating the conditions for a stable contact.

Your left side is free of vibrational contamination and you have a wide, open and accessible mind. This has been possible by the cleanliness and clarification of your soul, which is in order, reaching a more balanced and harmonious within your mental and emotional body. The balanced state between you and us allows us to communicate, since the frequency and vibration are maintained, stable and unalterable, qualities essential to understand each other.

179. Do you use the quartz crystals the way the brothers Seramitas do?

Communication with the brothers Ayaplianos-Volunteers of the space-craft and Seramitas is through palpable holograms or transmission of thoughts and ideas. We never stopped communicating with them in perfect harmony. Since we are living in a Spacecraft-City, we need not use quartz crystals in the process of communication. However, we know that these crystals are the origin of all existing in the universe, are *EL SER UNO*.

180. Is it you who appear projected by the palpable holograms?

Palpable holograms are replicates of ourselves that we launch and monitor from the Spacecraft-City. Holography is a highly advanced technology for projecting palpable physical shapes. One day this technology will be the substitute for human energy in many activities marking an era of monumental scientific and technological transformation on planet Tera.

181. How will palpable holograms substitute human activities?

Scientists some day will understand that exploring the cosmos will not be by interstellar spacecraft, even travelling at the speed of light, because the many realities of the universe confine life to its natural space of existence. Life as you know it emerged and developed in a specific environment. You and the planet are in a bubble-sphere called Earth that produces the electromagnetism necessary to preserve all that exists within that sphere.

To leave the Earth's sphere would demand creating a bubble-sphere inside the spacecraft identical to that of the planet. Since there is no way to reproduce the exact living conditions of the planet, space travel to remote places of the universe is impossible. The only way you can explore the vast universal body of *EL SER UNO* is using palpable holograms.

182. What will our future be like?

Tera lying ahead will be quite different from what it is today. From the year 2800 on, there will be profound changes. To begin with, the planet's population will considerably shrink, as increasing global insecurity will discourage people from having children. These changes come with great suffering, ecological disasters, wars etc. causing a significant slowdown of the planet's evolution.

Humans in the exterior will be in great distress, which, however, will lead them to a much better understanding of their reality. As never before, this awareness will be an enormous incentive to multiply their efforts to turn this planet into the so long dreamed of paradise. Our brothers Seramitas have explained everything relevant to your souls. We are going to enlighten you about evolution. Nowadays your evolution largely depends on economic interests. This is the main reason that instead of advancing as expected it seems to stagnate because of ambition, greed and incessant search for power.

There is an enormous number of investigations underway regarding new technologies promising great benefit for the population; nevertheless, many organizations adopt policies to limit or even block their implementation because they fear these technologies could curb their economic perspectives. Governments in many parts of the planet are drawing money in excess from the population based on improper legislation or even illegal schemes. Religious institutions depending economically on their followers secure their adherence by knowingly insisting on traditional and largely inconsistent messages.

Humans and the planet will have to face great energetic changes. There will be transformations at all levels. The planet's magnetic poles will reverse with such dramatic consequences as the separation of continents. You must realize that planet Tera is a cell that develops and before dying one day produces new cells in a steady process of reproduction like any living organism.

183. What is your part in the spiritual elevation humans will experience during the next 7 thousand years?

It certainly is a role of great responsibility. We Elohim have always been close to help your elevation occur in accordance with the universal laws transmitting the knowledge you need to reach the frequency for joining those other frequencies of Light and Love. During this important phase of evolution and elevation you will undergo, we also will protect you against the negative Reptilian energy that will do whatever in its power to keep you from breaking free.

184. Why will the Reptilian-Grays' energy spare no effort to keep us from freeing ourselves?

We must always keep in mind that the universe is Energy that works based on frequency, vibration, rhythm and colors. Our brothers Seramitas have shown you that high/low frequency energies attract other high/low frequency energies. Either thought-energies (souls) survive in the universe.

Nevertheless, low dense and dark frequency energies are restlessly trying to make humans generate dense and low thought-energy because this is how these souls of the dark survive. They are desperate to prevail and seek to encourage vice, degradation of feelings, corruption etc. since those negative thought-energies are the very energy source for their survival. They act like vampires keeping humans from gaining awareness to escape their fangs. A most devastating scourge today is the addiction to alcohol, drugs and sex. They are... Vampires of the Soul.

185. How can we fight these vampire-demons?

When I asked this question, the two Elohim looked at each other and kept silent. The brothers Seramitas then gave me the answer as this topic is of great concern to them. One of them turned to me and said... *Those human beings who live exposed to, surrounded by or, worse, involved with vampire-demons run a serious risk to becoming physically and psychologically ill. It is almost impossible that they can keep their souls from being involved one way or another by just striving for a certain distance from these harmful forces. Acquaintances, friends, relatives and family members, in some ways and in different grades, they will be affected and subjugated by them.*

These forms of addiction are a disease and need urgent treatment...

In many families, one way or another, a wife, a husband, a son or daughter have fallen victims to vampire-demons. What to do when you are living a painful and deplorable situation like that? How to deal objectively with the challenge of finding a solution? Before you start any cure, you should remember that humans have three bodies: the physical (matter), the psychical (soul) and the mental (spirit) body. This should be your guideline when looking for the correct treatment.

Any disease develops from low and dense energy attacking the physical and psychical body by using the energy that emanates from these two bodies. First, the disease attacks the psychical body (soul), then the physical body (matter). Regarding the mental body (spirit), we know that a person who suffers from severe and prolonged addiction is incapable of forming his spirit meaning his energetic being.

Humans develop addictions when their souls suffer continuous attacks from very ill, disincarnated anti-matter energy during long periods. Principal reasons are having been conceived with parents under the influence of alcohol and/or drugs, lack of affection (unwanted child), having grown up in an environment of harassment and physical abuse. When vampire energies of very low vibration invade a soul, this soul falls ill suffering Degradation, which means that the brain is processing negative thoughts of very low frequency only because it is assimilating ill negative energy. Under these conditions, humans' energy voltage drops and both their physical bodies and thought-energies deteriorate.

When the soul is possessed by vampire entities and very low vibration, gets sick and goes into Retroactive States. It means that the brain works only and exclusively with very low thought-energies frequently, because it feeds on sick-negative-thoughts. When human is in these conditions, lowers the energy voltage and at doing so, the thoughts and physical body deteriorate. Since he/she is not in a position to understand what is happening to him/her and by not taking the adequate measures, which would be analysis, reasoning, logic, knowledge, understanding, and love of themselves, of what is happening, supplies their deficiencies with chemical products that make them feel better.

Drugs occasionally do elevate the energy's voltage but mislead both the physical and psychical body and eventually create dependence. While the brain function starts to slow, the psychical body fails to guide the physical body causing it to work only with its primary zones 1 and 2 that represent: **Instinct** and **Sensation**.

The disincarnated vampire energies, that is, the souls of the humans who had been alcoholics and drug addicts, surround this physical body like parasites that live through their victim, enjoying the negative emotions that emanate from it. They feed on its anguish and pain, on the low vibration frequency energy of its soul. While dominated by energy vampires, alcoholics and drug addicts are unable to pay heed to healthy persons who endeavor to help them overcome their miserable life of dependence. What would be their cure? First thing to do is: **to strip them of physical dependence and to strip them of the psychological dependence.**

This entire process must be supervised and controlled under the direction of two types of doctors: A doctor of the physical body, who will be in charge of minimize the chemical dependency of the patient and another one who will need to take care of the soul. This doctor of the soul will initiate the process of exorcizing their vampire energies packed with energetic worms and parasites that dominate them by feeding on and subjugating their energy.

Talking of exorcizing we refer to professionals who specialize in dealing with vampire-thought-energies. The combined psychological and physical treatment is the way to proceed. You should remember that not love from those who want to help but only knowledge, understanding and love together can complete the cure, since each of these qualities relates to one of the three bodies as follows:

- Knowledge – physical body
- Understanding – psychical body
- Love – energetic body

It is the belief of many families that **Love** is enough to help their loved ones conquer the vice. Love is a wonderful feeling. No act of altruism is possible without it. However, many times treatments fail because feelings interfere with the need for decisions guided by **Knowledge** and **Understanding** to achieve positive results. Love *is* important but it takes knowledge and understanding to get a complete picture of the problem. You have to give treatment to both the physical and psychical body at the same time and only then have your energetic (spiritual) body develop and act.

Humans often fail to understand why **Love** guiding their acts does not produce the hoped-for results. The reason is that the love they show is one heavy with emotions. Real love means trying to comprehend the cause that generated an effect (problem) and do whatever you can to find the solution. Disincarnated suffering souls, ghosts and specters carry the effect of alcoholism and drugs using this energy to turn human beings into addicts. After that, they start drawing energy from them causing their psychological and eventual physical death.

Being souls without continuity, they keep wandering in the dark of their torment feeding on energy from "incarnated" souls. If you were to look at those vampire demons, you would be horrified!! Nevertheless, not only is addiction to alcohol and drugs multiplying across the planet, an infinitely greater threat to humanity is the morbid search for power giving rise to the corruption and a permanent unbalance and perversion of the external senses. This is the breeding ground for the energy vampires of the dark, the parasites of ill.

The important thing is that you understand the very nature of the disease. You therefore have to look at it from a different angle. The universe's reality is energy; everything works through frequency, vibration, rhythm and color. If you allow dense and ill negative energies to enter your brain and mind... physical and psychical disease will start to develop. Most patients with mental disorders have become victims of vampire energy leaving them with lifetime consequences.

Doctors who lack knowledge and understanding of parallel realities cannot but treat patients with conventional drugs. Consequently, many will get worse as the vampire-demons assimilate these same drugs neutralizing any treatment.

As long as doctors fail to understand how thought-energy works, or do not really comprehend the human soul nor have a clear notion of parallel reality, they will not be able to help their patients. If families of alcoholics and drug addicts, despite all their efforts using knowledge, understanding and love do not manage to help the addicts free themselves of their vice because they lack the willpower, those families will certainly suffer an immense frustration.

What they will have to do is to determine the degree of responsibility they might have had throughout this process. Psychoanalysis will help them reach important conclusion for the solution of some of their own problems and thus favor their transmutation and elevation. *"It is essential that you trace the origin of your problems to be able to face and solve them; otherwise, you will never really understand the cause-and-effect relationship"*.

186. How do you protect us against Reptilian thought-energies (souls)?

We have long been protecting you against those dark souls that are living by a deeply distorted ambition. Many have incarnated hiding under their human shape monstrous and malevolent forces. Our brothers Ayaplianos-Volunteers of the spacecraft and Seramitas have been relentlessly working with you for the past 150.000 years instilling in you high vibration thought-energies to help you transcend this reality and conquer those malignant forces.

We Elohim have aided your evolution transmitting advanced science and technology allowing you to activate your brain's left hemisphere and, in harmony with the right hemisphere, generate thought-energies of high frequency energy. We have always stimulated and guided those of your investigations, inventions, scientific and technological advances geared for the benefit of humanity. The general idea of the brothers Seramitas' actions and ours always was that of making advance your evolution and elevation simultaneously. We thus have been leading you on the Path of Return. The type and use of the science and technology as transmitted by the Reptilian-Grays, in turn, has always been in detriment of the planet and its population.

187. The Brothers Seramitas already gave a warning about projects like HAARP and LHC. Can you be more specific?

We have followed up closely on the projects and tests conducted by scientists whose souls are entirely Reptilians. Since Reptilian thought-energy was the first to settle on Tera, it always claimed the planet to be its exclusive habitat doing whatever in its power to preserve this status. It is the virus of the disease: distorted Ambition deeply rooted in many human souls that is reigning with enormous force and power.

Nonetheless, we never ceased fighting a force that originates from both the planetary and human electromagnetism; keep in mind that this is a confrontation in the anti-matter reality between the Ayapliano-forces of revelation and freedom and the Reptilian-forces of domination. Our brothers Seramitas and we Elohim are on the alert to block any Reptilian intent of interference that could have fatal consequences.

It is imperative that you elevate your souls' vibration frequency joining us to create a force that we will never succumb. We will be like the white blood cells the Tera- Cell needs to conquer this terrible pandemic forever. While we are taking care of you and the planet, nothing bad will happen. Have faith and work to elevate that additional part of your thought-energies we need to perfect the force of LIGHT and LOVE. When you see strange lights in the sky, accumulation of electric energy, erratic Orbs, huge earthquakes, very destructive torments and other meteorological phenomena it is because governments are testing machines for the ulterior control and domination of the human species in a not-too-distant future.

188. News are that Planet X is real and that Norway started storing food and seeds in the Svalbard and Arctic region for survival in coordination with the US and EU. Is it true that only the political elite and professionals such as scientists, doctors etc. needed for reconstruction will be safe?

Planet X is a fact but it will not be that close or affect life in the planet. Planet X is known by us as Alfa Nova, located in the Inferior Dimension, will be in the proximity of Tera during the 7 thousand years of the Cosmic Alignment. This planet will receive the disincarnated souls of very low vibration frequency from Tera to incarnate in the creature that started to develop there. We all know that with the beginning of the Cosmic Alignment galaxies and planets will be moving closer, allowing to the disembodied dense souls from Tera to be sheltered by the creature in Alfa Nova and Ebiares.

The incarnated Reptilian-force knows all about this and has been building secret shelters to hide and prevent "disincarnation". These incarnated human Reptilians have the knowledge of cloning. Their idea is to keep cloning, that is, leave their body for another adult one, copying thus the Reptilian-Grays' technique to live forever. However, their souls are bound to occupy a clone immediately because otherwise they can no longer stay on the planet.

The truth is that presidents, kings, owners of powerful organization, religious leaders etc. are preparing to live in those shelters as clones. The virus of Ambition developed great intelligence and will not surrender. While these human Reptilians will be safely cloning, an ever-larger number of humans will die. Nevertheless, many of these disincarnated souls will have AWAKED and feel attracted to the Internal City of the planet; afterwards, they will leave for the Internal City of Venus and live there until they are ready to continue their Journey of Return toward other realities of existence. These souls are safe because they will work for their elevation with true belief and great willpower.

At the end of the second phase of the Cosmic Alignment, that is, in the year 2800 many of the souls who are already living on Venus will return and incarnate on Tera to help awake those who had remained in the exterior to fight the Reptilian force. On the other hand, the Reptilian force, from 2300 until 2800 is going to dominate those who failed to awake and remained trapped in the exterior. They will be the work force for the construction of new premises to house those who had been living in secret shelters. Meanwhile, the overall population of the planet will be decreasing considerably. Along the 7 thousand years of the Cosmic Alignment, the total number of inhabitants will come down to about 600 million. At the end of it, the presence of the human species will be just a small fraction of that.

During the final phase of the alignment, the souls of Venus are preparing for the decisive confrontation with the Reptilian souls whose process of cloning will eventually prove useless for domination. They are going to lose this final battle and have to leave Tera for Mars from where they later will depart for the planets Alfa Nova and Ebiares of the Inferior Dimension. On the other hand, having almost completed its cycle to make room for the Yeti on planet Tera, the human species will turn the new Ayapliana-Human species, the objective of a task entrusted to us about 300 million years ago. *Allowing us all to accomplish elevation and, more, find the cure from distortion to return to where we came from... The Pleiades.*

189. Did any Reptilian-Grays incarnate in humans?

None of the 33 Reptilian-Grays who separated from us ever incarnated in humans. Nevertheless, the essence of their energy is present in those Reptilian-thought-energies from the Satien fragment that had leaked to the exterior taking root in the souls of humans and causing the distortion by absorbing ill and harmful energies.

To know who the real demons are, stay alert to the policies and performance of governments, religious institutions and the power of money. Do not blame the Reptilian-Grays, because these poor beings are confined to their habitat and watched by us to avoid they escape.

Some 22 mega-organizations control the planet and have enormous responsibilities for most of what is happening. They very cleverly use fear and ignorance to distract your attention by trying to make you believe that some superior alien power from outer space is threatening you.

You are bombarded 24 hours a day with: subliminal messages, movies that contain information that arouses the lower instincts: sex, lust, heartbreak, violence and much more. They show the aliens as diabolical creatures. The processed foods that you consume are made with chemicals that go directly to the brain, heightening the need and consumption. What we are telling you is not Science Fiction, it is a reality so raw, that the day you really wake up, you will be horrified to know how you live and how you have always lived.

190. The planet's climate is changing. Tera is under a constant bombardment of solar gamma rays and we have detected concentrations of gamma radiation in the center of our galaxy. Is there a relationship between gamma radiation and climate change?

Climate changes are cyclic. Remember that we all are inside an immense and ever dynamic mind, an energy that works through the electromagnetism. This mind creates and recycles the energy responsible for never ending cosmic reactions that you perceive as the creation or extinction of planets, stars or even galaxies. In reality, they are thought-energies that prepare for the creation of ideas. These thought-energies are crossing the universe (the mind) as gamma rays to settle in some planet where they take human shape and develop according to the ideas they have been creating.

Gamma Rays (as you know them)

Gamma ray or gamma radiation is a penetrating electromagnetic radiation consisting of photons and arising from radioactive decay of atomic nuclei or sub-atomic processes such as electron-positron annihilation. Quite a number of astrophysical processes generate g-rays with very high-energy electrons. Being ionizing they are biologically hazardous and capable of penetrating materials more profoundly than alpha and beta rays.

The main source of g-rays that reach Earth is the sun. If directly in contact with the planet surface these rays would be lethal to all living organisms even at a lower intensity rate after having traveled the distance of some 150 million km between the Sun and the Earth. Fortunately, the atmosphere's electromagnetism protects the planet by screening this radiation. This protection will last until the end of the Cosmic Alignment, that is, until the year 9 thousand. The planet's surface will then be subject to direct exposure of gamma radiation not only from the sun but also from some nearby Super Nova.

When this happens the human species, the Ayaplianos-Volunteers, the Seramitas-Ayaplianos and we, the Elohim, will already have departed for other planets and realities. The Yeti, future reigning species of the planet, will be living in caverns throughout the 7 thousand years of the alignment. When gaining the surface, he will find it ice and snow covered and start feeding on photons from the gamma radiation.

The Universal Mind engulfs everything, absolutely everything the One Principle has ever created. This means that you must realize that we all are inside the mind of *EL SER UNO* and that everything you observe is holographic creations of that infinite mind, the reality you live in. When you leave the physical for your anti-matter reality, you will be looking at the filaments of the Universal Mind, that is, the billions of neurons of this mind's brain that appear to be gamma rays or colorful energies and whose axons and dendrites you will perceive as constellations, galaxies and planets.

As the messages of this mind have to cover immense distances, they travel by waves, frequency, vibration, rhythm and colors. Myriads of dendrites extend across this mind reaching the body of planet-cells to have its neurons take messages from the axons of other nervous-planet-cells. Billions of nervous-planet-cells interconnect axons and dendrites that way, while glial cells surround the neurons nurturing, supporting and protecting them.

The various types of brain-cell-constellations of the Universal Mind have specific functions. Several cover the process of reasoning, learning and memorizing. Others handle the reception of sensory messages. Yet others communicate with the physical and psychical body stimulating the universe's actions and reactions. The brain of the Universal Mind has a metabolism of its own through which it turns chemical elements into electric energy (electromagnetism) to keep its nervous-cell-constellations functioning.

The metabolism of the Universal Mind's brain is a process the planet-cells and galaxy-molecules use to transform chemical and nutritional elements forming basic elements for the creation of new cell molecules (creation of supernovas). To be efficient the metabolism of the Universal Mind's brain must be guaranteed a stable blood circulation (energy flow) providing the planet-cells with oxygen and glucose (positive-thoughts). Positive thoughts are the energy source of the cosmic brain. Without them, the nervous-brain-cell-constellations cannot survive.

As you may have realized, the way the Universal Mind's brain works very much resembles the human brain. This should be no surprise since humans are the living image of the One Origin. Failing to see and recognize this reality would make it impossible for you to understand the true nature of your species.

191. What will planet Earth be like in the year 9000; will there be an atmosphere, water, food? On what will the Yeti feed?

Along the 7000 years of the Cosmic Alignment, humans will take every single measure using the science and technology we will provide to prepare for this scenario. To begin with, by 2800, the planet's population will already have dropped significantly and life in society be much different from nowadays. Solar energy's temperature will fall but its luminosity increase generating larger amounts of photons the Yeti will assimilate and thus turn a being of light. Unlike yours, his physical body will be subtle and transparent and shine with a fluorescent light.

Human science and technology will be well advanced and used for the benefit of all human beings. People will be living in autonomous cities under domes that offer shelter against Gamma and UV radiation. However, despite the precautions they adopt in their new habitat, humans will see themselves change into more delicate, hairless, big-eyed individuals, extremely sensible to photonic light. As they will feed on photons, they cannot risk exposure to sun light directly and will have to use special dark quartz glasses to protect their eyesight.

The domed cities that are located in the main centers, only will serve for young and working people, that is, for those who serve the productive work. The old and elderly will also work but in other dome-cities and in places outside the main centers. They will produce, but their work will not be physical, but intellectual. They will generate productive ideas for the young people to execute and work on.

Nutrition will be entirely different and plants be grown in hydroponics (in water) and processed without the addition of any synthetic chemical substance. The volume produced will always meet the requirements of consumption. Many of today's types of food will not exist anymore remaining a few appropriate ones for your future photonic body, a body of elevated frequency energy.

192. Are we approaching another Glacial Period?

Yes, you are. Some of today's climatic phenomena point in this direction. From 2300 on, the traditional four seasons will change to only two extremely marked summer and winter cycles causing many important cities to move to other locations or even rebuild on enormous marine platforms.

193. Will this climate change affect you?

No, it will not. As already outlined, our habitat is a Spacecraft-City designed for displacements that depend on the planet's rotation and passage as well as on its periodically unstable electromagnetism. This is why we have to look for locations with a strong and balanced electromagnetic force. We entirely depend on the electromagnetism and so will you in the future.

194. Where do you enter and exit the planet's caverns?

We do not enter or exit as our displacements may occur in any part of the planet's electromagnetism. At present, a large area covering Bolivia, Argentina, Brazil and Peru has the greatest electromagnetic stability and we therefore have taken a position in the proximity of Lake Titicaca between Peru and Bolivia from where we are sending you messages through holograms and orbs.

195. Why do you keep from interfering with the Reptilian-force's domination during the second phase of the Cosmic Alignment?

The concept of evolution and elevation of the species created by the Universal Mind and protected by the Interstellar Cosmic Federation determines that no alien force must interfere with another species' way of dealing with cause and effect, that is, creating and following procedures of their own to strive for evolution and elevation.

The human species' belief in the need for evolution and elevation must always be the driving force rather than inducement. This is how the energy in a natural way will fulfil its basic condition of creation. The Universal Mind will never accept imposition as nothing can question nor reverse the cosmic energy's established course. Ill negative energy has no place in this great mind because its standard or rhythm is incapable of adjusting to that of the universe. Those humans who let the negative Reptilian force occupy their minds will suffer the consequences of having failed to understand, to show self-confidence, to work their personality and to use the numerous opportunities they had in the course of their lives. Nevertheless, we have to respect the free will and decision of every being, the space of every creation.

196. It has called our attention that masculine and feminine soul energies incarnate in female and male bodies respectively. Has this to do with our evolution?

Yes, it has. In reality, there is no masculine or feminine energy; energy is asexual. So are we. On your planet, the energy has developed certain characteristics for a particular action in both male and female bodies. The human-species of other planets whose development has followed the general guidelines of the universe does not have this predicament. Either body will offer them the security of a harmonious development. Men and women have exactly the same status and they may be taking turns when it comes to decide either of whom will gestate a child.

It is the natural way for realities where procreation still exists. Other more elevated ones have immortal adult bodies who receive Energetic Beings (Spirits) to complete their elevation. The humans' energy in other parts of the universe is asexual. Thoughts and feelings do not differ because of hormonal effects since their brains' right and left sides are perfectly balanced.

On Tera, in turn, an increasing amount of sound positive energy from Venus is incarnating to reduce the enormous concentration of ill negative energy from Mars incarnated in you. The thought-energies from Venus will be choosing either sex for incarnation since both offer the shelter they need.

As to the situation of both energies, we are conscious that these massive incarnations will produce an energy imbalance, unfortunately inevitable for now. However, by unifying both energies in equal conditions you will be reaching the necessary equilibrium. This will be one reason for a significant drop in the planet's population during the next one thousand years. Future generations, especially those who are going to experience a permanent state of domination during the 500-years period, will be androgynous (with male and female features) individuals. Manipulation through mind control apparatus will neutralize their libido (sexual drive) and preservation of the species occur through fertilization in vitro, a process used for the one purpose of securing sufficient labor force.

197. A truly terrifying view of the future. What do we have to do to prevent this?

Much to our regret, there is nothing you can do. You will have to submit to this process, the same that created the human species in the universe. The human species of the future will be androgynous individuals whose physical body will change to shelter one single energy formed by both the Masculine and Feminine force. This process is already under way. In the future, human relations will obey the force of love rather than of passion.

Persons will feel attracted by the affinity of their souls (thought-energies), frequency, vibration, rhythm and colors. You should not feel shocked. We are like that and our existence has been an experience of joyfulness ever since. Sex is of no importance to us. We are feeling our energy emanate and mingle with that of the other person and together we are creating the most precious thought-energies any imagination could produce.

198. Do the Reptilian-Grays after all have a chance to manipulate and dominate the human race?

The Reptilians-Grays, those 33 brothers who went to live in the darkness of the caverns will stay forever where they are. For millions of years, they have been unable to leave their habitat. We nevertheless keep watching them closely.

The real threat – as we said earlier – is the ill negative Reptilian energy from the Satien fragment incarnated in humans...there are the 22 or so mega-corporations, governments and religious institutions that manipulate and control the planet. They are the heirs of Satien and Lucifer. They are the monstrous creatures of the dark, descendants of the first Reptilians to arrive on the planet with the Satien fragment. They are the ones you must fear, for they are the souls of darkness and evil is the master they worship.

There will be times of hardship and pain for most inhabitants of the planet. You will experience horror and darkness. BE ON THE ALERT, brothers, and beware of the tentation to believe in the fantasy of unreality.

Many of you will resist crediting us for this alert and think that we are extreme in our vision of the planet's situation in the near future. We are not. Immense changes will occur and they will occur in every one of you. Those who fail to understand that deep inside them a real change must take place and do not lift their frequency during the next 200 years, will fall behind in elevation and as descendants of the universe. They will be unable to free themselves of the planetary frequency and gravity because of the heaviness of their thought-energies (souls).

199. Is it true that certain very rich families, political leaders of advanced and developing countries... are incarnated Reptilians?

Yes. The Reptilian influence had passed from generation to generation way before we arrived on the planet. The Reptilian energy is very old and has preserved its lineage and descendance. Reptilians are the owners of this planet and masters of humanity. You work for them, for the Matrix. Few of you resisted its temptations. Those who did are helping others do likewise.

Trust us, brothers, and listen to our voice of alert. We do not mean to overdo this but you must know the truth. The Reptilian force camouflaged hiding in humans, do look closer, do perceive it, it is right there where you sense AMBITION y GREED... in the financial world, in governments, in the huge profits and the big cheats.

When reading this, many of you might consider the channel to magnify our message or even live in a fantasy world... it is nothing of that kind, brothers. We regret that the books *EL SER UNO* seem to offer no instant relief from fear, anguish and depression and, most certainly are of little use for entertainment and relax. You therefore have to use your free will and decide whether to continue pretending not to see and stay where you are or prepare to overcome domination and win freedom and dignity.

200. Did the 33 Reptilian-Grays ever communicate with the exterior?

There was a time when they did as the *Nephilim*.

The Nephilim

The Nephilim (the fallen or the giants) were the offspring from the mating of sons of God and daughters of humans (Genesis 6:1-4). There is much debate over the "sons of God". We believe that the "sons of God" were fallen angels (demons) who mated with human females giving rise to the Nephilim, a race of giants, the brave who since ancient times were considered men of renown (Genesis 6:4).

Why would the demons have acted like that? The Bible gives no clear answer. The demons are evil creatures and what they may do should not surprise us. Speculations go that another reason could have been the contamination of the humans' bloodline to prevent the arrival of the Messiah Jesus Christ. God had promised that the Messiah would carry the lineage of Eve (Genesis 3:15) who would injure the head of the serpent - Satan. The demons in all probability had tried to impede the appearance of an immaculate Messiah by contaminating the human bloodline. Again, the Bible does not refer to it in particular but there is a good chance as it is not in contradiction to what the Bible says.

Who are the Nephilim?

According to Hebrew and other legends (the book of Enoc and other non-biblical scriptures), the Nephilim were a race of giant superheroes who perpetrated acts of great evil. Their tallness and power seemed to have come from the combination of their DNA and human genes. The only direct mention in the Bible says that they were "the brave ones who since ancient times were said to be men of renown". (Genesis 6:4).

What happened to these Nephilim or giants? They seemed to have been the main reason for the big flood in times of Noah. When referring to the Nephilim the Bible says that Jehovah saw that humans' acts of evil on Earth were many and that deep in their hearts their only desire was to so continue". And Jehovah felt repentant to have created the human species and was very sad." Jehovah said I shall erase from the face of Earth the human species I have created and even the beasts, the reptiles and the birds in the sky; for I repent to have created them." (Genesis 6:5-7). And God proceeded to flood the planet killing every living creature including the giants but excepting Noah and his family and selected couples of all animal species who found shelter in the Ark (Genesis 6:11-22).

Were there any Nephilim or giants left after the big flood? In Genesis 6.4, we read there were giants on Earth in those times. They seemed to have continued with their sinful acts for some time after the flood but apparently to a lesser extent. Spies Moses had sent to the land of Canaan came back saying they also saw giants there, sons of Anac, the race of giants and felt that they were looking down on them. (Numbers 13:33) Now this chapter does not affirm that the Nephilim or giants were actually there but only that the spies thought they had seen them.

As likely as not, the spies had come across very tall people in Canaan and believed them to be Nephilim. It is also possible that the demons had mated again with human females giving birth to new giants. Whatever the case the Israelites during the invasion of Canaan likely destroyed the "giants" (according to Joshua 11:21-22, Deuteronomy 3:11 and 1 Samuel chapter 17).

What could hinder the demons to engender Nephilim or giants today? It looks like God ended all relations between demons and humans by eternally jailing the demons who had still been procreating. Judas in verse 6 tells us: "And the angels who failed to preserve their dignity by abandoning their abode are kept in prisons of darkness until judgement day". Obviously not all of the demons had been "imprisoned" and a number must have committed grave acts of perversion after the original fall. Yet the demons who supposedly have mated with human females are suffering eternal imprisonment to deter others from acting likewise.

(http://www.gotquestions.org/espanol/nefilim.html)

201. What can you say about this explanation the Nephilim?

In fact, the Reptilian-Grays are the Nephilim. Were they really giants? In those times, the Reptilian-Grays (Nephilim) still were Ayapliano size. They must have appeared very tall when compared to the much shorter humans. This could explain why these called them giants. This story took place when the cities of Lemur and Atlantis existed.

The Reptilian-Grays alias Nephilim surfaced from the center of the planet carrying the thought-energies from Satien. They conducted experiments with female humans, made humans worship them and even practiced human sacrifices. They were indeed abominable creatures, some with bat wings capable of flying, but strangely enough, believed gods that had descended from heaven to mix and procreate with humans. These demons intervened in the DNA of humans from the outside, changing the path of evolution and elevation.

The Nephilims did **NOT** achieve graft and procreation between themselves and the woman of the man, they could not do it, because of the difference in DNA, but they did manage to graft their thought-energy into the perverse minds of outside beings, they were able to entrench their wickedness in the soul of human by joining with the Reptilian heritage of the Satien´s fragment, evolved into becoming a Reptilian-Human... strength and illness tripled. This is how the Reptilian-Grays (Nephilims) caste, heritage and lineage began and this inheritance of thought-energies (soul) and negative-ill have been bequeathed to those human from abroad, who are still the energetic heirs of the first Nephilim or the Reptilian-Grays. Many of these demons incarnated in the man from the outside are the ones who until today, they continue dominating their victims through fear and terror: The Human.

Nothing seems to have changed ever since. Only instead of facing the horrible sight of the monstrous Nephilim, you are generally looking at respected human beings such as so many political and religious leaders, corporate presidents and kings. While human features hide the inheritance, theirs and most human souls continue prisoners of the Reptilian-Grays' frightening energy. What in ancient times began as openly cruel and inhuman domination has turned todays sophisticated influence... looks are deceiving.

202. What is the true story of Lemuria and Atlantida?

We will deal with this story in the fifth book where we, above all, are going to go into details about the Internal Cities of Lemur and Atlantis. There is reference in the sacred scriptures whose sources by word of mouth, however, hold great distortion. Therefore, much of what the scripts finally put down in writing is legend.

251

203. Why do you not use your technology to stop natural disasters on the planet?

We cannot interfere with the Tera-Cell's growth and development to turn an adult cell. Natural disasters are manifestations of the planet's evolution. If we did, we would get in the way of your evolution as well, which would be against the canons of the universe. In effect, our technology is well advanced but we cannot use it against the laws of nature. It is only for positive knowledge in strict accordance with the cosmic guidelines of wisdom.

We have to be very cautious when using universal knowledge, as it requires a clear understanding of the Cause-and-Effect relationship.

It is our task and that of our brothers Seramitas and Ayaplianos-Volunteers of the spacecraft to transmit knowledge, understanding and love for you and the Tera-Cell to succeed in completing the changes you will be facing. This is yours and the planet's natural process and we cannot act on your behalf to influence the course of your evolution and elevation.

204. Are the Nephilim the Annuakis?

No. The Annuakis belong to the Taurus Constellation, fourth grade, fourth plane, third dimension. Every 3800 years the proximity of this constellation allowed them to descend on Earth. However, the Cosmic Confederation will not authorize these visits any more. The Annuakis' physical body is similar to the humans' but purer and their energy is more subtle. In the planet's history, they are Cyclopes or Cicelos, creatures of reptiloid features, almost three meters tall, with slightly greenish hairless skin, long slim members and big dark eyes. A humans' legend describes them as creatures with one eye in the middle of the forehead.

Cyclopes
In Greek mythology, Cyclopes of the first generation were the offspring of Uranus and Gaia, artisans and builders of renown. According to Hesiodos, they were strong and stubborn giants of unstable emotions and brusque behavior. Eventually their species was associated with strength, power and especially with well-made arms. Yet legends

tend to distort reality. The Annuakis arrived on the planet in times of Lemur. They had the gift of clairvoyance and divination and what people perceived as being just one eye was in reality their third spiritual eye, the Rima Gland, located between the eyes on their forehead's center part.

While their legend spread by word of mouth, the knowledge that they were a species from outer space got lost. Ancient writers like Homer saw them as angelic beings out of heaven but to others they were the opposite, demons descending in their carriages of fire. Most writers for obvious religious motives described them as winged beings of angelic beauty and genuine human traits.

Many books actually reveal authors' ignorance of their times, but even the better writers very often did not go beyond personal impressions and religious convictions. The Annuakis species has an active presence in the universe and is free of any disease, as their energy has developed following the guidelines of the universe. Being dedicated investigators and scientists of vast knowledge and understanding, they intensely use their brain's left side but do not seem to know the feeling of love. They work with the positive force of the universe and are members of the Cosmic Confederation.

The Annuakis are the scientists who escaped Satien's destruction. Reading the signs of alert – *EL SER UNO – Planet 333 – The Guardians of Tera* – they left on spacecraft for other planets where they continued evolution according to the universal concepts. Many events in the history of Earth relate to the era when the Annuakis settled on the planet and you believed them to be the Reptilian-Grays. Coexistence between humans and the Annuakis did not work out as humans started to worship them as gods.

The Cosmic Confederation will surely withdraw the Annuakis from the planet, because they cannot control the men from the outside. Humans began to worship them as gods and history was repeating just like Satien. They belong to the constellation of Taurus, fourth degree, fourth plane, third dimension. Every 3800 years, this constellation approaches Earth, it is there, they have the opportunity to come to the Earth, but this is not going to happen, since the Cosmic Confederation already wouldn't let them in. They have a dense material body, it is more sophisticated, refined, slightly and subtle, they have a material body and dense energy like yours.

205. Did the Annuakis experiment with our DNA?

No. Their task was to cure you by extracting the harmful Reptilian energy called Ambition that had invaded you. Unfortunately, their efforts were in vain. Those who conducted experiments with humans were the Reptilian-Grays.

They first tried to procreate with female humans. When this failed owing to the incompatibility of DNA, they turned to experiments with the metaphysical DNA by introducing engraved crystals into the minds of a number of males and females. As a result, the energy of many descendants suffered mutation.

Thought-energies of these descendants have been incarnating ever since in humans and been claiming the right to establish the sovereignty of Satien on Earth.

206. Could you not have taken action against the Nephilim while they implanted their crystals in human minds?

There was a time when heaven witnessed a battle. We Elohim fought a war against the Nephilim. The Bible tells this story as follows: *"A war broke out in heaven. Michael and his angels fought the dragon and the dragon and his angels fought back but succumbed. There was then no place in heaven for them anymore and the dragon, the serpent or Satan along with his angels fell deep down to live among the humans. I heard a strong voice in heaven, saying:*

Now the power and the reign of God and the authority of Christ are safe because God expelled the accuser of our brothers. The blood of the lamb and their word of testimony has conquered him and they were not even worried about their souls while facing death. Therefore, be joyful heavens and all who reside there. Oh! Poor land and sea, for the Devil has descended in anger knowing that his time is short."

We Elohim won this war and from that moment on, the Nephilim were unable to ascend to the planet's surface remaining confined to their habitat (hell) until the end of their days. Our brothers Seramitas and we have worked with you ever since sending you millions of engraved thought-crystals to cure you from the Reptilian-Nephilim' harmful energy.

207. Is the Avatar Abigahel or Michael (Mikael) one of you?

No. He is not an Elohim. Abigahel (earthly name Michael or Miguel in Spanish) is the Avatar who will arrive at the end of the year 2800. He is a Solar Spirit who will make his appearance on Earth after going past Mercury and Venus. Mikael is a Hebrew name and stands for *"He who is like God"*

- MI=he
- KA=like
- EL=God

To incarnate Abigahel will need the help of a human being who uses his brain's left side (Elohim), right side (Seramita) and Pineal Gland (Ayapliano-Volunteer or Spirit) in a balanced manner. From the Bible you know the ***Archangel Saint Michael***, the Elohim who fought and conquered the Nephilim. The Old Testament refers to him four times Two times in the Book of Daniel calling him prince and protector of the chosen people and two more times in the letters of Judas who calls him "Archangel" because of his struggle against Satan.

Books and history refer to him as Commander of the Celestial Forces and leader of the good angels (Elohim) who defeated Lucifer (Reptilian thought-energies) and the bad angels (Nephilim) expelling them from heaven. The Catholic church is greatly devoted to him calling upon him when feeling attacked by infernal spirits because of his Divine Power to conquer the "Serpent" (Reptilian-Grays).

208. If Michael is Elohim will he come back to conquer the incarnated Reptilians?

Yes, he will, since his name stands for a general concept and thus represents us Elohim. This means that we shall return to defeat finally the demons and the ill negative energy from Satien. Once we disincarnate and renounce cloning, every one of our crystals is going to incarnate in the brain's left side of a human. The same human is going to receive on his brain's right side a crystal of our brothers Seramitas called **Gabriel**. The names of Michael and Gabriel, however, have a broader meaning since they do not refer to beings or entities only.

Gabriel: Is a male Hebrew name and means: "He who is a strong and brave man of God" Some authors define it as "He who has received God's power" or "He who is God's power".

In ancient times, he who was a chaste and wise man had a name that distinguished him from an average person. Those who failed to have these virtues, instead, bore the names of demons or entities denoting illness, scourges and wickedness. When a human shows the qualities and strength the names Michael and Gabriel represent, he is ready to receive an Avatar (Abigahel) and start to walk the path of Light and Love. The solar spirit Abigahel is a Sephiroth called Binah, which means UNDERSTANDING and stands for the Tree of Life.

Sephiroth Binah is the energy of Love and Compassion, the archetype of feminine love (Venus-Love) and mainstay of rigorous judgement. It stands for divine intellect (Knowledge and Understanding) and denotes acceptance of tradition and reason in humans.

209. How much truth is there in the story of Adam and Eve?

Ancient books narrate historical events. However, the authors' biggest problem was not to have the science or the technology to properly investigate and analyze many of those events and the descriptions suffered distortions or changes from generation to generation.

Consequently, authors described events to the best of their ability but tended to add personal impressions, philosophical and religious interpretations introducing many times angels, demons, dragons, witches, fairies, etc. Thus, to understand those scriptures you need to study ancient cultures and the symbols they use.

The Story of Adam and Eve

- **Adam:** male Hebrew name, which means *"He who is earthly"* or *"He who is male"*.

- ***Eve***: female Hebrew name meaning *"She who has life". Mother of Humanity, wife of the first male.*

At first sight, these are just names. However, by referring to them you realize the signification they have in history. In the first three books *EL SER UNO*, we explained how distorted and ill thought energy led you to succumb to Ambition. This is where the allegorical story of Adam and Eve comes in... "And God prohibits Adam and Eve to taste the apple. You may taste any one of the garden's fruit, but you are not to taste the fruit of the Tree that holds the Knowledge of Good and Evil". Eve, deluded by the Serpent of Satan (Reptilian energy of Satien) into eating fruit from the forbidden tree, disobeys God and gives some of the fruit to Adam who accepts knowing it that he is doing wrong.

By disobeying God's explicit order, they had chosen to obey Satan. This disobedience is the beginning of their spiritual and ulterior physical death. God expels them from the Garden of Eden for having followed their desires instead of his commandment. It is the original sin of humanity. Let us see how this story appears in the message of *EL SER UNO*.

Adam represents the first man and Eve the first woman on the planet but they are not the ancestors of humankind. Both are living off the wrong knowledge (the apple) the Reptilian energy has transmitted and are taken ill by ambition. They are expelled from paradise (because their thought-energy-soul has been contaminated) and are incapable of forming the spirit that would take them back to the universe. In consequence, the human species is a victim of Reptilian-energy (the serpent) right from the beginning.

Ancient books tell the story giving the characters therein names that tended to be the meaning of a representation the authors wished to perpetuate. Michael and Gabriel, for that matter, are elevated thought-energies, that is, spirits of Light represented by the Elohim and Seramitas, rather than angels.

210. Why do you use Hebrew terminology when dealing with our history?

We use it because Occident knows us by our Hebrew names. We are aware of the existence of much older books than the Bible and the Coran written in other languages like the Chinese for instance but prefer to communicate with you using the background of occidental history for better understanding. Occident and, above all, the American continent are places of very active channels whose qualities allow communication with their inner self and memory of the past. This recollection gives humans the chance to rediscover the truth of long hidden realities.

211. You say the Reptilian-Grays are in confinement. We have testimony of persons having suffered abduction with very unpleasant experiences. Could you please comment on this?

As we have assured you earlier, the Reptilian-Grays (Nephilim) do live in confinement. However, in a distant past they had practiced abductions and experiments with humans. We always have to remember the intimate relationship of Cause and Effect in all life cycles. Any of your acts (causes) will produce an effect of some sort. If we accept the existence of repeating incarnations, that is, the fact that souls incarnate more than once, we become aware that the souls along these incarnations will activate memories that mix or alternate.

When a soul disincarnates, it takes with it the experience of a lifetime that it stores in its memory. This experience surfaces during a new incarnation when a genetic code activates this memory. Many abductions remain stored in inactive memories during past lives until some occurrence revives them so intensely that a person believes having suffered an abduction in his present life.

There are also cases where a person has captured the memory of another soul rather than having relived a personal past life abduction. As a rule, however, the memory a soul carries is what you know as Inheritance of the DNA. The legacy from ancestors to descendants is both energetic-physical and genetic-metaphysical. What we do guarantee you is that there are not nor will be any abductions involving the Reptilian-Grays (Nephilim). Instead, we do not tire to repeat that, while the threat of being abducted has vanished, many of you are in real and immediate danger of being harmed by those Reptilian-Humans who operate advanced technologies using them to conduct genetic experiments with human beings, particularly women. They are the creatures of the dark hiding behind human features.

Trust us, Brothers! Whom you must fear are the Reptilian-Humans who are wolves in sheep's clothing such as innumerable leading politicians, religious leaders, etc... rather than "extraterrestrials" who all they want is to see you free yourselves from manipulation and control.

212. I understand that one could remember an abduction from a past life experience. However, what happens to individuals who had suffered abduction for hours or days only or to others whose bodies show signs of the experiments?

To answer this question, we have to refer to the fact that your science and technologies have reached an advanced state, in many cases under strictest measures of security and camouflaged by holograms. If, for instance, a commercial airplane overflies a jungle area, the crew and passengers might actually be looking at the projection of a holographic image hiding an area with infrastructure for secret scientific and technological investigations such as laboratories, hangars, engineering and construction facilities, housing for personnel etc. The same goes for mountains, lakes and rivers frequently used in the form of holographic images to camouflage restricted areas.

In these places such as: Norway, Sweden, Denmark, Greenland, Alaska, New Zealand, Antarctica and the Arctic and other places, are camouflaged, but in reality, there are secret bases where governments develop very advanced technologies not known by most of the common population. We want you to realize that many sightings of "UFOS" are advanced human technology rather than evidence of extraterrestrial activity. Many nations have developed the technology to operate the spacecraft you believe alien. You need to awake and realize what in reality is occurring. Governments and mega-organizations that control the planet, using multimedia at their service, do everything in their power to make you believe that we, Elohim and Seramitas, are abominable aliens who abduct humans to submit them to experiments. You, Brothers and Sisters, must be Awakened, because it is they who belong to the darkness and the plot, are hatching a long time ago in order to make you believe the 7 billion inhabitants will be conquered and abducted by malevolent and infernal entities that do not belong to this world. They want to make you believe that aliens are going to come to this planet to conquer and dominate you. Actually, they are the ones who want to do it.

We know of the formidable procedures they are preparing. Religious organizations will unite to project holographical images across the planet announcing the advent of a luminous being, bearer of a new religion with the promise to save those who firmly believe in his teachings.

Brothers! The moment you awake, you will understand that you have suffered abductions for millions of years. They were not physical but in the form of thought-energies of "other humans" invading and controlling your minds. There is a current of fundamentalism in all religions stressing strict adherence to a set of basic beliefs. Fundamentalism intends to impose radical ideas or concepts impeding the free exchange of arguments and opinions thus seriously compromising the search for truth. Those of you who may have turned unconditional followers are in great danger to fall victims of fantasy, manipulation and control.

213. You say that you will intercede on our behalf only in cases of extreme danger. How will you know?

We are part of you and have the means to realize what occurs to you and the planet. We have been collecting detailed information ever since we came to the planet and have full knowledge of all your thought-energies and their energetic quality. Right from the day of birth, we Elohim and Seramitas have integrated you into our historic register of lives and existence since we all are tied to each other through thought-energies. The thought-energies (souls) are split into millions of parts.

All of us: Ayaplianos-Volunteers of the spacecraft, Ayaplianos-Seramitas, The Elohim, Ayaplianos-Humans, Reptilian-Humans and

Nephilim... are part of the Tera-planet-brain. One way or another we are interconnected by thought-energies that have occupied their space in the electromagnetism. By working his emotions every one of you is making great efforts to elevate the energetic frequency and vibration of his Micro-Cosmos... likewise the planet's brain is struggling for the elevation of its Macro-Cosmos' frequency and vibration.

It is right here where we all must become extremely active because it is we who create the thought-energies (souls) to construct this Macro-Cosmos. When pondering this immense number of thought-energies we have to conclude that the positive ones are majority. And that is the reason we can be confident to conquer evil. The disease is no match and shall be eradicated.

214. What is your idea of us when looking at so many different countries, languages, mentalities, customs etc.?

The accelerated population growth seems to be the root of an infinite number of conflicts and caused your evolution and elevation to become stagnant. This has led to the formation of opposing ideologies and divergence and disorientation of thought-energies which then occupied humans' brains in a disorderly manner losing at the same time energy and remaining with a cell nucleus of quite particular characteristics.

Our most difficult task has been... TO BRING YOU TOGETHER... by reordering your thought-energies according to knowledge, understanding and love. That is why we, Elohim and Seramitas, have been instilling in you thought-energies of union, fraternity and affection and provided also technological support through advanced science, medicine and, above all, global communication (internet, cellphones), so that thought-energies may begin to gather through this same knowledge, understanding and love.

Ours is the responsibility to encourage you to look for this UNION through evolution as well as energetic-spiritual elevation. In this way you will be able to connect your cognitive capacity with the diverse brain zones of the planet and start following the guidelines to evolution and elevation. The divergence of thought-energies will cease and their multiplication occur in order. Thoughts without context (wandering souls) will begin to gather and articulate ideas (spirits), ideas your brains will feed on in the near future. Today the thoughts you produce are greatly disassociated, tomorrow these same thoughts will emerge in the form of ideas. An essential difference.

Today you think with thoughts, which swarm in the environment, in the future, you will form those thoughts because they will come out of the brain in the form of ideas. It is very different to think only with thoughts to think with ideas. Sometimes when you think only with thoughts these do not concretize, they leave the brain, disperse and occupy useless space within of the planet-Tera brain. On the other hand, ideas join thoughts, unite them and when they leave the brain, they concretize occupying the minimum space inside of the brain-planet-Tera.

When diverging thoughts produce disorder, opposing ideologies and conflicting mentalities which pass from generation to generation. Chaos and anarchy rather than fraternity, union and harmony are the consequences.

The Reptilian-energy has always been the driving force in this. It is using the multimedia to divide nations, communities and people using fear, raising distrust and sowing hatred. Affinity of ideas and solidarity among humans is what it fears most. But until now the Reptilian-force appears to be in the lead by preventing humans from generating ideas and by keeping them busy with the generation of thoughts for mere survival.

215. How do you feel about the disease we are suffering?

The disease as you call it is the malfunctioning of your thought-energy (soul) whose symptoms start to show with the emanation of thought-energies of low frequency and vibration as a consequence of the brain's totally instable electromagnetic waves. This is where distortion occurs.

We know that planet Earth is surrounded by a brain with nine zones and nine energy centers (chakras) just like all existing in the universe. All human beings of the planet are this brain's thought-energies and occupy the zone and energy center according to their evolution and elevation:

Brain Zone and Energy Center:

Energetic Center and Zone 1	The Nephilim Creatures
Energetic Center and Zone 2	The Reptilian-Humans
Energetic Center and Zone 3	The Ayaplianos-Humans
Energetic Center and Zone 3-4	The Ayaplianos-Elohim
Energetic Center and Zone 5-6	The Ayaplianos-Seramitas
Energetic Center and Zone 7	The Ayaplianos-Volunteers (Spacecraft)
Energetic Center and Zone 8-9	The Ayaplianos of Alpha-Centauri

Up to zone and energy center 3 the thought-energies are in a state of imbalance. Consequently, we are working with you so as to equalize them with the more elevated zones and centers, for this imbalance of energy is the cause of distortion, that is, disease. The thought-energies of the planet's population are vibrating in a range of frequency and are tied to the respective zone of the planet Earth's brain. According to its particular frequency each thought-energy is attracted to the corresponding brain zone suffering the degree of distortion and disease this same zone stands for.

216. What is your idea of spirituality?

To us everything is energy. What you call spirituality is the frequency and vibration with which this energy becomes effective or communicates with other realities of the same grade. What complicates your process of communication is the use of innumerable languages and terminologies dividing rather than uniting you. This does not happen to us because we communicate through telepathy with an interlocutor of equal frequency, vibration and intention. This form of communication helps us prevent misunderstandings and favors a coexistence of peace, harmony and wellbeing.

217. In what way does an eclipse affect the planet, humans and other living organisms?

An eclipse is the total or partial obscuring of a celestial body by another. Lunar eclipses for instance occur when the moon enters the shade of the earth failing to receive the light of the sun. THE BEING ONE has shown you that the moon is a crystal that receives and allows sunrays to pass through it. During the process the moon absorbs rays turning them photons. These photons bathe planet Earth providing it with elevated energy. Breathing the energy your thought-energies tend to be clearer and your understanding broader.

During an eclipse, the moon functions like a prism and the photons emanating from it are strong and radiant. This means that you and the Earth assimilate very special photons. For better understanding, we have to remember that everything in the universal body of THE BEING ONE is based on chemical processes and consequently the photons are chemical elements which you call: Particles. Scientists have already proof that the photons form waves but behave like particles when submitted to corpuscular studies. Photons are fundamental particles that travel at the speed of light.

218. Do you, like our Brothers Seramitas, continue to communicate with other realities and beings of other planets?

Yes, we always have had communication of that kind and in particular with the Interstellar Cosmic Federation. Exchanging energy with other beings of Light and Love of the universe is part of our nature. We are and always will be time travelers.

219. You seem to be incapable of forming your spirit or Energetic Being. How do you then manage to communicate with the Light and Love of the universe?

We all have the gift of telepathic communication. But our frequency and vibration are different and we cannot occupy a place for which we are not yet prepared. The universe is very orderly and to incarnate as beings of light we need to obtain further mathematic and chemical elements. Energy never ends, it just transforms. To be part of these transformations we have to continue working and properly preparing with Knowledge, Understanding and Love.

But having perhaps been trapped does not necessarily mean that we, Elohim, are unable to leave this planet. The means to do so are to use all of the Knowledge (we ourselves), Understanding (the Ayaplianos-Seramitas) and Love (the Ayaplianos-Volunteers of the spacecraft).

220. How do you read us, do you know and understand the thought-energy of humans?

We have been studying you for millions of years and are familiar with your innermost thoughts which we have analyzed together with our Brothers Seramitas. There is an astounding proliferation of thoughts on Tera with billions of thought-energies circling the planet and human beings feeding on them to keep their brains working. This myriad of thoughts has created a strong energetic shield encapsulating the Tera-Cell.

We deliberately use the term encapsulate because the shield around the planet is so complicated and disorderly that we have had great trouble analyzing it. We have been studying it from our anti-matter position and during our extensive process of evolution only gradually been able to comprehend it. The reason is your complicated emotional form of thinking. During the past 150.000 years we have been working extremely hard to get a clear picture of the layers of thought-energies that surround the planet. Every one of these layers holds the same frequency and vibration your brains do.

We do not have emotions but we study and distinguish them according to frequency, vibration, rhythm and colors. This is how we made "Contact" and are speaking with you in this interview. Much of what you experience and feel we do not. But we have come to understand it and are conscious of your sufferings, needs and moments of happiness. *"I then asked not only the Elohim but also the Seramitas and Ayaplianos-Volunteers present in the interview the following question. I would very much like to know whether our requests for support are actually paid attention to and by whom?"*

221. Do you keep a record of each one of us...do you really listen when asked for help?

Yes, we do – They all respond – And we very closely listen and do come to your rescue when there is true need of it. But there are many factors – the Seramitas remarked – we have to analyze before we can accept a call for support. It is a matter of Cause and Effect as we have to consider human lives involved, the environment etc. Besides, calls for assistance are entering the planet's electromagnetism by the millions and must be classified to prevent from adding to the existing density.

And the Ayaplianos-Volunteers added – there is a joint task with the Seramitas, Elohim and the non-incarnated souls who occupy their respective zones within the planet's electromagnetic brain. This work – he went on – never stops as we are permanently treating souls by having them change from one side of the brain to the other.

The fulfilment of this task – an Elohim observed – has been assigned to the existing hierarchies in accordance with their specialization. Our society emphasizes order and an efficient organization. In this way the Anti-matter reality is working for the wellbeing, elevation and transcendence of both incarnated and non-incarnated souls (thought-energies). When receiving requests – one Seramita noted – we pass them on to the non-incarnated hierarchies (Seramitas and Ayaplianos-Volunteers) who will prioritize them according to their nature. A great many of these requests are inconsistent, unbalanced, selfish, emotional etc. Others in turn are considered important and passed on to the respective area for study and execution if necessary.

If the requests were of spiritual nature – observed the Ayapliano-Volunteer – it is we who take care of them. If they were psychological the Seramitas will deal with them. In case they concern the physical body, the Elohim will try to be of help. But in any of the calls both incarnated as well as non-incarnated souls of the planet will collaborate with us. As you can see, the Internal City is organized in a way that absolutely all incoming requests are recorded. But most have to be turned down because they do not justify our intervention.

222. Then it is not God who listens?

God? – The Ayapliano-Volunteer thoughtfully remarked – we understand him as being a theological, philosophical and anthropological concept. We comprehend that the word God makes reference to a supreme deity. There are humans – he went on – who according to their innermost faith and philosophy believe in the existence of a personal God. Others believe in God as a supreme force without the need to communicate with him through religion. And there are those who think that God is anthropomorphic (of human shape) and expect him to take action for the salvation of humankind.

While you are praying to "God" – he continued – we who are his children and thoughts listen to you. For example: If you listen to someone's request who is listening? Your mind or the thoughts of your mind? The correct answer would be – "The thoughts of your mind" – but your thoughts without your mind would not be able to listen nor would your mind without your thoughts. In conclusion: We the thoughts and "God" the mind are one. Therefore, it is we who are listening to your requests because we have been destined to look after the planet and are close to you.

223. When we ask for help against a disease, that is, against something that affects our physical body, how you, brothers Elohim, would aid us?

It is not easy for us to see you suffer and implore for help from above for your families, children, friends, acquaintances and yourselves. Most times we have to cope with it from a scientific point of view to an extent that you might consider us insensible or even indifferent. But this is the only way to look at it objectively and understand it. The problem is that it is you who originate the disease. This disease begins to develop in your thought-energies (souls) despite all the knowledge you have already assimilated and you are absolutely aware of it. Nevertheless, failing to make proper use of that knowledge, you continue to cause distortions.

These distortions threaten to lead you toward a point of no return. Most times we abstain from interfering since this is a process that helps you with your energetic development and is the only way for you to understand and grow. The task of receiving and classifying requests has been assigned to the non-incarnated souls who study them to see whether they need further attention. It is they who are responsible to take care of the brothers of their species and who will interfere with every individual case if necessary. We, the Elohim, are to serve the cosmos. Our specific task is to shelter the Tera-Cell from falling ill, maintain its electromagnetism stable and have the rays of the Star Sun bathe the planet constantly. We also see to it that the planet's energy be distributed in a balanced way and permanently keep the atmosphere free from any interference that could damage it.

224. Do you create thoughts the way humans do?

No, we do not. We are ideas, that is, we create ideas using combined thoughts while in our communications we employ symbols. Each symbol holds a number of interconnected thoughts. Together these symbols have a meaning, represent an idea.

225. Do you have contacts with other civilizations?

Yes, we have and always had. Communication with other civilizations beyond planet Earth is necessary as evolution continues and we therefore never lost contact with the Universal Knowledge. We are very actively collaborating with the Interstellar Cosmic Federation exchanging knowledge with them. All these communications have been extremely useful during our studies and investigations to find a cure for yours and other planets.

As already outlined our contacts are through palpable-holograms and so are the communications of other brothers in the cosmos who visit your planet for reasons of investigation. They are from galaxies such as: Alpha Centauri, Orion, Andromeda, Cyrius, Great Bear, the Pleiades and others. None of us do interplanetary traveling on board of spacecraft as you may think. We all use the technology of the holograms to prevent the risks of long and energetically dangerous space journeys.

226. Knowing what we are and the disease we are suffering, do you think we have a chance to save ourselves?

Of course you have. Major proof that we are positive about this is our presence here. There will come the day when you will enter the Internal City and learn about everything we have gone through and how hard we have been working to get where we stand today. There are many who do not recall because the past remains hidden deep down in your memories. But the moment you abandon your physical bodies you will clearly see what your lives had been like.

227. Are you the "Extraterrestrials" who, according to some channels, are circling the planet on board a "Spacecraft" and waiting to take us to the Internal City?

Yes, that is us. But we are not waiting for you in our "Spacecraft" to take you to the Internal City. For that you first have to give up living in a fantasy. From the year 2014 on those who will be leaving their bodies during the next 200 years and are ready will enter the Anti-Matter World and be conducted by us to the Internal City of the planet. There we, the Elohim, will be together with our brothers Seramitas. When that moment comes you will see for the first time what we look like: Ayaplianos. And you will really know and accept us. There will then be no need of communicating through holograms any more simulating human features.

228. How will this passage occur?

As announced the Cosmic Alignment will begin in the year 2014. You already are receiving the signs: Cosmic Bubbles, Subatomic Particles, stronger UV and Gamma Rays from the Star Sun, High Energy Electrons and radio waves from the center of the Galaxy, increase of the planet's electromagnetism, heavier solar winds and violent climate changes.

This whole process of changes strengthens the planet's electromagnetism which allows us: to leave the planet and head for Venus. In the first three books we have explained that when your soul abandons the physical body, it makes an energetic passage to another being's brain. Now those who as of 2014 are reaching a predetermined energy elevation are directly received by the planetary brain and prepared to enter the planet's Internal City.

From the year 2014 on, those souls who reach the frequency and vibration of zone 9 will be preparing for the departure as follows: They abandon their bodies heading for the planet's electromagnetism where they are received by us. We, the Elohim, in the meantime will have launched millions of orbs heavy with protons (ships) to which the energy of the souls will feel attracted and use for a womb as shelter from any possible interference.

When the souls have accumulated a certain number, they will unite by frequency and vibration, leave through the Northern-Cone to head first for the Internal City of the planet and then for the Internal City of Venus. Venus will receive and transform them into positronic energy. A positron is an antiparticle and combines with an electron. Either will take an opposite direction and form two photons of gamma rays. In other words, on Venus the souls' energy will turn photonic by a nuclear chemical transformation and show a three-dimensional image.

229. Do souls who undergo this process cease to be individual?

Yes, in a way, because these souls carry thought-energies of a high frequency who are destined to form the spirit. To reach Venus means having thought-energies with elevated frequency and vibration since they are the chemical elements needed to create the Energetic Being. Souls will unite and form spirits. And the spirits will remember every detail of the souls who joined to form a: SER UNO (ONE BEING). The individuality and memories accumulated life after life by each soul will not be lost, will not cease to exist but rather turn a single one with the union of all these souls.

230. Can you give us an example?

If you prepare a meal you will have to use a number of ingredients. If you look at these ingredients one by one you realize that they are just that, ingredients with no effect on one another. The moment you put them together and cook them they will interact and become a menu. The Energetic Being or Spirit is formed of thousands of single souls. When these souls unite and start to interact, they are the expression of a different existence. It is the same with the universe. We all are an infinity of memories and energetic formulas created by the union of thousands of souls who together eventually form EL SER UNO (THE ONE BEING).

Failing to understand this process is the source of many of your problems. What you call individuality is your EGO that does not allow you to be part of something greater. You do not manage to free yourselves from the Ego and thus lose the chance to become part of a greater and more elevated expression. This lack of comprehension still holds you prisoners. You constantly repeat to yourselves: We are All, We are One. But do you really know what this means? It means DETACHMENT AND UNDESTANDING. It means to be aware that you have to make a decision because there is too much at stake. And your decision is either to keep on with your apparently satisfying life or strive to fill your soul with the highest possible frequency and vibration of an existence really worth living.

231. Having helped us you, the Elohim, with our evolution, what would be your answer to why sex without love is out of control?

We, your elder Brothers, on this planet have transmitted to you the Universal Knowledge in multiple ways. The books EL SER UNO have constantly been calling your attention to what is occurring in your reality. You have been asked to elevate your frequency and that of the planet's electromagnetism so that you may break free from domination.

Fantasy? Overreaction? Many of you think so but do not perceive the danger of what lies ahead, fail to listen and hide behind illusions and lack of realism. You should long have understood that while there are beings of light like us who work for everything positive in creation, there are ill-negative incarnated and non-incarnated thought-energies that: Stir up aggressiveness and violence, cause disorder, injustice, anarchy and great suffering and praise the satisfaction of sexual pleasures merely as such developing a dense and annoying energy which hampers the electromagnetism and covers you with an energetic layer of unbalanced and distorted vibrations.

This dense negative energy leaves the brain producing uncontrolled electric discharges across the atmosphere and surface of the planet. You at the same time function as receptors of these discharges of energy assimilating them. Therefore, you must protect yourselves creating a strong gravitational-spiritual shield to prevent those discharges from further causing the physical and mental disease you have been suffering for so long.

The ever present ill-negative force of enslaving consumism stirred by the ego, drug addiction, unhealthy food etc. trigger and stimulate sex without love, indifference, imbalance, disease and wickedness, that is, all that degrades the human species. Look and see for yourselves... propaganda, cinema, television, food, clothes, etc. arousing morbid habits and degrading natural instincts. Why? You may be wondering. It is one of the most effective forms of control.

232. What about sex with Love?

This, Brothers, is the most beautiful and noblest form of loving each other. It is the union of two human beings in love who in complete unison reach an orgasm of plenitude. Why slavery has been able to advance? Why, you, good beings, have not been able to control many ill-negative situations that today have advanced uncontrollably? The ill-negative force has been gaining ground because it denies you access to the Universal Knowledge. Even when you do not believe this, the reptilian-energy-thought never allowed you the right to have the real knowledge and understanding. Thera are papyri, books and very ancient teachings that have been hidden by the controllers, whether they are governments and religions.

In ancient times, in Lemur and Atlantis could readily avail themselves of this knowledge transmitted to them by us, the Elohim, and our bothers Seramitas, that showed them how to handle, control and project the energy. However, leading political and religious factions such as priest and scripts only interested in power and domination started to restrict its use and eventually hid it from the public. Many of today's governments and global organizations are the incarnation of those priests and scripts. In those times, we taught you the sexual energy made with love, which was an important shield for you and earth planet.

During the sexual act, two people in love produce a discharge of electrical energy, which originates in the sexual chakra at the lower part of the spinal column. Now this energy goes up through the spine (Kundalini) until reaching the brain where it reproduces an orgasmic explosion. After that, the energy loaded with protons heads for the planet's electromagnetism with the protons surrounding the planet and joining with electrons to maintain the nucleus of the planet-Earth-atom stable.

Sex without love is producing the imbalance. Why? Because the orgasm without the elements quarks (love) produces many electrons (negative) since we know that protons are composed of two quarks up (Atmosphere) and a down quark (Earth) and together they form the atomic nucleus (the core of planet Earth). Sex without love is producing a lot of electrons and this is causing imbalance in the brain-planet-Earth and some of the disasters ecological, atmospheric and planetary. We are going to ask all of you human beings who help us raise the planet's electromagnetism and from now on you will do the following when you make love:

When you are close to this supreme instant and feel the emanation of the brilliant white energy of love... embrace the planet in your imagination and let the energy: flow into its electromagnetism. Doing so you will contribute to elevate frequency and vibration of the planet and every single living being because all of them will be assimilating this energy which carries a very special element... Love.

So, start working not only for yourselves but in conscience for the planet as the war of the sound-positive against the ill-negative forces has just begun.

MAKE LOVE USING YOUR CONSCIENCE.

Spread this knowledge. It is of great importance to all... From now on, brothers, and particularly in the fifth book EL SER UNO, we shall give you: the Shield, the Sword and the Power of the Knowledge to fight the ill-negative force. You are the Warriors of Light and united we shall overcome.

233. Do you feel an orgasm when uniting with another being?

Beings like we who are living in a different reality do not have orgasms any more the way you do. Instead, we feel overwhelmed with immense harmony, peace and universal love throughout the cosmos. Your sexual instincts and the way you perceive and live them will have to change for the sake of transcendency. When elevating your sensation of sexual pleasure will become one of plentifulness and immense spiritual satisfaction. This a characteristic of the energy's process of evolution and elevation.

234. Coming back to the process of domination, we have always been slaves then and still are today?

Yes, that is true but evolution has sophisticated you and also those who exert control over you. Today's slavery is using an arsenal of psychological traps rather than the chains and forced labor of former times to guarantee the widest possible domination. As already referred to you have been slaves from the age of Lemur and Atlantis. The Elohim, our brothers Seramitas and we have accompanied you at all times and been conscious of the density and distortion you were suffering. There was a moment when we together started to combine the DNA of both to help you free yourselves.

It is true when you ask if we abducted you or have abducted. We answer yes, but it has always been to save you, not to obtain benefits of control or enslavement. We knew what we were doing and we know what we do until today. Abduction as you call it is done with the permission of the Interstellar Cosmic Confederation, we follow a pattern of investigation and we can tell you, that each one of you is filed in our genetic record, we know who you are and what is the descent of each one of you.

Slavery exists abroad and is carried out by the Reptilians who are incarnated from generation to generation. They have human shape, but they are not in real. You are slaves, you always were, slaves to: Consumerism, pharmaceuticals, wrong diet, fashion, beliefs, governments, idiosyncrasies, customs, jobs, financial system, money etc. These modalities are imposed by the control and manipulation of those who keep you slaves. These do not let you free yourself, because you have to work for collective and that means...Perform...to the fullest. As you can see, slavery is not coarse as in the past, today it is a slavery demands, subtle and disguised as progress, which makes you believe that you are enjoying it, only you must work for it and "They" make you work to have it.

235. Is it you, the Elohim, who make appear the crop circles?

Our brothers Seramitas and we conceived and started to realize the crop circles in the mid-seventies of the 20th century as another important means of communication and proof of our existence. We started out with simple circles to call your attention using them later on as a language of geometrical, mathematical, oneiric and psychological symbols with the hope that many of you would dedicate time and efforts to interpret them so that they might become common knowledge.

The circles' symbolism refers to the Material, Ethereal and Spiritual body, that is, to a three-dimensional image (3D). Reading the circles in order to understand the symbols has always to be made from the circumference toward the center. Putting them on a 3D program you will note that the image shows the material covering the ethereal and finally the spiritual body. The spiritual body is always located in the center of the circle.

The symbols we use to characterize matter relate to its mathematical and chemical elements; those for the ethereal body base on the interpretation of dreams; and finally the image of the Electromagnetic Field holding all the knowledge and understanding of the thought-energies is the symbol of the Spirit. All these symbols are well known to you but have to be interpreted from diverse angles. To do this, knowledge of Mathematics, Chemistry, Psychology, the Interpretation of Dreams and a broad understanding of spiritual reality is necessary.

The electromagnetic field of planet Earth observed from the distance shows an intense bright luminosity. This is where the Seramitas of the

Eighth Hierarchy-Anti-Matter Reality, the Elohim and we live. It is the Internal City of the planet from where we communicate with many of you. This may explain why we always have stressed the importance the electromagnetism has for you, the planet and the Solar System. We communicate with you, the Material World, by means of the electro-magnetism. It holds the force that enables us to use telepathy for the transmission of messages, knowledge, Orbs and for the realization of the Crop Circles. This language has helped us come closer and will also be the way of communicating with you in the future.

236. Would it not be more practical to communicate directly with scientists and investigators instead of using symbols?

Yes, we could do it without any problem, but to do that we need the being who is channeling contains in itself the knowledge of all the sub-jects that we named before: Mathematics, Chemistry, Psychology, Dream Interpretation and a high knowledge of spiritual reality. You may believe that we exaggerate, but among the 7 billion inhabitants there is not a single one who has that united element capacity. Between you there are many elevated and very open-minded special-beings, but they not possess joint knowledge of the above subjects.

As a rule, scientists are dedicated to their specialty and have little or no interest in spending time and prestige on probable cosmic realities. Only few have the broad-mindedness, imagination and, above all, are prepared for the risk to accept such realities without scientific proof, for the time being. This makes it very difficult to communicate with them. On the other hand, humans who nowadays are receiving our messages are open-minded, straightforward and have an extraordinarily elevated soul. The communication with them allows us to send you messages with elevated frequency and vibration so that you after studying them are able to engrave them on your thought-energies.

In ancient times, those who captured our messages were always in-terlocutors such as priests, hermits and mystics but never Kings, Phar-aohs, Presidents or inveterate Scientists. Why? Because of their Ego, Pride and Vanity. Their primary interest has always been the knowledge of the planet rather than the cosmos.

237. Would it not be best to present yourselves before us to prove that you are extraterrestrials?

We want you to understand that: we, Ayaplianos-Volunteers of the spacecraft, Seramitas-Internal City and Elohim have actively been sending you for the last 40 years the message of EL SER UNO through Ascended Masters from our Magnetic-Anti-Matter reality. We have had no chance to communicate with you physically because of the disease that attacked you and the electromagnetic instability of the planet caused by the distortion of the thought-energies. Up to now, we have only been able to make contact with a certain number of humans who managed to capture the frequency of our telepathic waves. This was possible because of their elevated thought-energies and stable electro-magnetism. We are Energetic Beings and you, Psychical Beings. Unless you advance on the formation of your spirit by adjusting to the frequency, vibration and speed of our waves a face-to-face communication will not be possible.

To communicate with you we need to slow down and emit a lower frequency, we can do it to a certain extent and that's where we can make ourselves visible and communicate with some of you because the beings that capture us have raised their frequency, we have down and we met halfway. Many of you are picking up on us telepathically, you are elevated energetically, but you do not have the knowledge of science and technology. Therefore, they are only receiving our psychological and philosophical messages, this way, we are getting the elevation and the "Contact".

238. For better understanding, we would like to know how you create the Crop Circles.

Crop Circles are formed by Electromagnetism we subtract from the atmosphere and the Astro Sun, whose magnetic waves work through frequency. First of all, what we want to convey through the drawings is a language that unites symbols: mathematical, chemical, oneiric, psychic and spiritual. They are formed by us: The Seramitas-Ayaplianos of the Inner City and by the Elohim. Our minds work from various angles, we are privileged beings, because we dominate several subjects at the same time.

At the Internal City, we communicate through telepathy rather than spoken words. While thinking our minds shape the thought-energies and make them accumulate appropriate crystals to express these thoughts. Our thoughts form just like the Crop Circles and those who are able to capture them will understand the meaning of the circles. Crop Circles originate from universal thoughts, which are a combination of crystals. These crystals form geometrical figures according to the message they will transmit. The process compares to that of the water crystals, which form crystalized figures when submitted to a low or high tone music source nearby. The same happens with salt grains, which form figures when exposed to sound waves of diverse frequencies.

The language of the Internal City is: Electromagnetic Frequency. This is how we communicate with each other and with you. We are Beings of Energy able to enter and leave the electromagnetism of the planets of the Solar System and live in the luminosity of Earth, Venus, Mercury and the Star Sun. Our reality is different from yours as we are made of the four basic elements plus Ether and Helium. Living in the electromagnetism means that we can form thoughts and express them through figures by shaping and combining elements within the electromagnetism in accordance with our needs.

239. Could we shape our thoughts, create Crop Circles or other symbols the way you do?

No, you are not yet capable of concentrating your thought-energies to give the thoughts an adequate form. The reason is the oscillation of thought-energy between your brain's left and right side as well as the existing ethereal-electromagnetic instability. On the other hand, you personally suffer from this instability. So, when you form an emotional thought the crystals of this thought appear deformed and with no clear expression.

Even if it were an elevated thought, the figure of its crystals would not show much of a definition since you just now are forming your Baby-Spirit who does not yet have the capability to properly unify the thought-crystals. It is the spirit who gathers the thought-crystals, which for an appropriate expression extract the necessary elements from the electro-magnetism. We use the following three steps to form a Crop Circle: we, the Ayaplianos-Volunteers, create the thought-energy of an idea, our brothers Seramitas install this idea in the electromagnetism and our brothers Elohim receive and provide it with the required elements and compress it to form the Crop Circle.

240. How do you communicate with the channels?

We use symbols for communication. When a being forms his spirit, this spirit carries crystals with the engraved formulas, the DNA of the universe. Thus, the spirit comes totally prepared and without having to study and assimilate anything, new to be able to function whereas the souls are bound to undergo the process of experience, instruction and assimilation. We communicate with the channelers of the planet through symbols and these are interpreted with the existing vocabulary that is found in the memory of the being. Who is interpreting and translating the sym-bols is the spirit, which shapes them adequately in the language that finds to communicate correctly, taking from it what is necessary.

These symbols are exactly the same as Crop Circles that you will find in the future in the City: Atlantida. If we say that it is spirit who inter-prets the symbols, you may be wondering why not are we achieving? They are not succeeding because many of the researchers, scientists and scholars, have to do it through the spirit, and not through of the intel-lectuality that belongs to the soul. If they interpreted the Crop Circles with the inner senses, they would not make mistakes, because it would be the spirit that would guide them to make an elevated and cosmic reading, but they insist on interpreting them with the intellectualized and planetary knowledge and this is not enough.

241. Having formed his spirit, will a person then be able to read the Crop Circles?

Yes, but in addition this person needs to have a notion of mathemat-ics and chemistry, a good comprehension of human psyche and be experienced in the interpretation of dreams. We are aware that as for now few humans have the required abilities. Therefore, a correct reading of the Crop Circles would be possible by gathering small groups of five people, each a specialist in one of the areas but all with their spirits formed to work together and advance on interpretation and communication. Given this situation, only in a distant future you will be able to make a complete reading of the symbols we are transmitting. Today's isolated interpretations are not sufficient to establish a regular communication with us.

242. Then my communication with you is a limited one?

Yes, because our communication with you and thousands of other humans is a psychological and philosophical dialog. Most channels act in accordance with the knowledge of these two disciplines accumulated during several incarnations. This makes them specialists in these areas and very relevant contacts for us. Yet our communication with you does not include science nor technology. This does not mean you're being incapable of learning to deal with both. It is because your spiritual memory does not hold the formulas needed so that we can understand each other.

Thus, every channel is to perform in his particular area and in this way gain the Universal Knowledge. Once you find yourselves in the Internal City you will extend your knowledge to all areas, that is, there will be no more need for specialists.

243. Given the difficulty to gather those five persons, why do you keep on sending us symbols we do not understand?

We do this to call your attention in the first place so you may awake and realize our presence. Despite your knowing about it, we find it surprising that your minds are still blocking this information. After all, the Crop Circles' function is to approximate us to humans. We are aware that you perhaps do not yet manage to understand the whole meaning of the Crop Circles but are sure that little by little you will. There will be further information, though many are already awaking, and the moment will come that you will be forming the groups of five as mentioned all across the planet and together accomplish the interpretation of the codified messages contained in the symbols. We are already preparing those who will form the groups. They all are channels who after a certain time will be working together.

244. What is it you intend to transmit through codified messages?

The messages and symbols are the language you will be using when finding yourselves in the Internal City. They will help you change from your virtual state of life into a true reality of existence. It is of importance that you start to conceptualize a different way of existing. When we say that you are living a virtual life, we refer to the fact that you conceive your reality using the parameters of certain rigid concepts. Based on these parameters your thought-energy has created an entirely unreal existence.

The spiritual reality you are supposed to live has 3 dimensions necessary to understand the language of the universe but you just live and move in one of these dimensions. The messages are subliminal. While observing them you will feel that they engrave in your minds. After leaving your physical body and entering the Internal City, you will begin to study and understand them. Our way of working with you has always been to fix the symbols in your memories. Our Brothers Seramitas have been doing most of the work guiding you in your dreams on the path of your energy's evolution and elevation.

Let us take the following Crop Circle as an example and analyze it (see image in page 280):

What is the first thing you see?

You respond: We observe three larger, three smaller overlapping circles and a triangular figure with one larger and one smaller circle in its center. Everything in the figure seems to represent the numbers 3 and 6. We comment: The three smaller overlapping circles (number 3) represent the trilogy: physical, ethereal and mental Body guided by its inner sun (Pineal Gland) in the center (triangular figure with one larger and one smaller circle).

The overlapping of the circles denotes that you have to unify both the 3 larger and the 3 smaller overlapping circles to be commanded by your inner sun (number 6). The 3 major circles to the naked eye also show the figure of three waning moons symbolizing your source of photons since the rays of the Star Sun pass through the moon bathing the earth with their intense radiant light.

The number 3 refers to the DNA while the number 6 points to the evolution of the human species in the future. The three inner circles with their center at the same time indicate the unification of the three bodies (trilogy) inside the innermost circle as one single reality that will command all existing. The symbols of the Crop Circles will be opening to understanding with the advance of science and many of you will then be capable of reading them.

245. How do you create the Crop Circles?

Our brothers Ayaplianos Seramitas mentally designed the Crop Circles. We Elohim produce and control them by using static electromagnetism and remote control through Orbs. These electrostatically charged and monitored Orbs descend and execute the recorded commands through electromagnetic impulses without touching physical matter. We also use palpable holograms for the same purpose.

246. Why do you always use crops to form the circles?

Crops are very appropriate for this task because like the Orbs they hold an electrical charge and moisture, which favor the action of the magnetism to form the circles. We proceed with their formation when the crops are almost due for harvest and their stems easy to bend. We could also produce the circles on sandy or icy ground. The figures, however, would suffer the effect of wind or water and rapidly vanish.

247. Why is it that most Crop Circles have appeared in Great Britain?

We have chosen this country because of the position of its magnetic meridian, which very much favors the correct functioning of Orbs and Holograms. There are regions on the planet where the circles are less frequent. Nevertheless, local governments and other organizations who refuse to accept our presence always seek to distract the population's awareness.

From 2014 on, however, the number of Crop Circles in South America will increase considerably as the ethereal point of the six-pointed star will make its appearance there. Places such as Bolivia, Peru, Argentina, Brazil, Uruguay and Paraguay where the planet's electromagnetism is rising will attract the Orbs we are launching into the atmosphere. This rise is the result of a massive migration of thought-energies (souls) to the Southern-Cone for healing and a new incarnation to continue their cycle of existence and eventually depart via the Northern-Cone.

The Cosmic Alignment along with other dimensions of the universe has added to the process of the souls' preparation by reinforcing the planet's electromagnetism. To get a clearer picture, you must think of the planet as being a compass the needle of which indicates the position of the most powerful magnetic field. The day this happens, you will be aware that the position of the planet's axis has reversed. you will feel like you are upside down, but it is not like that, it is the magnetic force that will play tricks on you.

248. How will the electromagnetism affect the aforementioned countries?

In reality, there will be a positive effect. South America will become a center of magnetism and will represent the western since Europe, Central and North America will be magnetized in such a way that the power of this magnetism will open and vigorously activate the magnetic circuits of the brain. The population of this vast area will awake to new and advanced consciousness, subtle and intelligent.

At the same time, all negative energy will transform since it has to adjust to the frequency and vibration of the planet's axis. The Western hemisphere will rise like Phoenix and have the great responsibility to receive the energies of the Eastern hemisphere and introduce them in the electromagnetism for treatment and cure. Changes will start to occur. Science and technology will have to step forward to explain our presence. We will make our appearance everywhere and you will start to believe. There is nothing to stop the revelation of the truth. The energy of the Cosmic Alignment will be immense. You will sense it physically and in all your thoughts and actions. You will see changes for the better in health, wealth, clearness of mind, justice, compassion. It will be an extraordinary and unparalleled transformation. You will begin to listen to your inner voice to guide you on the path of return. Though you perceive the energetic transformation as mainly being a spiritual one, we evidently have to add some scientific explanations to have you realize that this process, this phenomenon does not only occur here and now...

The solar winds launching Gamma rays will become more intense triggering heavy climate changes across the planet as well as electromagnetic phenomena such as: Rainbows and Auroras Borealis (Northern hemisphere) and Australis (Southern hemisphere) in areas where they have never been observed before. Children will marvel you with their extraordinary gifts, people start speaking languages they do not know and some extinct languages resurge. Memories of a distant past emerge. All these phenomena will occur while you awake to conscience. Millions of planets and beings in the universe will benefit from the changes to come. We all are in the body of *EL SER UNO* and this is where everything is occurring and will continue to occur.

249. You always told us that everything is holograms. How have we to understand our existence, our reality?

Let us for a moment go back in time and have a look at the first book *EL SER UNO I – The Arcana of Toth*. Do you remember when the giant *SER UNO* took a crystal from the Pineal Gland, installed it in a bubble sphere, had it exploded and created a universe in miniature like the one in which they were existing calling it the Odd Reality? This is the universe where we all are, a mental laboratory of a bubble-sphere that we observe from the Even Anti-Matter reality.

We who find ourselves in this reality are *Ayaplianos Ser Uno*. That is why they say: We are they and they are we. We who are in the Odd Reality of the mental laboratory are a virtual reality, palpable holograms; for the Even Antimatter Reality is our true reality.

250. What were the reasons for this experiment?

We needed to know who we are and what our place in the universe is. We, The Beings One belong to the Regular Dimension-even of the Orion Constellation. We are the creators of every tangible and intangible reality. We are very subtle energy called: Anti-Matter. We are direct descendants of the Superior Dimensions and our thought-energies originate from the dualism between the superior and inferior reality. The Perfect Dimension created us to investigate the dense and dark reality and provide it with full information.

To be able to take on this mission we underwent a process of preparation in the Regular Dimension but all the same found ourselves with the problem of being unable to descend to the Inferior Dimensions. To resolve the situation, it occurred to us to create a duplicate of ourselves in a mental-laboratory by extracting a crystal from one of our Pineal

Glands and install it in an artificial bubble-sphere. This crystal suffered exposure to a chemical reaction under an extremely elevated temperature, which made it explode and form another universe parallel to ours. The explosion literally resembled the universe the One Origin had created and to which we belong. We thus became creators of a new universal expression, which we termed Odd Matter Reality.

Through this new reality, we had been able to investigate everything we needed to know about the inferior dimensions including the development of an infinity of animal species and plants, but above all, of the humans and ourselves. However, while installing a supposedly "perfect" crystal in the course of the experiment we found that this crystal had not at all been perfect because it contained chemical elements quite different from all we knew about ourselves. We discovered that our ideas still carried corrosive elements. This neatly appeared when planet Satien started to ionize its atmosphere and everything we had implanted on its surface.

We, the Seres uno, who thought to be perfect had to face imperfection and to remedy it had to enter the same universe we had created. Consequently, we proceeded to form the human mold (material body) in this miniature universe laboratory and incarnated in him to be able to penetrate the density and fight the harmful elements. Therefore, you as well as the Ayaplianos-Volunteers, the Ayaplianos-Seramitas and the Elohim... are us... *SERES UNO.*

251. Are we all SERES UNO (BEINGS ONE)? Are we in a universe created by ourselves in a laboratory?

Yes, you the universe's odd reality and we, the even reality are *SERES UNO.* At this very moment, you and we are in telepathic communication because we are *SERES UNO.*

252. This giant even universe where you are now, has it been explored?

Not yet. In fact, the only universe that we have studied is the Micro-universe created in the laboratory where we *SERES UNO* enter and leave. For the time being, we are exploring the Micro-universe and will do the same in the future with the Even Macro-universe of our creator, the One Origin.

253. What actually was the reason to first explore the micro-universe and then the macro-universe. Why not at the same time?

There was a risk since we could have perished for lack of knowledge. Nowadays we can affirm that our wisdom is almost complete and this has helped us advance. This lack of knowledge could have annihilated us. That is why we created palpable-Holograms traveling a long way to explore the Micro-Universe. We all, absolutely all, are Holograms. Our true reality is the Regular Dimension. We are Anti-Matter beings, extremely subtle energy with elevated frequency.

254. Did you therefore say that we all are palpable holograms?

Yes, but we also said that you live in an unreality, in a world of phantasy. Because when coming to planet Earth you suffered distortion and lost the memory of your origin.

255. What is then the reason of the process of elevating, transmuting, becoming spiritual, turning Energetic Beings?

The reason is to return to *EL SER UNO*, to which every one of you belongs. To find the way back to the One Origin that gave us life and existence. We do not belong to this reality. We only came here to investigate and became prisoners. You must regain your memory in order to know where you now are and why. Only after forming your Energetic Being, which is a sophisticated and very advanced Hologram, will you be able to explore the universe, return to *EL SER UNO* and be part of its thoughts. However, every time we depart from and return to our origin, we provide our *SER UNO* with millions of data gathered during our cosmic journey.

287

256. Do we ever stop entering and leaving our SER UNO?

Never. We will not cease to enter and leave until we know about creation to the last detail. You have to have complete knowledge before we can head for the Even Giant Reality.

257. If we are Seres Uno, what are our features?

We all are Ayaplianos and have universal features. The millions of palpable-holograms in the vastness of the universe are alike. Yet, distortion changed the holographic characteristics of planet Earth and the other 6 planets. While you advance and conquer distortion, we are working to help you restore the original form of your holograms.

258. I imagine that we will learn the "Truth" about it all in the Internal City... is this the only reason we have to go there?

The Internal City is transmutation of energy and a dimensional portal to go from odd to even reality and vice versa. Passing through the various grades of the Internal City is a process of purification to avoid contamination of other realities. You must therefore keep your hologram in perfect operating conditions. If the hologram does not show the image the mind has designed, the mind will consider it a virus. In this condition, it cannot return and be again part of the mind of its *SER UNO*, that is, its origin.

259. If we are Holograms, is then everything else Holograms, too?

From your palpable-holographic perspective, you perceive chemical elements of the Odd Micro-Universe created in laboratory. In a way, this Universe is partly holographic and partly physical. What you, for instance, call Planet Earth is a cell. The Star Sun is energy resulting from chemical reactions the *SERES UNO* of the lab conducted to "light up" the darkness. The Suns of the Primary Dimension are powerful sources of light that make these realities visible. Thus, the Seres Uno know exactly where they are and already visualize what darkness still conceals.

You have to enter the Internal City to understand the true meaning of reality and essence of existence.

260. There is news of fish and birds massively dying across the planet. Do you know why?

Humans often fail to be conscious of what they do and seem not to care about the planet and its creatures. The apparently inexplicable death of animals is the consequence of experiments of the LHC and HAARP projects referred to several times in this book. The equipment used on these projects affect the planet's electromagnetism by destabilizing frequency and vibration of the Earth-Cell thus seriously threatening the living conditions of many species. Migrating birds for instance may lose their sense of orientation and die of exhaustion during a flight. In the case of fish, sudden peaks of electromagnetic waves can cause brain damage and death. Experiments with HAARP and many other tests are unknown to the public and will be an increasing threat to all species in the future.

What has happened now with the birds and the fish will be repeated many times. Falling planes, appearances of spirals, unexplained deaths, programmed wars, experiences with human beings, genetic mutations with Reptilian DNA, experiments with animals and the more, that you do not they come to imagine. The only way to get rid of, it is by raising the frequency of thought. Brothers, it is not a story that we are telling you, it is the truth of what exists on the planet.

Dark, malevolent and reptilian forces have subjugated you in the necessity of consumerism and in the drug of living. You will discover and see so much, that you will be horrified when the truth begins to be revealed. This is nothing, in the next few years countless revelations will come to light, so crude that only the energy of the spirit could protect you.

261. What about global warming of the planet?

In these times the warming of the Planet will be inevitable. This will bring many problems and disasters to the planet and to you. It is already perceived the consequences such as: Droughts, melting of the Poles, climatic changes, skin diseases etc. We are at the beginning of time, where this will continue for almost 200 years, while the Cosmic Alignment is getting under way. Once aligned, heating will tend to decrease, bringing about a number of effects, some positive, others not quite so.

There will be only two clearly distinguishable seasons: Winter and Summer. The population of many urban centers will have to move to other locations because extreme climate changes and the breakdown of water supply will make them inhabitable. The Star Sun's emanation of heat, light and luminosity will suffer a decline marking the beginning of a new Glacial Period. All these changes are imminent since they characterize the development of the Earth-Cell, part of a natural process that occurs within this immense body of *EL SER UNO*. We ourselves, despite our level of science and technology, have no way of escaping this process having to contribute to the perfection of this immense *SER UNO*.

262. If the Earth poles suffer inversion, what will be the consequences for the navigation of ships and airplanes?

Air traffic and sea travel routes will have to change to prevent accidents. From 2014 on, your scientists will be observing stunning visible and palpable changes of the electromagnetism that will oblige them to adopt a series of drastic preventive measures. Many accidents in the past, in particular the disappearance of airplanes and ships in the Bermuda Triangle, were a consequence of electromagnetic instability. Therefore, scientists and specialist in international traffic in close collaboration already introduced numerous changes into the system.

Fluctuation of the electromagnetism will make the planet enter the Cosmic Alignment. The poles will reverse and become the centers of the gravitational force formerly located in the center of the planet. This will allow souls to depart in accordance with their evolution and elevation from the Southern or Northern Cone. Furthermore, tide levels will change and most animals feel the effect of new frequencies that will have them migrate to other regions of the planet. Auras Borealis and Australis will start to be out of place forming expressive images related to the Crop Circles.

The Spirits of Light of Venus will come the planet Tera to incarnate and continue their elevation. Only those who have awakened will realize this occurrence. Scientists immersed in their material world will be unable of interpreting it unless they lend an open mind to these divine events of the universe.

263. I do not understand why the Seres Uno observing us in a laboratory seem be unwilling to prevent what is occurring to the planet and its inhabitants.

On the contrary, they are doing what they can to help your energy transcend this reality to depart and enter the Internal City. It is an *Evacuation Project organized by the SERES UNO*. The Solar System has been very ill. As part of the Odd Micro-Universe holding contagious elements that could affect this and the Even Reality, the SERES UNO decided to withdraw it from the Laboratory-Project.

264. Do you wish to transmit information we should have?

Yes. We would like you to receive a great deal of scientific information but encounter a telepathic barrier because the minds of most scientists are not open to this kind of communication. For that reason, we are trying to send codified messages via Crop Circles, the only way we have so far to make contact with them. In this book, our Brothers Ayaplianos-Seramitas and we the Elohim have tried to enlighten you about present and future events. It is therefore of great importance that you reach a state of broadmindedness. Without this condition, you will have no chance to awake to conscience and thus fail to elevate your energy frequency.

You must realize that you are holograms, which for proper functioning need the connection to electric vibration thus activating all its circuits in accordance with the vibration of the universe. This electric-vibration carries a predetermined voltage, which have to match to prevent short-circuits of the holograms. Elevating frequency denotes thoughts of elevated vibration frequency. There will have to be friction among the energy crystals so that they produce a very high-pitched sound. An equal sound of the universe will attract it and jointly they will depart for other realities.

During this journey, the energy will be suffering a chemical transformation to adjust to the conditions of its place of destination. It is through the Cosmic Alignment that the SERES UNO support and enable us to depart and return to our origin. The Cosmic Alignment will create the conditions for our passage by forming an energetic stairway the thought-energies (souls) will gradually be ascending until they reach their destination. We, your brothers, will stay until the end of the Cosmic Alignment to help the souls (thought-energies) transcend, pass, ascend and transform. We will always be close. We are the Guardians of Tera and responsible for what is our part in this great event.

265. How will you help us with the passage?

As of 2014, the souls who disincarnate and whose energy has the required vibration frequency will prepare for the passage to the Internal City of the planet. This is always an energetic passage (passage of souls). Do not pay attention when there is talk of alien spacecraft waiting to take your physical bodies. It does not work that way. The physical body is just a palpable-hologram that has failed to function correctly and your thought-energies (souls) will therefore create a new correct hologram.

In other words, when awaking you start projecting a hologram from a real mental image. This image will allow you to leave the planet. The departure will occur when your soul abandons the body in a "natural" way and feels attracted to the electromagnetic frequency circling the planet. The electromagnetism of the planet-brain is the place that will receive the soul in accordance with its vibration, rhythm and colors.

When referring to the "natural" departure of the soul we wish to make it clear that suicide has no part in energetic elevation. The electromagnetism or the Internal City is our habitat where you will prepare by passing several grades of energetic purification to eliminate an amount of dense energies your soul still carries. The Internal City is also the place where you will initiate a process of chemical and energetic transformation necessary for your cosmic journey. We, your brothers Ayaplianos-Seramitas, the Elohim and volunteer-souls will join to help you with a gentle and orderly departure.

Leaving the planet in a state of energy means to be born again. You are being born into a different reality of existence. You will become beings of great transparency and have new physical bodies. This is when the children of the Internal City of Venus will receive you and when they give birth to their children, it will be you to be born again as true Crystal, Indigo and Rainbow children. While you clearly realize that drastic changes are necessary, you fail to know when and where they will take place. Knowledge is present in your lives but it is obsolete and you have to update it. You consider the effects of many past events valid to explain possible causes of the future, whereas for still unknown events of the future you hope to see the cause for them in the present. This is why there is great confusion.

To adapt to a new reality such as the Internal City of Venus you cannot expect your souls to enter it in an adult state and just continue as before. Your thought-energies (souls) have to undergo a process of adjustment and you therefore will have to begin a new life cycle, develop and adapt your energy to this reality.

The changes largely referred to are part of a natural process involving the species and *EL SER UNO*. Everything tangible and intangible and we ourselves are in constant movement, recycling, adapting, transforming and transmuting. The mental-energy of *EL SER UNO* is never static, never was and never will be. The answers you have long been seeking will emerge during the process of studying, learning and understanding.

To do this you have to be part of different realities, each one offering you a universe of possibilities and knowledge. Yet, if you want more you have to embark on your Cosmic Journey, going from one reality to another. The vehicle you will have to use to realize this enormous effort with satisfaction certainly is not an intergalactic spacecraft but the merit from hard work of your energy. There is a moment when you will find out. Brothers, we love you and want you to transcend. We are here to help. Do not fear. WE ARE YOUR BROTHERS OF LIGHT AND LOVE... We are the past, the present and the future... with your belief and inner

293

strength, together we will advance. Do not be doubtful of your inherent abilities and even in moments of weakness or idleness do not ever surrender to evil.

Do not feel captivated by intellectualism. What you need is to understand what you desire and use a positive attitude with everything you do elevating your frequency. Do not be too hard on yourselves, do not be rude in your judgements, be real brothers, be always yourselves and straightforward in your way of thinking doing the best you possibly can at all times.

Do not chase after false promises and illusions that will soon be gone. Be sincere when you love, do not abuse of criticism and quit believing in fantasies. Immerse in your Inner self, observe, listen and feel the Internal City. Be wise when using your knowledge for yourselves and start perceiving your innermost life. Everything, absolutely everything you are looking for on the outside lives and exists inside yourselves. Therefore, shape your Inner World so you may depart and start walking the eternal path of LIGHT and LOVE...

The Elohim continued to speak asking me to communicate with them whenever necessary as they would be always close accompanying our evolution and be with all who needed their knowledge. They asked me to tell all readers and people of science that they are available for any scientific and technological enlightenment if required. They left no doubt that if we trusted; they would begin to give us the Science of the Universe but with the condition to keep on working our inner senses with broadmindedness so that they could activate their channel of telepathy. They also told me not to fear the Reptilians since those had no chance fighting the LIGHT and to prepare consciously for the realization of what we had learned during our many incarnations since this would be of great help when finally entering the Internal City. We looked at each other with Love – and they kept affirming – that all those who work and live showing Belief and Love would have nothing to be afraid of and be victorious. They asked for patience but that things would gain momentum in the course of time.

I said – There is still so much to talk about – they replied while withdrawing – Indeed, there is, there are yet two more books where we shall keep on – Will we meet again? I asked – Yes, we certainly will.

While they were getting ready to depart, the luminosity of their bodies became more intense showing iridescent flashes of colors. It was a moving sight to see them slowly walk surrounded by their own radiant light. Already distant they turned and gave me a last look from their clear bright eyes and said...

WE ARE THE ELOHIM!!... and so, they said goodbye.

END OF THE INTERVIEW

Concluded this interview with our energies of LIGHT and LOVE in unison, we bid farewell like brothers knowing that one day we would be ONE with EL SER UNO. It has been an extraordinary and memorable experience. After the Elohim had left, I stayed with the other brothers in the hall. I went to a large window to the right... the sight my eyes caught was almost unimaginable... The City of Crystals... filled with LIGHT and colors I so often had seen in my dreams. I had never looked at anything more beautiful before.

Looking at my brothers Ayaplianos-Volunteers and Seramitas I asked them – Is this the Internal City? – They exchanged a look and the Seramitas replied – It is one of two... the City of Atlantis at the South Pole, the first we built after we descended from the spacecraft. In the fifth book, we will explain how we built it and what life was like while you lived there. We still owe you a good deal of explanations – they added – One is the true story of Lemur and Atlantis. During that age, your hearts were pure and unconscious of evil. Although you already had suffered distortion the Reptilian seed had not yet found the way to your souls.

When the Reptilian-Grays (Nephilim) emerged from the deep of the planet your journey of darkness ambition and distortion began taking you to that sinister reality you are struggling to overcome ever since. Do not fear, brothers – they went on – you came from the LIGHT and that is where you will return. Having faith will make you victorious because you are LIGHT and LOVE... never forget this. We looked at each other, smiled and bid farewell.

With this book finished – I mused – there are two more to go. We still have a lot to remember, discover and study. Hard work doing away with lies and made-up stories, which had us all but, live a life of amnesia and suffering. I gave the City-Spacecraft another look to be sure to have its image engraved on my mind. I did not want to miss any detail. I realized that many of us carry the truth in their memory thinking that it is a dream or fantasy. It is neither one; what we carry is a solid memory in our souls and hearts.

We will be again, what we were one day. I do not have the slightest doubt about this. We will be pure again. Some day we will be part of the universe and return to our creator EL SER UNO. However, when this occurs it will be in a very different way... Pure in our hearts...With absolute consciousness, for we neatly remember all of it and we finally will know... Whom we were, whom we are and where we are heading...

WITHOUT KNOWLEDGE I DO NOT LIVE

WITHOUT UNDERSTANDING I DO NOT EXIST

WITHOUT LOVE I AM NOT

FRANCA CANONICO DE SCHRAMM became a channel for the Masters of Orion, Alpha Centaury and the Pleiades who started preparing her for this communication when she was 33 years old. This preparation culminated in 2002 when she started channeling the Knowledge of *EL SER UNO* in six books dictated via telepathy by the Elder Brothers Ayaplianos of the Sixth, Seventh, Eighth and Ninth Dimension of the Universe. *EL SER UNO* is a Philosophical, Psychologic and Spiritual knowledge.

Made in the USA
Monee, IL
08 January 2023

24783338R00173